Cooking
for
Company

WINIFRED GREEN CHENEY

Oxmoor
House®

Library of Congress Catalog Number: 84-60290
Hardcover ISBN: 0-8487-0632-3
Softcover ISBN: 0-8487-1197-1

Manufactured in the United States of America
Fifth Printing 1993

Executive Editor: Ann H. Harvey
Southern Living Foods Editor: Jean W. Liles
Senior Editor: Joan E. Denman
Senior Foods Editor: Katherine M. Eakin
Production Manager: Jerry R. Higdon
Art Director: Bob Nance

Cooking for Company

Book Editor: Helen R. Turk
Director, Test Kitchen: Laura N. Massey
Test Kitchen Home Economists: Kay E. Clarke, Rebecca J. Riddle,
   Elizabeth J. Taliaferro, Dee Waller, Elise Wright Walker
Editorial Assistants: Donna Rumbarger, Karen Hardegree
Photographer: Jim Bathie
Photo Stylist: Sara Jane Ball
Designer: Faith Nance
Artist: Robin Sarvis
Editorial Consultant: Nao Hauser

Cover: *A Small Dinner Party (menu on page 77).*

Page i: *Easter Dinner (menu on page 112).*

Page ii: *Crêpes for Brunch or Lunch (menu on page 14).*

Contents

Dedicated to my two beloved friends
Beauty Luckett and Elly Launius
whose unselfish devotion and untiring
efforts made this book a reality.

Acknowledgments are gratefully made to Miss Eudora Welty for her inspirational help, to Mrs. John Bookhart, Mrs. Frank Hagaman, Mrs. Elly Launius, and Mrs. Hugh Luckett for their valuable assistance, and to the friends and restaurants around the world who shared their prize recipes with me.

Author's Note

We Southerners continue to live at a leisurely pace, and sharing our hospitality with our family, friends, and the stranger within our gate is still one of our greatest joys. However, with the changing times we have had to make many adjustments in our everyday living. Frequently, both parents work, and the planning of nutritious and tempting food which is easy to prepare and quick to complete is almost a necessity.

In planning this book, I tried to think of food that could be prepared in advance and either refrigerated or frozen, to be reheated later. As much as possible, I used ingredients common to most pantries with only the addition of fresh fruit, vegetables, meat, or fish. I enjoy having company at my table, but I like to plan and prepare my menus ahead and leave the last minute details until just before serving time. The menus included here are designed for home entertaining without the aid of caterers. For Sunday dinner guests, which I have often, I prepare almost everything myself that morning. When I return home from church, everything is ready to serve within 20 minutes. I will admit, though, that I am a fast worker.

I want you to sample the full range of Southern cookery as well as that of other regions and other lands. My recipes are time-tested. I learned through experience. I enjoy dreaming up new creations and unusual combinations of foods; the majority of my recipes are my own brainchildren.

From Rosemount, the Glover family's antebellum home in Alabama, comes the delectable, yet inexpensive Chocolate Bread Pudding that has been enjoyed there for seven generations. From neighboring Georgia comes Sea Island Shrimp.

In my own Mississippi Delta, a visiting guest might savor Charlotte Caper's Elegant Quail and hot Sally Lunn. Or going on to Natchez for dinner, we may finish our meal with Lemon Meringue Pie.

From the southern part of my state in the homes of some fine Italian families, you will find unsurpassable food brought from their native shores: Bracciolini, Cauliflower Frittata, and Biscuit Tortoni alla Mandora.

When visiting Texas, we dined in a stately home on King William Street, part of

San Antonio's old German section, and enjoyed German Potato Soup, a marvelous meal in itself, with a fresh green salad and German rye bread. At a ranch near Comfort, celebrating a family gathering, we feasted on Pepper Steak, Snappy Cole Slaw, and Rum-Yum Apples. And where else can you find such an abundance of Mexican food as that of Chimi-Changas, Salsa, Chili con Carne, and refreshing Sangria?

From Joe Middleton, a fine teacher, comes the distinction between Cajun and Creole cooking in Louisiana. The Creoles of the New Orleans area blend herbs and spices to enhance, not drown the taste of the naural food, such as a new version of Shrimp Creole where the shrimp are first sautéed in butter, put aside, and later added back to the Creole sauce. The Cajuns, on the other hand, give you the robust country cooking found in Ratatouille, Jambalaya, and boudin.

And from Master Chef Jacques Pepin comes the lesson in haute cuisine. Jacques places great emphasis on fresh food, natural ingredients, and the avoidance of the heavy use of salts. In listing ingredients for a dish he said, "Use fresh food; there is no such thing as fresh frozen food. It's either fresh or frozen. Butter is nature's gift to us; use it wisely. Just take plenty of exercise, and you will have no problem."

In my cooking school classes, I have always emphasized that good food around a common table welds a family together with strong bonds of affection and comaraderie. In essence, good nourishing food may be a way of showing the family your love for them by preparing their favorite dishes. It may provide a time of fellowship for the family. Or it may be a way to welcome friends or guests to your family circle. The table is indeed the center of a happy home, the lure and sustainer of a loving heart. Make your own table such a center of happiness, and rejoice with me.

Winifred Green Cheney

Ready for Company

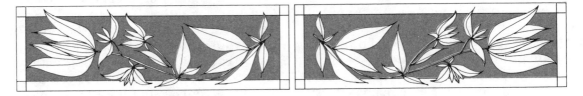

Warm hospitality starts by putting the company ahead of the cooking, and that's the way *Cooking for Company* has been arranged. What comes first is the occasion for getting together—whether an impromptu brunch or barbecue, a luncheon or dinner planned long in advance, a holiday feast, or a family supper. Then comes the cooking, in a menu especially designed to match the invitation.

There are sixty-three complete menus in *Cooking for Company*, and many more ways to make guests feel welcome. Some of the menus anticipate popular events. Whether you are planning a New Year's Eve party, a birthday dinner, or a July Fourth cookout, you'll find appropriate fare. Many others are tied to the delights of the season—the fresh produce in the market and the pleasures of light or hearty food. Perhaps the most intriguing menus are those that suggest a mood, such as A Relaxed Evening or A Small Dinner Party, for these will lead you to think about the context in which you and your guests would feel most comfortable. And sometimes the friendliest greeting is coffee and cake; you'll find that one chapter of *Cooking for Company* is devoted to coffee accompaniments that invite relaxed conversation anytime.

The menus have been composed with two major concerns in mind: how the foods will look and taste together, and whether they can be served without a great deal of last-minute fuss. Some menus include a choice of main course or dessert recipes. Usually, one of these is much simpler to prepare than the other or calls for more readily available ingredients, allowing you to choose according to your schedule and what the supermarket can supply. But even when choices are not specified, all of the menus allow for complete flexibility, since each recipe can stand on its own. If peaches look most tempting in the market, you should feel free to substitute a luscious pie for the dessert listed in a given menu. Or, if you're planning a dinner party but lack the time to make a fancy cake or custard, don't hesitate to look for simpler versions of these desserts in the lunch or quick supper chapters. In both instances, the Index can guide you to appropriate substitutions. It includes recipes for most seasonal fruits and

1

vegetables, and the fresh tastes of these can enter easily into any meal. Look under the key ingredient of a dish, such as asparagus or orange, and you'll find suitable alternatives to the recipes featured in any specific menu.

Another good guide to substitutions is the regional accent of the menu; if it highlights Italian, French, Creole, Chinese, or Mexican flavors you can borrow recipes from another menu of similar origins.

Each menu chapter is based on certain popular expectations—such as light food for brunch or lunch and extra side dishes for a holiday feast, but there are no firm rules. Some of the menus in "Come for Brunch or Lunch" would be just right for a patio supper on a hot summer's day. Many of the menus for "Holidays and Celebrations" would qualify as "Perfect Dinner Parties," and vice versa. The portability of picnic fare makes it perfect for covered dish suppers; its informality also makes it ideal snack fare for weekend guests. The chapter called "Ready When You Are" is devoted to convenient, family-style suppers, but many of the recipes in "Cooking for a Crowd" are just as easy, since quantity cooking also calls for streamlined, do-ahead preparations. Throughout the book there are breads and desserts that can be added to the selection in "Come for Coffee and . . ."

Comfort is the key to hospitality, but surprise also has a role to play. When everyone's convinced that spring will never come, you might lighten the mood considerably by serving an indoor "barbecue" instead of a more formal dinner. The intriguing flavors of an Indian or Chinese dinner can be just the change of pace everyone craves after Christmas turkeys and hams. Days with too much work and not much else could be the best dates to declare time out for a tabletop trip to Italy or Spain, or a romantic dinner for two.

The Look of the Table

Honesty and individuality are important keys to hospitality. After all, guests come to your house to socialize with you. They will feel most welcome if you feel comfortable with all aspects of the meal. Table settings should reflect your tastes and preferences. You can create an attractive setting with a wide variety of dishes, linens, and decorative accents, using these principles.

The Basic Settings. The arrangement of dishes and silverware has one objective—the diner's convenience. The customary setting is: dinner plate in the center, forks to the left, knives and spoons to the right. If an appetizer is served, the appetizer fork is placed to the outside of the spoons. Silverware should be placed in the order of use with the napkin to the far left. Standard variations are: butter spreaders on bread and butter plates; appetizer forks placed on appetizer plates; and dessert forks and spoons placed above and parallel to the dinner plate with the fork next to the dish, pointed right, and the spoon above it pointed left. If used, bread and butter or salad plates are placed to the left of the dinner plate and slightly above it.

If you are serving only one beverage, the glass goes directly above the point of the knife. To serve water and wine, place the water glass to the left of the knife and the wine glass to the right, slightly below the water glass. If two wines will be served, place the wine glasses to the right of the knife in the order of use, one slightly above the other. Wine glasses should be removed after the appropriate course.

It's perfectly all right to mix and

match dishes, glasses, and silverware if the overall effect is attractive. Eight unmatched wine goblets can look spectacular if each is an interesting antique. You can use china dinner plates with glass or plastic salad plates if the designs match well. As with all dimensions of tablesetting, the thought that goes into a harmonious and creative ensemble can be more impressive and much more entertaining than fancy sets of china and crystal.

Colors. The colors you choose can set the tone of the whole meal. At one extreme, pale colors suggest formality, and bright colors invite informality. But there are infinite options in between. Think of a white cloth set with white china and silver candlesticks. Sounds formal, doesn't it? Now think how the mood could be relaxed by adding red napkins and green candles.

Red, white, and green are the colors of the Italian flag—an appropriate scheme for a relaxed Italian meal. Think of a striped cloth, colored napkins, and wooden candleholders. An informal arrangement? Not necessarily. If the stripes and napkins are in muted shades, such as sea greens or mauves, and contemporary in design, the look can be utterly elegant.

You can create a very pleasant effect that's neither formal nor informal by keying the color scheme to a single focal point. If lilacs or tiger lilies are blooming in your yard, set a big bouquet on the sideboard. Then set the table as simply as possible, with perhaps lavender candles to reflect the lilacs or yellow napkins to complement the lilies. A nice way to get better acquainted with new friends is to arrange something that has special meaning to

Table setting for a formal dinner.

you, such as a collection of seashells or antique bottles, on a sideboard. Pick up one or two of the colors for the table.

Another color cue may come from the food itself. If the menu has the flavor of, say, New Orleans, then continue the theme with the festive colors of Mardi Gras.

Texture and Contours. The essential dining accessories—dishes and silverware—are made of hard materials. To make a table look inviting, you have to add elements that soften their look. A tablecloth and napkins help, but they don't counter the flatness or the angularity of the implements. Add a small vase of flowers and you'll see a dramatic difference. The delicate texture and shapes of the flowers make all the lines and surfaces seem softer.

Keep in mind the need for diverse textures and contours, and you'll recognize other ways to create the harmony. Nubby placemats or napkins can work well, especially if you gather the napkins into rings. Baskets and woodenware are softening elements; candleholders, stemmed goblets, salt and pepper shakers vary the contours. Food can be just as effective as flowers. Sometimes all you need to do to make the table attractive is to set out the first course before guests enter the dining room. A basket of rolls and breadsticks can present interesting contours. A bowl of vegetable relishes or fruit, if they suit the menu, can do the same. In a pinch, you may have to resort to a bit of artifice, such as placing rolled napkins in goblets or using a small green plant as a centerpiece, just for the visual effect.

Garnishes

Garnishes that relate to the foods you're serving or that would complement their flavors, can do much to enhance the meal presentation. Here are some general garnishing ideas you might want to keep in mind when you're shopping and cooking:

Herbs and Leaves. Any herb used in a recipe in fresh or dried form makes an appropriate garnish in fresh form. Parsley comes immediately to mind, of course. A sprig or sprinkling of fresh dill, rosemary, basil, thyme—any fresh herb in season—will have the same refreshing effect. Use watercress and curly endive when the tanginess and crunch of the leaves might perk up a creamy or mild dish. And don't overlook things you might otherwise discard, such as celery leaves, carrot fronds, and chopped beet greens or broccoli leaves—all are natural garnishing assets.

Fruit and Vegetable Peels. Cooks with a flair for garnishing tend to save everything! Remember that the next time you peel an orange, lemon, lime, tomato, cucumber, zucchini, yellow squash, or turnip. All of these parings can be turned into curls or "flowers." Using a vegetable peeler, remove the peel in long strips. To make curls, just roll up the peel, secure with a toothpick, and drop in ice water; for long-term storage, freeze the curls in water in ice cube trays and thaw as needed. There's really nothing to it. A spiral of lemon or orange peel set off by some greenery can make a platter of fish look special. Curls of cucumber or zucchini peel can attract attention to a pallid bowl of dip or dressing on a buffet table. The delicacy of tomato, yellow squash, and turnip peels makes them suitable for "roses." Roll up one strip loosely; then fit a second tightly rolled strip inside it. Add a "stem" of watercress or flat-leaf parsley, if you wish. "Roses" set off meat platters especially well.

Grated Vegetables. Grate a carrot or

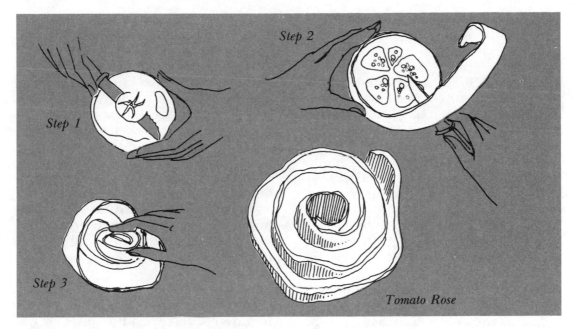

Step 1

Step 2

Step 3

Tomato Rose

a few radishes over a salad or pale dish that could be perked up by the orange or red-and-white color contrast.

Chopped Vegetables. When a recipe calls for chopped tomato, pepper, olives, celery, or green onions, you can highlight it by chopping some extra to garnish the top. This is a good tip to follow with soups, casseroles, dips, sauces, and other foods where ingredients lose their separate colors when cooked together.

Diced and Sliced Vegetables. Remember while you're shopping that vegetables come in so many colors that there are numerous choices for natural contrast. Think of diced red peppers on a dish of cooked corn, fresh peas on a seafood casserole, or a rim of shredded red cabbage for a platter of pork chops. In fact, it's safe to say that any tempting vegetable can be turned into a garnish, but some may need to be cooked a bit. Imagine roast beef garlanded with blanched broccoli flowerets and cherry tomatoes; mashed potatoes topped with steamed shredded sweet potato and a sprin-

kling of nutmeg; or any egg dish accented with cooked asparagus tips. To turn a small amount of a raw cut-up vegetable into a garnish, microwave it with a few spoonfuls of water, covered, on High for a minute or two.

Chopped Nuts. Any recipe that calls for chopped nuts can be garnished with the same kind of nuts left whole or in large pieces. The crunchiness of nuts also makes them a nice accent for foods of smooth consistency, such as soups and creamy salads. Spread the nuts on a baking sheet and toast them in a moderate oven for a few minutes to bring out the flavor.

Seafood. Cooked shrimp and crabmeat are so appealing all by themselves that it makes sense to set some aside to top any casserole or salad made with them. Butterfly the shrimp, if you wish, by splitting them lengthwise along the inner curve, to but not through the back; then open them flat.

Chopped Hard Cooked Eggs. Chop the whites and yolks separately so that you can frame a circle of the yellow with a ring of the white. Not only is the color effect lovely, but the soft taste and texture of the egg will blend well with any vinaigrette-dressed salad or vegetable.

Chopped Olives and Pimiento. Surround a circle of chopped black olives with chopped green olives or pimiento and you'll have a tangy "bull's-eye" to perk up bland foods.

Green Onions. Especially versatile because their flavor blends well with so many foods, green onions yield a bonus of delicate green and white rings when sliced for a garnish. Green onion brushes are the perfect garnish for Chinese food, since they may be used as "serving dippers" for sweet-and-sour sauce and other condiments. But they go equally well with Western-style dips and sauces. To make a brush, trim the root end and make six to ten one-inch slits in the white part of the onion; trim the green end but leave some of it attached. Place the brushes in a bowl of ice water and refrigerate; the white part will curl out into a brush shape.

Frosted Grapes and Cranberries. Nobody needs a reminder to use fresh berries to garnish desserts when the harvests are ripe. But grapes and cranberries can bring the same beautiful burst of color to fall and winter tables. To make them sparkle, dip small bunches of grapes or handfuls of berries first in lightly beaten egg white and then in superfine sugar; dry on wire racks. Arrange frosted green and red grapes or cranberries on a "wreath" of grape leaves or holly sprigs to frame a holiday fruit cake.

A Choice of Beverages

The best choice of beverage is the one a guest will most enjoy. Some people will be touched by your thoughtfulness if you stock their favorite soft drink. Others welcome a bottle of mineral water more than anything else. A tall glass of orange juice "on the rocks" can be the kindest offering when friends arrive thirsty after a long trip to your house. These supplies are so easy to overlook when you're worrying about which wine to serve or how much bourbon to buy that this reminder belongs ahead of the following discussion of alcoholic beverages.

Cocktails and Aperitifs. The trend toward lighter pre-dinner drinks has altered the standards of a well-stocked bar. White wine and light beer have joined the ranks of commonly requested drinks such as bourbon, scotch, gin, vodka, rum, rye, and blended whiskey. The concern for lighter tastes has also increased the appeal of popular European aperitifs, such as dry vermouth, Campari, Dubonnet, and Lillet. Chances are that no one will request a specific aperitif, but it's nice to be able to offer one.

To strike a note of informal congeniality as soon as guests arrive, have a pitcher of cocktails—such as Bloody Mary's, whiskey sours, daiquiris, or margaritas—waiting. The drink may not be everyone's first choice, but sipping the same great-tasting cocktail sets a party mood immediately. If you think that some guests might not want an alcoholic drink, blend all the ingredients except the liquor before pouring their drink.

Champagne. If yours is not a cocktail crowd, you might consider a bottle of champagne instead of a pitcher of cocktails for pre-dinner sipping. It will have the same festive effect. There are so many inexpensive sparkling wines available, both domestic and imported, that you don't need a special event to justify popping a cork. Not only does champagne fit the trend toward lighter drinking, but it is also compatible with the tastes of most foods.

For aperitif purposes, you might prefer a sweeter "extra dry" champagne to the very dry "brut" champagne. Brut champagne can be served throughout a meal, while extra dry is only appropriate beforehand or with dessert.

The only true Champagne, in the traditional sense, is made in the district of the same name in northern France, and the best champagne is labeled with a vintage year. But excellent sparkling wines are also made in other parts of France as well as in the United States, Spain, Italy, Germany, and other countries. These may be called either champagne or sparkling wine. The Italian product is often labeled "spumante," the German "sekt." Champagne that has been colored pink naturally, by allowing the grapes to begin fermenting with the skins intact, can be extra festive and delicious, but beware of the sweetness of sparkling wines colored pink with additives.

The classic champagne glass is flute-shaped, its narrow contours designed to minimize the rate at which bubbles escape. But any wine glass can be used. The only champagne rule that should always be observed is to keep the bottle pointed away from people when you're removing the cork. To minimize chances of spillage, hold the bottle at a 45-degree angle, remove the wire around the cork, grasp the cork firmly, and slowly twist the bottle and cork apart.

Wine with Dinner. The custom of drinking wine with dinner is relatively new to many Americans. So there's a lot of confusion attached to the rite. Therefore, you'll find wine suggestions given with the menus in this book whenever appropriate. The suggestions are quite general, and they are not exclusive. They will mention a type of wine, such as a red Burgundy or a Chardonnay. But these names cover a vast range of quality and price. It's up to you to make the final selection. The best way to proceed is to mention the type of wine to your wine merchant and let the merchant present the options available in that category. A reliable and knowledgeable merchant will point out that Chardonnay, for example, refers only to a kind of grape. The

From left: champagne, red burgundy, white wine, and sherry glasses.

wine made from that grape may be an inexpensive Italian table wine, a medium-priced white French Burgundy, or a top-vintage California Chardonnay. A red Burgundy may be a California jug wine or a vintage bottle from one of the best châteaus in the Burgundy region of France. The wine recommendations in this book have been designed so that any of these selections will be compatible with the food.

Americans are fortunate to find wines from so many countries stocked in local stores. This makes it possible to enhance many ethnic meals with wines that come from the same region as the recipes. Such matches have been proposed whenever appropriate, not only because the wines will taste especially good with the food but also because many of them offer good price value. The most time-honored wine custom, however, is simply to drink what is readily available and affordable. Europeans customarily drink the wines made locally, whether red or white. They don't worry too much about precise flavor matings, and neither should you. There are white wines robust enough to flatter beef and pork, and red wines light enough for chicken and fish. You can stick with one or the other, if that's what you prefer.

One bottle of wine or champagne will provide two three-ounce glasses each for four diners. Most people use all-purpose wine glasses nowadays. But tradition calls for larger-mouthed glasses for red wines to allow them to breathe and smaller glasses for white wine. Fill glasses only two-thirds full. White wines and sweet wines should be chilled. Full-bodied red wines should stand at room temperature, uncorked, for about 30 minutes before pouring. Light and fruity red wines benefit from brief chilling in the refrigerator.

After Dinner. Dessert wines are gaining in popularity as people discover their mellow sweetness. A glass of French Sauternes or Barsac; late-harvest German, Alsatian, or California Gewurtztraminer; sweet spumante or other sparkling wine; or Port, Madeira, or Marsala wine will provide a wonderful excuse to linger around the table after dinner. With fruit and plain cookies, they offer a fine substitute for more elaborate desserts.

A choice of brandies and liqueurs with coffee will also invite conversation to continue after the table has been cleared. These, too, can be turned into ad hoc desserts, just by spooning them over ice cream or drizzling some over coffee dolloped with whipped cream.

The Difference a Crowd Makes

Every aspect of party planning becomes magnified when you're cooking for more than twelve. Obviously, you need more food, more seating area, and more dishes, silverware, napkins, and glasses. You might also need more coat hangers, ash trays, guest towels, ice cubes, coasters, and paper products than you normally keep on hand. The best way to keep track of it all is to make more detailed lists than you would for a smaller group, with the following considerations in mind.

Seating and Type of Service. You have to anticipate how guests will be seated before you can start thinking about the food. The two concerns are inseparable. If guests will be balancing plates on their laps, then you should be certain that the food doesn't require knives. But this doesn't mean finger food only. You could also serve chili, a casserole, or a hearty soup. If there will be a place setting for each guest, you have to calculate whether the food can arrive at the table in prime condition. You might be courting disaster to attempt fish for twenty, for example, because fish overcooks so easily. Chicken and ham would be more cautious choices.

Once you've decided how guests will dine, you can make up the list of seating and serving requirements. Start with tables and chairs—will you need to rent or borrow them? What surfaces do you have available for buffet service—can you divide the food among appetizer, main course, and dessert tables? Whatever the answers, you'll need to add to the list tablecloths, dishes, dining implements, napkins, salt and pepper shakers, and appropriate decorations. Write down the source of each item as you list it—to remind yourself to rent or borrow in plenty of time—and whatever cleaning or arranging will need to be done.

Serving Dishes and Utensils. Weeks before the party, write down the serving dishes and utensils you'll need for each dish. Then borrow or improvise whatever you may lack, and make sure that what you do have is cleaned and polished long before you get caught up in the last day or so of preparations. You can turn large baking sheets into attractive serving trays by covering them with aluminum foil or gold metallic wrapping paper and placing fresh lemon or grape leaves (remember to order from florist) over the paper. A large bread board or marble pastry slab can also be pressed into service. Baskets are extremely versatile because you can place otherwise plain-looking dishes inside them. Sometimes you'll need to create a border of lettuce or other greenery around the dish to conceal an unattractive gap between the sides of the dish and the basket. You might also need to raise the dish inside the basket by placing a folded cloth or another dish, up-side down, underneath.

Party Presentation

All the considerations of color, textures, and contours discussed in "The Look of the Table" apply to party settings, but there's one big difference: You should be much bolder. A pleasant-looking table set for eight can look downright dull when the same settings are repeated for 20. And by the same token, decorative accents that would interrupt the serenity of a small dinner can be just what you need to make a party room look festive.

The Total Party Space. Imagine the party area as a grouping of smaller spaces. If you're setting up four tables of six settings each, for example, think about how you could decorate each table a little differently and still achieve a harmonious look. You might use cloths of complementary colors or varied flower arrangements. Everything should still match, but the room will look more inviting if everything isn't exactly the same. This overall approach to the space will also enable you to fit unmatched dishes and utensils into an attractive context, such as patterned dishes on white cloths and white dishes on colored cloths that match a color in the patterned dishes.

The principle is the same, but the applications differ when you're serving buffet-style. It often makes sense to divide the food among two or more serving areas rather than invite a traffic jam around one table. Look at the entire party space—living room, dining room, and kitchen or den, too, if appropriate—and think of the areas convenient for mingling. Then treat each one as a separate focal point of the party but as a part of a unified decorating scheme. If you have a dip and vegetable relishes on one table, for example, and desserts on another, both will look more tempting if the decorating motifs are coordinated. This doesn't mean that if there's a vase of roses near the desserts that there should also be one next to the appetizers. But everything will look brighter if the appetizer table matches or complements the rose motif in some way—perhaps with a cloth that's a paler shade of the green of the leaves, or with a garnish of tomato roses. The details can be extremely subtle, but they will succeed in linking the foods in a lavish-looking presentation.

Consider the height of your presentation. Be aware that people in a large group tend to remain standing longer than they would in a small group. So you should raise some things to their level of vision, just to make the setting more interesting. You might use taller arrangements of flowers and fruit than usual and rearrange vases, candlesticks, and other decorative accents to fit the stand-up perspective.

An Inviting Buffet. Pay close attention to the scale of foods on a buffet table. Small dishes tend to get lost if they're placed next to a large platter or chafing dish. So think about ways to make them stand out. If you have a small bowl of a cooked vegetable, you might place it in a larger bowl or on a platter and make a garland around the small bowl with other kinds of vegetables—a wreath of cooked broccoli or brussels sprouts around a dish of carrots or a border of celery sticks and radishes around a dish of peas. This is the kind of artifice that might look out of place at a regular dinner table, but fits the more dramatic dimensions of a buffet.

Give the food an aura of overabundance. This is a trick that requires little extra preparation and needn't cost very much. But it will make people feel that your party is a special occasion. The trick can be as simple as a big basketful of shiny red apples, golden pears, or long loaves of French bread placed near the prepared food. It can be a matter of filling a basket with raw vegetables—cabbages, eggplants, carrots, peppers, or any garden variety—and placing a platter of crudités on top of the "cornucopia." It could even be a big bowl of fresh cranberries to frame a dish of cranberry sauce. Whatever foods you use this way will no doubt be left over for other uses. But they will have made an important visual statement—not only in colors and shapes, but also, intangibly, about the spirit of generosity in your home. And that, too, is the guiding spirit in the menus and recipes that follow.

Page 11: *A profusion of flowers rises above guests' line of vision at a table set with Shrimp-Stuffed Artichokes to begin the Elegant Fish Dinner (page 88).*

Page 12: *Surprise your guests with the Tropical Flavor Luncheon (page 38) of Curried Chicken Salad with Avocado-Pecan Bread and Mango Bread spread with cream cheese, Appleade Fizz, and Key Lime Pie.*

Come For Brunch or Lunch

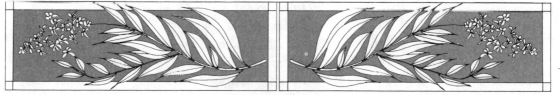

You can gather guests for brunch or lunch after a game of tennis or before a club meeting, after weekend chores are done or before the big game. It's the easiest invitation to fit into hectic schedules.

It's also by far the easiest meal for a cook to prepare and serve. Daylight sets the mood for informal place settings—preferably bright—and streamlined menus. Focus on a single dish with fresh fruit or a salad and a light dessert to round it out. Add a loaf of homemade bread and a good cup of coffee, and success is assured.

Because the fragrance of hot coffee and bread can be the best lunchtime greeting, you may want to make some extra provisions for these. Be prepared to offer decaffeinated coffee and a pot of good-quality tea, in addition to regular coffee. A standby batch of bread or muffins can always be kept frozen, thawed overnight in the refrigerator, and popped into the oven when the doorbell rings.

The menus in this chapter have been developed around a single convenient strategy. The breads and desserts are all do-ahead and the side dishes have been kept simple. This allows you to feature an entrée that's a bit festive and fun, such as crêpes, quiche, or a seafood bisque, without getting up at the crack of dawn to pull a midday meal together.

Crêpes for Brunch or Lunch

Peach-Berry Compote
Tuna Crêpes
or
Crab Crêpes with Shrimp Sauce
Herbed Tomato Aspic with Asparagus
Brown Sugar Muffins
Cream Cheese Squares

Serves 8

You can almost wake up to this brunch ready-made. Even the crêpe fillings can be made the night before and refrigerated, but they're so easy that there's no reason to worry about doing them ahead.

Peach-Berry Compote

Raspberries, blueberries, and peaches have a definite affinity; together they make a light, delicious way to start or end a meal.

5 large ripe peaches, peeled and
 sliced
1 cup fresh blueberries or frozen
 and thawed
1 cup fresh raspberries or frozen
 and thawed

¾ cup superfine sugar or ⅔ cup
 granulated sugar
6 fresh mint leaves

Place peaches and blueberries in 1-quart casserole dish. Mash raspberries through a sieve. Combine raspberries and sugar in blender, and blend 3 minutes, or beat at high speed of electric mixer in a deep narrow bowl for 8 minutes. Pour puree over fruit. Bake at 350° for 12 minutes; cool and refrigerate. Do not stir until ready to serve. Spoon into individual serving bowls and top with fresh mint leaves. Yield: 6 to 8 servings.

Note: To serve as a dessert, top with sweetened whipped cream.

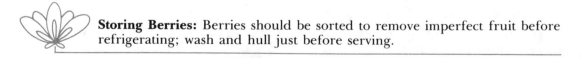

Storing Berries: Berries should be sorted to remove imperfect fruit before refrigerating; wash and hull just before serving.

Basic Crêpes

1 cup plus 2 tablespoons
   all-purpose flour
1½ cups milk
3 eggs

1 tablespoon butter or margarine,
   melted
⅛ teaspoon salt
Vegetable oil

Combine all ingredients except vegetable oil in container of electric blender; process until smooth. Refrigerate batter 1 to 2 hours.

Brush the bottom of a 6-inch crêpe pan or heavy skillet with vegetable oil; place pan over medium heat until oil is just hot, not smoking.

Pour 3 tablespoons batter into pan; quickly tilt pan in all directions so that batter covers the pan in a thin film. Cook about 1 minute.

Lift edge of crêpe to test for doneness. Crêpe is ready for flipping when it can be shaken loose from the pan. Flip the crêpe, and cook about 30 seconds on the other side. (This side is rarely more than spotty brown and is the side on which the filling is placed.) Place on a towel to cool. Stack between layers of waxed paper to prevent sticking. Repeat until all batter is used. Yield: 16 crêpes.

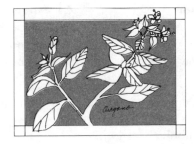

Tuna Crêpes

½ cup slivered almonds
3 tablespoons butter
1 (13-ounce) can water-packed tuna
¼ cup lemon juice
¼ teaspoon hot sauce
1 tablespoon chopped parsley
¼ teaspoon salt
⅛ teaspoon mace

1 (6-ounce) can sliced mushrooms,
   drained
¼ teaspoon dried green onion
1 (10¾-ounce) can cream of
   mushroom soup, undiluted
¼ cup sherry
Basic Crêpes

Sauté almonds in butter in a heavy skillet for 8 to 10 minutes. Drain on paper towels and set aside.

Drain tuna in colander and place in large mixing bowl. Pour lemon juice and hot sauce over tuna; add parsley, salt, mace, mushrooms, dried green onion, and enough mushroom soup to hold mixture together. Spoon ¼ cup tuna mixture in center of each crêpe; roll up and place seam side down in a greased 12- x 8- x 2-inch baking dish. Dribble sherry over each crêpe and sprinkle 1 tablespoon reserved almonds over each. Bake at 350° for 30 minutes. Serve hot. Yield: 8 servings.

Crab Crêpes with Shrimp Sauce

1 pound lump or flake crabmeat,
    drained
1 cup finely chopped celery
½ cup mayonnaise
¼ cup chopped green onions with
    tops
2 teaspoons lemon juice

1 (2-ounce) jar diced pimiento,
    drained
1 teaspoon Worcestershire sauce
½ teaspoon curry powder
Basic Crêpes (page 15)
Shrimp Sauce

Combine all ingredients, except crêpes and Shrimp Sauce, in a medium mixing bowl; mix well. Spread 2 tablespoons of crab mixture evenly over each crêpe; roll up, and place seam side down in a lightly greased 13- x 9- x 2-inch baking dish. Bake, covered, at 350° for 25 minutes or until thoroughly heated.

Place 2 crêpes on each warmed serving dish; spoon Shrimp Sauce over crêpes. Serve immediately. Yield: 8 servings.

Shrimp Sauce

¼ cup butter or margarine
¼ cup all-purpose flour
2 cups milk
1 cup peeled, cooked, and deveined
    shrimp, chopped

2 teaspoons lemon juice
1½ teaspoons tomato paste
½ teaspoon salt
⅛ teaspoon red pepper

Melt butter in a heavy saucepan over low heat; add flour, stirring until smooth. Cook 1 minute, stirring constantly. Gradually add milk; cook over medium heat, stirring constantly, until thickened and bubbly.

Add remaining ingredients; mix well. Continue to cook over medium heat until thoroughly heated. Serve immediately. Yield: about 2 cups.

Herbed Tomato Aspic with Asparagus

3 envelopes unflavored gelatin
¾ cup cold water
2½ cups tomato juice, divided
1 (6-ounce) can tomato paste
¼ cup vinegar
3 tablespoons lemon juice
1½ teaspoons dried whole basil

1 teaspoon sugar
1 teaspoon salt
⅛ teaspoon black pepper
⅛ teaspoon onion powder
½ teaspoon Worcestershire sauce
1 (10½-ounce) can tender green cut
    asparagus spears, drained

Soften gelatin in water. Bring 1 cup tomato juice to a boil in a small saucepan; remove from heat and add gelatin, stirring until dissolved. Transfer gelatin mixture to a large mixing bowl; add tomato paste, and stir until blended. Add remaining ingredients except asparagus; stir well. Chill until consistency of unbeaten egg white. Fold in asparagus. Spoon into a lightly oiled 6-cup mold; chill until firm. Yield: 8 servings.

Brown Sugar Muffins

Hot bread was an essential part of a plantation breakfast. This very old recipe comes from Georgia Plantation, in the heart of the Louisiana sugar country on Bayou La Fourche. Exceptionally light, with an unusual flavor, the muffin is delicious with coffee for a brunch.

½ cup butter, softened
1 cup firmly packed dark brown
    sugar
1 egg, beaten
2 cups all-purpose flour
1 teaspoon baking soda

1 teaspoon baking powder
¼ teaspoon salt
1 cup milk
2 teaspoons vanilla extract
½ cup chopped pecans

Cream butter in a large mixing bowl; gradually add sugar and egg. Beat until fluffy.

Sift together flour, soda, baking powder, and salt; add to creamed mixture alternately with milk, beginning and ending with flour mixture. Stir well after each addition. Stir in vanilla and pecans.

Spoon into greased muffin pans, filling two-thirds full. Bake at 400° for 15 minutes. Yield: 24 muffins.

Lisa Walker Turner's Cream Cheese Squares

These vanish so quickly in my home, I can't tell you how long they will keep! But they can be refrigerated a day or two and are wonderful for any kind of party.

½ cup margarine, melted
3 eggs, divided
1 (18.25-ounce) package yellow
    cake mix
1 (8-ounce) package cream cheese,
    softened

1 (16-ounce) package powdered
    sugar, sifted
1 tablespoon vanilla extract

Combine margarine, 1 egg, and cake mix in a large bowl; mix well. Press mixture into an ungreased 13- x 9- x 2-inch baking pan. Set aside.

Combine 2 eggs, cream cheese, powdered sugar, and vanilla; beat until smooth. Spread topping over cake layer. Bake at 350° for 50 minutes. Cool on wire rack. Chill. Cut into 2-inch squares. Yield: approximately 2 dozen squares.

Quiche for Brunch or Lunch

Chilled Melon
Salmon Mushroom Quiche
or
Chicken Liver and Mushroom Pie
Fresh Spinach Salad
Sugar Crust Cake

Serves 6 to 8

---

uiche is at its best warm from the oven; it tends to toughen a bit if reheated. But you can pre-bake the pastry anytime and refrigerate or freeze it — no need to thaw before filling. The cake and salad dressing are do-ahead recipes.

Salmon Mushroom Quiche

This quiche will freeze well prior to baking. Do not thaw; bake as directed below, adding 10 to 15 minutes as needed.

Pastry for 9-inch quiche dish or
    pieplate
¼ pound fresh mushrooms,
    chopped
2 green onions, minced
2 tablespoons butter, melted
1 (7¾-ounce) can salmon, drained
3 eggs, lightly beaten
1½ cups whipping cream
1 teaspoon lemon juice

½ teaspoon salt
⅛ teaspoon pepper
Pinch of nutmeg
2 tablespoons fresh chives, finely
    minced, or 2½ teaspoons dried
3 tablespoons grated Gruyère or
    Swiss cheese
2 pitted ripe olives, thinly sliced
    (optional)
Parsley sprigs (optional)

Line a 9-inch quiche dish or pieplate with pastry; trim excess pastry around edges. Prick bottom and sides of pastry with a fork. Bake at 400° for 3 minutes; remove from oven, and gently prick with a fork. Bake 5 minutes longer. Remove from oven and set aside.

Sauté mushrooms and green onions in a heavy skillet in melted butter about 7 minutes. Remove from heat and mix with salmon. Beat salmon mixture with a heavy wire whisk until smooth. Pour mixture into pastry shell.

Combine eggs, cream, lemon juice, salt, pepper, nutmeg, and chives. Pour over salmon mixture; sprinkle with cheese. Bake at 350° for 30 to 35 minutes or until set. Garnish with olives and parsley sprigs, if desired. Yield: 8 servings.

Chicken Liver and Mushroom Pie

3 slices bacon
1 pound chicken livers, coarsely
    chopped
2 tablespoons butter or margarine
½ pound mushrooms, sliced
2 green onions, chopped
3 eggs, beaten
1 (5.33-ounce) can evaporated milk,
    undiluted

½ cup grated Parmesan cheese
¼ teaspoon salt
¼ teaspoon dried basil leaves
⅛ teaspoon ground nutmeg
⅛ teaspoon hot sauce
Pastry for 9-inch quiche dish or
    pieplate

Cook bacon in a large skillet until crisp; drain on paper towels. Crumble and set aside, reserving drippings in skillet.

Sauté livers in reserved drippings. Remove livers and keep warm. Add butter to skillet; sauté mushrooms and onion until tender. Remove from heat.

Combine eggs, milk, cheese, salt, basil, nutmeg, and hot sauce in a large mixing bowl; beat well. Set aside.

Arrange livers, mushrooms, and onion in prepared pastry shell; sprinkle with reserved bacon. Pour egg mixture over bacon. Bake at 325° for 30 to 35 minutes. Cut into wedges to serve. Yield: 8 servings.

Pastry

1¼ cups all-purpose flour
¼ teaspoon salt
⅓ cup shortening

1 egg, beaten
1 teaspoon lemon juice
1 teaspoon Dijon mustard

Combine flour and salt in a medium mixing bowl; cut in shortening with a pastry blender until mixture resembles coarse meal. Combine egg and lemon juice in a small mixing bowl; add to flour mixture and stir with a fork until dry ingredients are moistened.

Roll dough to ⅛-inch thickness on a lightly floured surface. Place in a 9-inch pieplate or quiche pan; trim excess pastry around edges. Fold edges under and flute. Brush bottom of pastry shell with mustard. Bake at 450° for 8 minutes or until pastry is set. Yield: one 9-inch pastry shell.

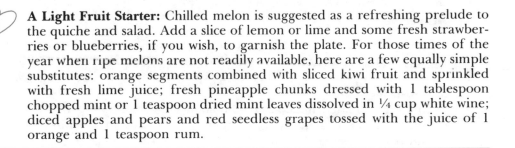

A Light Fruit Starter: Chilled melon is suggested as a refreshing prelude to the quiche and salad. Add a slice of lemon or lime and some fresh strawberries or blueberries, if you wish, to garnish the plate. For those times of the year when ripe melons are not readily available, here are a few equally simple substitutes: orange segments combined with sliced kiwi fruit and sprinkled with fresh lime juice; fresh pineapple chunks dressed with 1 tablespoon chopped mint or 1 teaspoon dried mint leaves dissolved in ¼ cup white wine; diced apples and pears and red seedless grapes tossed with the juice of 1 orange and 1 teaspoon rum.

Fresh Spinach Salad

1 pound fresh spinach, torn into
  bite-size pieces
6 slices bacon, cooked and
  crumbled
6 medium-size fresh mushrooms,
  sliced

Spinach Salad Dressing
1 hard-cooked egg, chopped
2 tablespoons grated Parmesan
  cheese

Combine spinach, bacon, and mushrooms in a large bowl. Add dressing and toss well. Place salad in individual serving bowls and sprinkle with egg and Parmesan cheese. Yield: 6 to 8 servings.

Spinach Salad Dressing

¾ cup vegetable oil
¼ cup white wine vinegar

½ teaspoon salt
½ teaspoon dry mustard

Combine all ingredients in a jar. Cover tightly and shake vigorously. Chill several hours. Yield: about 1 cup.

Sonia Nosser's Sugar Crust Cake

A delightful cake with a lovely texture and crunchy crust.

1 cup shortening
1¾ cups sugar
6 eggs
2 cups all-purpose flour, sifted 3
  times

⅛ teaspoon salt
1 teaspoon vanilla extract
½ teaspoon almond extract

Cream shortening; gradually add sugar, beating at medium speed of an electric mixer until light and fluffy. Add eggs, one at a time, beating well after each addition.

Combine flour and salt; add to creamed mixture ½ cup at a time. Mix well after each addition. Stir in flavorings.

Pour batter into a greased and floured 10-inch tube pan or Bundt pan. Bake at 325° for 1 hour or until a wooden pick inserted in center comes out clean. Cool in pan 10 minutes; remove from pan and let cool completely. Yield: one 10-inch cake.

Down Home Brunch

Fruit Juice
Easy-Does-It Casserole
Fried Ham Slices
Nectarine Sauté
Corn Fritters
Sourdough Coffee Cake

Serves 4 to 6

---

asy-Does-It Casserole offers a delicious change from plain eggs and saves you from last-minute scrambling. The ham, nectarines, and corn fritters can all be cooked while the casserole is in the oven. If your timing is off a bit, don't worry — the casserole will hold for 30 minutes out of the oven. Make the fritter batter the night before, if you wish, but bring it to room temperature before frying; extra batter can be put back in the refrigerator for the next day.

Make the Sourdough Starter at least 2 days ahead or keep a batch in the refrigerator and replenish it with "Food" once a week. Remember to stir the starter every day. Or you may choose a quick dessert from "Come for Coffee and . . ." such as Honeycomb Coffee Cake (page 256) or Pineapple Pound Cake (page 268).

Easy-Does-It Casserole

Mary Alice Bookhart's Easy-Does-It Casserole inspired this savory variation. It's like a quiche without a crust—tantalizing and creamy.

4 eggs	Pinch of red pepper
2 cups small curd cottage cheese	⅓ cup chopped parsley
½ teaspoon salt	2 teaspoons to 1 tablespoon Dijon
¼ teaspoon black pepper	mustard
½ teaspoon nutmeg	1 tablespoon butter or margarine,
Dash of paprika	cut into pieces

Beat the eggs in large mixing bowl until light; stir in remaining ingredients. Pour into a lightly buttered 1-quart casserole, and bake at 325° for 50 to 60 minutes until firm to the touch. Serve hot or warm. Yield: 4 to 6 servings.

Note: This recipe can be doubled and baked in a 2-quart casserole.

Nectarine Sauté

When nectarines are abundant, try this breakfast treat. At other times of the year, substitute two or three sweet red apples, thinly sliced. Either way, it's also a wonderful accompaniment for lamb, pork, or chicken.

3 or 4 firm ripe nectarines, unpeeled
2 tablespoons butter

2 tablespoons dark brown sugar
1 tablespoon lemon juice

Slice nectarines. Heat butter and brown sugar in a small skillet over medium-high heat until bubbly. Add nectarines; cook until heated through and glazed, about 15 minutes. Sprinkle with lemon juice and serve hot. This dish does not reheat successfully. Yield: about 4 to 6 servings.

Corn Fritters

They're fine for dinner too, especially with ham or chicken.

½ cup plus 2 tablespoons all-purpose flour
⅓ cup cornmeal
1½ teaspoons baking powder
1 teaspoon sugar
½ teaspoon salt
1 (7-ounce) can whole kernel corn, undrained

2 eggs
1 tablespoon vegetable oil
1 (8.5-ounce) can cream-style corn
Vegetable oil
Maple syrup or honey (optional)

Sift together flour, cornmeal, baking powder, sugar, and salt in a small mixing bowl; set aside. Drain corn, reserving 2 tablespoons plus 1½ teaspoons liquid. Set aside.

Combine eggs, 1 tablespoon vegetable oil, and reserved corn liquid in a medium mixing bowl; beat on medium speed of electric mixer until thoroughly blended. Add cream-style corn, beating well. Gradually add flour mixture, stirring until well blended. Fold in drained whole kernel corn.

Drop mixture by tablespoonfuls into deep, hot oil (375°); cook until golden brown, turning once. Drain on paper towels; serve hot with maple syrup or honey, if desired. Yield: about 2 dozen.

Sue Busby's Sourdough Coffee Cake

A tasty treat for the sourdough lover.

¼ cup firmly packed dark brown
    sugar
1 cup plus 1 tablespoon all-purpose
    flour, divided
½ teaspoon ground cinnamon
¼ cup finely chopped pecans
½ cup sugar
¾ teaspoon baking soda

1 cup Sourdough Starter
½ cup vegetable oil
1 egg, lightly beaten
1½ teaspoons vanilla extract
⅛ teaspoon salt
2 tablespoons butter or margarine,
    melted

Combine dark brown sugar, 1 tablespoon flour, cinnamon, and pecans in a small mixing bowl; stir well and set aside.

Combine remaining flour, sugar, soda, Sourdough Starter, and oil in a medium mixing bowl; beat on medium speed of electric mixer until well-blended. Stir in egg, vanilla, and salt; mix well.

Heavily grease a 6-cup Bundt pan; sprinkle one-third of reserved sugar mixture over pan. Drizzle melted butter over sugar mixture in pan. Pour one-half of batter into pan; sprinkle another one-third of sugar mixture over batter. Gently pour remaining batter into pan, and sprinkle with remaining sugar mixture.

Bake at 350° for 35 minutes or until a wooden pick inserted in center comes out clean. Cool 10 minutes in pan on a wire rack; invert onto serving platter. Remove pan; slice and serve warm. Yield: 1 coffeecake.

Sourdough Starter

1 package dry yeast
2½ cups warm water (105° to 115°),
    divided
2 cups all-purpose flour

1 teaspoon salt
3 tablespoons sugar
Food (recipe follows)

Dissolve yeast in ½ cup warm water; let stand 5 minutes. Combine next 3 ingredients in a medium-size nonmetal bowl; mix well. Gradually stir in 2 cups warm water. Add yeast mixture, and mix well. Cover loosely with plastic wrap or cheesecloth, and let stand in a warm place (80° to 85°) for 72 hours, stirring 2 to 3 times daily. Place fermented mixture in refrigerator, and stir daily; use within 11 days.

Remove Sourdough Starter from refrigerator and let stand at room temperature at least 1 hour. Stir well, and measure amount of starter needed for recipe. Replenish remaining starter with Food, and return to refrigerator; use within 2 to 14 days, stirring daily.

Repeat the procedure for using and replenishing starter. Yield: about 2 cups.

Food

½ cup sugar
1 cup all-purpose flour

1 cup milk
1 cup instant potato flakes

Stir all ingredients into remaining Sourdough Starter and refrigerate.

American Classics Luncheon

Maryland Escalloped Oysters
Broiled Tomatoes
Fresh Plum Cobbler

Serves 6

The flavors of oysters and fresh summer tomatoes go together well. But scalloped oysters are also a warming dish on a winter's night when you may want to substitute an all-season side dish, such as Green Beans with Chive Butter (page 143) or Sautéed Spinach (page 244) and baked or fried potatoes.

Maryland Escalloped Oysters

A quickly prepared, satisfying dish.

3 (12-ounce) containers Standard
    oysters, undrained
2 chicken-flavored bouillon cubes
¼ teaspoon mace (optional)
1 cup milk
3 tablespoons butter or margarine,
    melted

¼ teaspoon hot sauce
40 saltine crackers, crushed
⅛ teaspoon pepper
¼ teaspoon paprika
2 tablespoons chopped fresh
    parsley

Drain oysters, reserving ½ cup liquor; set oysters aside.

Combine reserved liquor, bouillon cubes, and mace, if desired, in a small saucepan; cook over medium heat, stirring constantly, until bouillon cubes dissolve. Remove from heat; add milk, melted butter, and hot sauce, stirring well. Set aside.

Combine crushed crackers and pepper in a small mixing bowl; mix well. Layer half of cracker mixture in bottom of a buttered 2-quart shallow baking dish. Arrange reserved oysters over crackers, and sprinkle with remaining cracker mixture.

Pour oyster liquor-milk mixture over casserole. Bake at 325° for 35 minutes. Sprinkle with paprika and parsley. Serve hot. Yield: 6 servings.

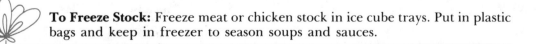 **To Freeze Stock:** Freeze meat or chicken stock in ice cube trays. Put in plastic bags and keep in freezer to season soups and sauces.

Broiled Tomatoes

3 large tomatoes
½ cup fine dry breadcrumbs
1 teaspoon dried whole oregano
2 tablespoons lemon juice

2 teaspoons vegetable oil
1 tablespoon grated Parmesan
  cheese

Remove stems from tomatoes; cut in half crosswise. Combine remaining ingredients; lightly press mixture over top of tomato halves. Broil 6 inches from heat about 7 minutes or until topping is lightly browned. Yield: 6 servings.

Fresh Plum Cobbler

1 cup sugar
¼ teaspoon salt
½ cup butter or margarine
1¼ cups all-purpose flour
¾ teaspoon ground cinnamon,
  divided
¼ teaspoon baking powder
1 egg, lightly beaten
1½ teaspoons almond extract,
  divided

1½ pounds ripe, fresh plums,
  halved and seeded
½ cup whipping cream
¼ cup sugar
1 egg, lightly beaten
½ teaspoon vanilla extract
2 tablespoons sugar
Vanilla ice cream (optional)

Combine sugar and salt in a medium mixing bowl. Cut in butter with a pastry blender until mixture is crumbly. Add flour, ½ teaspoon cinnamon, and baking powder; mix with pastry blender until mixture resembles coarse meal. Remove and reserve 1 cup mixture. Combine 1 beaten egg and 1 teaspoon almond extract; stir into remaining flour mixture to form a soft dough.

Pat dough evenly into a greased 9-inch square baking dish. (Dough may be sticky; flour hands if needed.) Bake at 350° for 10 minutes.

Arrange plums over baked mixture. Combine whipping cream, ¼ cup sugar, 1 beaten egg, vanilla, and remaining almond extract; beat well. Pour cream mixture over plums. Sprinkle with reserved crumb mixture. Combine 2 tablespoons sugar and remaining cinnamon; sprinkle over crumb mixture. Bake at 350° for 45 minutes or until browned and bubbly. Serve warm with ice cream, if desired. Yield: 8 servings.

A Welcoming Luncheon

Wine Coolers
Fresh Vegetable Relishes
Gems of the Ocean Shrimp with Rice Mold
or
Shrimp Eudora
Avocado-Grapefruit Salad
Chocolate-Raspberry Dessert

Serves 6

This menu will leave you ample time to get acquainted with a new friend or neighbor. The only thing to leave for last minute attention is the salad, since the avocado should be peeled and cut just before serving. Try the Easy Bellini wine coolers described in the note; sip them while you're reheating the entrée.

Gems of the Ocean Shrimp with Rice Mold

Hot cooked rice can be molded by packing it tightly into a well buttered mold of desired shape. Turn rice mold out onto serving platter and surround with shrimp mixture.

1 cup (4 ounces) sliced fresh
    mushrooms
½ cup finely chopped green onion
¼ cup finely chopped green pepper
1 stalk celery, finely chopped
2 tablespoons butter or margarine
¼ cup instant-blending flour
1 cup whipping cream
3 pounds uncooked medium
    shrimp, peeled and deveined

½ cup (2 ounces) shredded Colby
    cheese
½ teaspoon salt
½ teaspoon white pepper
½ teaspoon paprika
¼ teaspoon hot sauce
Rice Mold
Parsley sprigs

Sauté mushrooms, green onion, green pepper, and celery in butter in a large skillet until vegetables are tender. Add flour, stirring well. Cook 1 minute, stirring constantly. Gradually add cream; cook over medium heat, stirring constantly, until thickened and bubbly. Stir in shrimp, cheese, salt, pepper, paprika, and hot sauce; cook over medium heat 5 minutes or until shrimp turn pink. Serve hot with rice mold; garnish with parsley. Yield: 6 servings.

Shrimp Eudora

I prepared this to honor my neighbor Eudora Welty on the occasion of the world premiere of
The Ponder Heart, *a new comic opera based on her novel.*

1 cup milk
1 slice onion
1 sprig parsley
¼ cup butter, divided
2 tablespoons all-purpose flour
2 tablespoons whipping cream
Salt to taste
⅛ teaspoon white pepper
⅛ teaspoon nutmeg
⅛ teaspoon ginger
3 dashes hot sauce

½ teaspoon dried green onion
3 cups (12 ounces) fresh
   mushrooms
½ teaspoon chopped fresh parsley
1½ pounds uncooked medium
   shrimp, peeled and deveined
1 tablespoon sherry
1 loaf French bread, cut into
   half-inch slices and lightly
   toasted
Paprika

Scald milk in saucepan with 1 slice onion and 1 parsley sprig. Strain and set aside.

Melt 2 tablespoons butter in a heavy skillet over low heat; add flour, stirring until smooth. Cook 1 minute, stirring constantly. Gradually add strained milk; cook over medium heat, stirring constantly, until mixture is thickened and bubbly. Stir in whipping cream, salt to taste, white pepper, nutmeg, ginger, hot sauce, and green onion. Set aside.

Sauté mushrooms in remaining 2 tablespoons butter in medium skillet.

Combine sauce, mushrooms, parsley, and shrimp; cook over low heat until shrimp turn pink, about 4 to 5 minutes. Stir in sherry before serving. Serve over toasted French bread and sprinkle with paprika. Yield: 6 servings.

Note: This dish reheats well; however, I do not recommend freezing.

Avocado-Grapefruit Salad

2 large grapefruit, peeled, seeded,
   and sectioned
2 ripe avocados, peeled and sliced

Boston lettuce leaves
French Dressing

Arrange grapefruit sections and avocado slices on a lettuce-lined serving platter. Serve with French Dressing. Yield: 6 servings.

French Dressing

1 cup vegetable oil
¼ cup white wine vinegar
¼ cup orange juice
2 tablespoons lemon juice
¼ cup sifted powdered sugar

¼ teaspoon salt
¾ teaspoon dry mustard
1 teaspoon paprika
¾ teaspoon Worcestershire sauce
1 small clove garlic, minced

Process all ingredients in electric blender on medium speed 2 minutes or until thickened. Refrigerate in a covered container. Yield: about 1½ cups.

Chocolate-Raspberry Dessert

This dessert can be layered in parfait glasses or molded in a 5-cup decorative mold.

2⅔ cups milk, divided
⅔ cup plus 2 teaspoons sugar,
   divided
⅓ cup cocoa
1 tablespoon light corn syrup
½ teaspoon vanilla extract
1 (10-ounce) package frozen
   raspberries

3 tablespoons raspberry preserves
⅛ teaspoon almond extract
1½ cups vanilla ice cream, softened
2 envelopes unflavored gelatin
Whipped Cream Topping

Combine ⅔ cup milk, ⅔ cup sugar, cocoa, and corn syrup in a medium saucepan; mix well. Bring to a boil over medium heat, stirring constantly. Remove from heat; stir in vanilla, and set aside.

Thaw raspberries according to package directions. Drain thoroughly and chop.

Combine chopped raspberries, raspberry preserves, and remaining sugar in a medium saucepan; mix well. Bring to a boil over medium heat, stirring constantly. Remove from heat; stir in almond extract, and set aside.

Combine ice cream and 1 cup milk in a large mixing bowl, stirring well; set aside.

Combine remaining 1 cup milk and gelatin in a small saucepan; mix well. Cook, stirring constantly, over low heat until gelatin is dissolved. Remove from heat, and combine with ice cream mixture. Stir until ice cream melts. Add ¾ cup gelatin mixture to reserved raspberry mixture; stir well, and let stand at room temperature. Add remaining gelatin mixture to reserved chocolate mixture; stir well, and let stand at room temperature.

Place 2 cups of chocolate-gelatin mixture in a lightly oiled 5-cup mold; chill until partially set. Gently spoon raspberry-gelatin mixture on top of chocolate layer; chill until partially set. Repeat with remaining chocolate mixture. Cover and chill overnight.

Unmold onto serving platter; garnish with Whipped Cream Topping. Yield: 6 servings.

Whipped Cream Topping

1 cup whipping cream
2 tablespoons sugar
½ teaspoon vanilla extract

1 tablespoon Chambord or other
   raspberry-flavored liqueur

Beat whipping cream in a medium mixing bowl until foamy; gradually add sugar, beating until soft peaks form. Gently fold in vanilla and raspberry liqueur. Chill until ready to use. Yield: about 2 cups.

Wine Coolers: A fizzy light alcoholic beverage can put a lunch or brunch crowd into a party mood. Easy Bellini is a classic feature. Puree unsweetened frozen or fresh peaches; press through sieve. Add superfine sugar to taste, if desired. Place 2 tablespoons juice in each wine glass; fill with chilled sparkling wine.

Salad Luncheon

Chilled Carrot Soup
Salmon Salad
Hot Rolls
Strawberry Shortcake

Serves 6

---

*P*erfect for a summer day—a menu of light fare that benefits from being made and chilled a day ahead. Even the strawberries for the shortcake will taste better if sliced and sweetened in advance, but leave the final assembly of each dessert portion until just before serving.

Chilled Carrot Soup

Even people who claim not to like carrots enjoy this orange-spiked soup. Serve it chilled or hot. For an informal dinner party, carrot soup may be served on the patio in punch cups, allowing the host to complete last minute kitchen jobs.

1 pound carrots	**⅛ teaspoon white pepper**
2 tablespoons butter	**½ cup fresh orange juice**
2 (13¾-ounce) cans chicken broth	**1 cup light cream**
1 medium onion, chopped	**1 tablespoon Cointreau (optional)**
1 bay leaf	**Parsley sprigs**
1¾ teaspoons salt	

Scrape carrots and chop into small pieces. Melt butter in large saucepan; add chicken broth, carrots, onion, bay leaf, salt and pepper. Bring to a boil; cover and simmer until carrots are tender, about 30 to 35 minutes. Puree carrot mixture in blender. Cool. Add orange juice, cream, and Cointreau, if desired. Chill at least 6 hours. Serve in chilled bowls and garnish with a sprig of parsley. Yield: 6 servings.

Note: This soup is also delicious served hot. Pour mixture from blender into a large saucepan to serve hot. Place over low heat, stirring gently until heated.

To Serve Chilled Soups: Pour into long-stemmed crystal goblets, and garnish with parsley, cucumber, sour cream, or chopped dill.

Zollie Kimbrough's Salmon Salad

1 (15½-ounce) can pink or red
　salmon, drained and flaked
1 teaspoon prepared mustard
1 tablespoon lemon juice
2 hard cooked eggs, chopped
2 tablespoons mayonnaise

⅛ teaspoon pepper
2 tablespoons chopped dill pickle
6 medium tomatoes, peeled
Mayonnaise
Paprika
Leaf lettuce

Combine salmon, mustard, lemon juice, eggs, mayonnaise, pepper, and dill pickle in a medium mixing bowl, stirring well. Cover and refrigerate until chilled.

Cut each tomato into 8 wedges, cutting to, but not through, base of tomato. Spread wedges apart to form shell. Spoon salmon salad into tomato shells. Top with a dollop of mayonnaise, and sprinkle with paprika. Serve on lettuce-lined plates. Yield: 6 servings.

Strawberry Shortcake

2 pints ripe strawberries, washed
　and sliced
½ cup sugar, more if berries are
　very tart
2 cups all-purpose flour
1 tablespoon baking powder
½ teaspoon salt
3 tablespoons sugar
3 tablespoons butter or margarine,
　softened

1 (3-ounce) package cream cheese,
　softened
1 egg, lightly beaten
¼ to ½ cup milk
2 tablespoons melted butter
1 pint whipping cream, whipped
　and sweetened

Combine sliced strawberries and ½ cup sugar, stirring gently; chill 1 to 2 hours or overnight.

Combine flour, baking powder, salt, and sugar in a large mixing bowl; cut in butter and cream cheese with a pastry blender. Combine beaten egg with enough milk to make ¾ cup liquid. Gradually stir milk mixture into the flour mixture.

Turn dough out onto a lightly floured board, and knead lightly about 1 minute; divide dough in half and roll each half into a 13-x 9-inch rectangle. Cut each rectangle into 8 strips, approximately 3-x 4-inches. Place on a lightly greased cookie sheet, spread with melted butter, and bake at 425° for 12 to 15 minutes.

Place 1 shortcake strip on individual serving plate; cover with ¼ cup strawberries. Top with another strip and additional ¼ cup strawberries. Repeat procedure with remaining pastry and strawberries. Top with a dollop of whipped cream before serving. Yield: 8 servings.

Spring Luncheon

Chilled Green Pepper Soup
Chicken Carottes
or
Bayou La Fourche Orange Chicken
Sweet Potato Biscuits
Macaroon Dainty
or
Praline Ice Cream Roll

Serves 6 to 8

---

*S*tart with cold soup to take the heat off other preparations. Serve it while the chicken is still in the oven and the rice is cooking. Then you'll need only a few minutes to finish either chicken dish and heat the biscuits.

Chilled Green Pepper Soup

This colorful soup came from Jonathan Naindy-Luxmore, a charming English visitor to Jackson, Mississippi.

8 medium-size green peppers, finely chopped	1 quart boiling water
2 large onions, finely chopped	1 tablespoon all-purpose flour
3 tablespoons butter or margarine, divided	1 cup milk
	¼ teaspoon salt
	⅛ teaspoon pepper
4 chicken-flavored bouillon cubes	1 small red pepper, finely chopped

Sauté green pepper and onion in 2 tablespoons butter in a large skillet until tender. Dissolve bouillon cubes in boiling water.

Melt remaining 1 tablespoon butter in a heavy saucepan over low heat; add flour, stirring until smooth. Cook 1 minute, stirring constantly. Gradually add milk; cook over medium heat, stirring constantly, until thickened and bubbly. Stir in salt and pepper.

Combine chicken-flavored bouillon cubes, white sauce, and green pepper mixture. Pour about one-third of mixture into the container of an electric blender; process until smooth. Pour pureed mixture into a bowl or pitcher and repeat procedure with remaining mixture. Cover and chill. Spoon into individual serving bowls and sprinkle with chopped red pepper to serve. Yield: about 8 cups.

Chicken Carottes

8 chicken breast halves, skinned
2½ teaspoons salt, divided
⅛ teaspoon coarsely ground pepper
¼ cup butter
3 chicken-flavored bouillon cubes
3 cups boiling water
2 tablespoons lemon juice
1 teaspoon dried green onion
1 pound carrots, thinly sliced
1 (3-ounce) package cream cheese, softened

1 (8-ounce) carton commercial sour cream
3 tablespoons finely chopped green pepper
2 tablespoons finely chopped green onion
1 (2-ounce) jar sliced pimiento
½ teaspoon Worcestershire sauce
¼ teaspoon hot sauce
Hot cooked rice

Sprinkle 1¼ teaspoons salt and pepper on chicken. Melt butter in large heavy skillet. Add chicken and cook about 10 minutes or until golden brown on both sides. Remove chicken and place in 3-½-quart shallow baking dish.

Dissolve bouillon cubes in boiling water. Pour half of bouillon in skillet. Stir well and pour over chicken in baking pan. Sprinkle lemon juice and green onion over chicken. Cover and bake at 350° for 1 hour or until tender.

Add carrots and ½ teaspoon salt to remaining bouillon in saucepan. Cover and simmer about 25 minutes or until carrots are tender. Drain; add remaining ¾ teaspoon salt, cream cheese, sour cream, green pepper, green onion, pimiento, Worcestershire sauce and hot sauce. Stir to blend.

Remove chicken from baking pan and place on serving platter. Add carrot mixture to juices in baking pan and stir to mix thoroughly. Pour over chicken. Serve with hot cooked rice. Yield: 8 servings.

Bayou La Fourche Orange Chicken

1 (3½-pound) chicken, skinned and cut into serving pieces
1 cup dry white wine
2 tablespoons grated orange rind
1½ cups fresh orange juice
1 large onion, thinly sliced
2 stalks celery, thinly sliced
4 carrots, thinly sliced

3 tablespoons vegetable oil
1 teaspoon ground cumin
1 teaspoon paprika
1½ teaspoons salt
¼ teaspoon black pepper
⅛ teaspoon red pepper
Hot cooked rice or pasta

Arrange chicken in 12- x 8- x 2-inch casserole dish. Combine remaining ingredients except rice in large bowl; pour mixture over chicken. Cover and refrigerate overnight.

Bake, covered, at 350° for 1 hour or until chicken is tender. Transfer chicken and vegetables to a warm serving platter and cover. Reduce cooking liquid over high heat, stirring for 1 or 2 minutes or until slightly thickened. Serve chicken on a bed of cooked rice or pasta. Arrange vegetables over chicken; spoon sauce over chicken and vegetables. Yield: 6 servings.

Sweet Potato Biscuits

1 very large or 2 medium-size
   sweet potatoes (about 1 pound)
1 cup plus 2 tablespoons
   all-purpose flour

1 tablespoon baking powder
½ teaspoon salt
¼ cup plus 1 tablespoon shortening
½ to ¾ cup milk

Place sweet potatoes in a medium saucepan; cover with water and boil for 20 minutes or until tender. Drain, peel, and beat with electric mixer for 2 to 3 minutes to remove strings. Measure 1 cup potatoes; set remainder aside for other uses.

Sift flour, baking powder, and salt into large mixing bowl. Cut in shortening until mixture resembles coarse meal. Add sweet potatoes and enough milk to make dough stiff enough to roll.

Turn dough out onto a lightly floured surface; knead 10 to 12 times. Roll dough to ½-inch thickness; cut with a 2-inch biscuit cutter. Place biscuits on greased baking sheets. Bake at 450° for 12 to 13 minutes. Yield: 18 (2-inch) biscuits.

Note: These will keep 2 or 3 days in a plastic bag and re-heat nicely. Pat top of biscuits with cold water and place in toaster oven for 10 minutes at 350°.

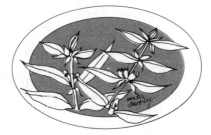

Sarah Pate's Macaroon Dainty

6 eggs, separated
¾ cup plus 2 tablespoons sugar,
   divided
1 tablespoon all-purpose flour
¾ cup milk

¼ cup dry sherry
16 almond macaroons
¼ teaspoon cream of tartar
½ teaspoon vanilla extract
Sliced almonds

Beat egg yolks until light and lemon colored. Gradually add ½ cup sugar, flour, and milk; beat well. Cook mixture in the top of a double boiler, stirring constantly until smooth and thickened. Remove from heat, and gradually stir in sherry.

Arrange macaroons in a shallow 13- x 9- x 2-inch baking dish. Pour cooked egg yolk mixture over macaroons; set aside.

Beat egg whites (at room temperature) with cream of tartar until foamy. Gradually add remaining sugar and vanilla; continue beating until stiff peaks form. Spoon over egg yolk mixture and sprinkle with almonds. Bake at 425° for 5 to 7 minutes or until meringue is lightly browned. Yield: 8 to 10 servings.

Cissy Coleman's Praline Ice Cream Roll

This recipe breaks down into three easy steps—baking a delicate pecan sponge cake, rolling it around ice cream, and spreading it with a simple topping. The steps can be done on separate days.

Vegetable oil
4 cups pecans, divided
2 tablespoons all-purpose flour
½ teaspoon baking powder
4 eggs, separated
1 cup sugar
1 teaspoon vanilla
⅛ teaspoon maple flavoring

⅛ teaspoon cream of tartar
½ cup powdered sugar
1½ quarts Praline 'N Cream ice
  cream, softened
1 cup brown sugar
1 tablespoon butter
2 tablespoons Kahlua
2 tablespoons water

Grease a 15- x 10- x 2-inch jellyroll pan with vegetable oil, and line with waxed paper. Grease waxed paper lightly with vegetable oil, and set aside.

Coarsely grind 2 cups pecans; reserve for topping. Finely grind remaining 2 cups pecans. Combine finely ground pecans, flour, and baking powder; set aside.

Beat egg yolks until light and lemon colored; gradually add ½ cup sugar, vanilla, and maple flavoring, stirring well. Set aside.

Beat egg whites (at room temperature) and cream of tartar until foamy; gradually add ½ cup sugar, 1 tablespoon at a time, beating until stiff but not dry. Fold in egg yolk mixture. Fold pecan mixture into egg mixture. Spread batter evenly in prepared pan. Bake at 350° about 12 minutes.

Sift powdered sugar in a 15- x 10-inch rectangle on a linen towel. When cake is done, immediately loosen from sides of pan, and turn out onto sugar. Peel off waxed paper. Starting at narrow end, roll up cake and towel together; cool on a wire rack, seam side down.

Unroll cake, and remove the towel. Quickly spread cake with softened ice cream, leaving a 1-inch margin around edges. Immediately reroll cake, and wrap in aluminum foil. Freeze.

Combine brown sugar, butter, Kahlua, and water in small saucepan. Bring to a boil, stirring constantly. Boil 1 minute. Cool to lukewarm.

Spread topping on frozen cake and press reserved coarsely chopped pecans over surface. Cover and freeze until ready to serve. Slice cake with an electric or serrated knife. Yield: 8 to 10 servings.

 For Best Baking Results: Use shiny baking sheets and cakepans for baking. Dark pans absorb more heat and cause baked products to overbrown.

Crab Season Luncheon

Crabmeat Bisque
or
Crabmeat Salad
or
Crabmeat à la Winifred
Tomatoes Rellenos
Buttered Lima Beans
or
Corn on the Cob
Fresh Blueberry Pudding

Serves 6 to 8

These three ways to celebrate fresh crabmeat all come together quickly at lunchtime. Fresh Blueberry Pudding is a tasty, yet quick dessert, and the lemon sauce can be refrigerated up to 1 week. Prepare Tomatoes Rellenos up to 1 hour in advance; keep the dressing refrigerated for all kinds of salads. Heat water to steam the lima beans or boil the corn while you're cooking the crab, and the meal will come together smoothly.

Crabmeat Bisque

Fast cooking, fresh crab flavor.

½ pound fresh mushrooms, sliced
3 tablespoons finely chopped green
    onion
¼ cup plus 2 tablespoons butter or
    margarine
¼ cup instant-blending flour
4½ cups warm milk

1 pound lump crabmeat, drained
    and flaked
1 tablespoon seasoned salt
¾ teaspoon ground mace
¾ teaspoon hot sauce
½ teaspoon paprika
French bread

Sauté mushrooms and onion in butter in a large Dutch oven until vegetables are tender. Stir in flour. Gradually add warm milk; cook over medium heat, stirring constantly, until slightly thickened. Add crabmeat, salt, mace, hot sauce, and paprika; stir well. Cook over medium heat until just heated through. (Do not allow to boil.) Serve in heated soup bowls with hot French bread. Yield: about 2 quarts.

Crabmeat Salad

1 cup mayonnaise
2 tablespoons seafood cocktail or
   chili sauce
2 tablespoons wine vinegar
1 tablespoon olive oil
½ teaspoon Worcestershire sauce
⅛ teaspoon salt
2 tablespoons diced green onion or
   1 tablespoon dried green onion

2 tablespoons chopped parsley
6 drops hot sauce
¼ cup heavy cream, whipped
1 pound crabmeat
6 medium tomatoes, peeled
2 tablespoons green olives, finely
   chopped (optional)
Leaf lettuce

Blend first 9 ingredients in a mixing bowl. Combine sauce, whipped cream, and crabmeat about an hour before serving; refrigerate.

Cut each tomato into 8 wedges, cutting to, but not through, base of tomato. Spread wedges apart to form a shell. Spoon crab salad into tomato shells; garnish with chopped olives, if desired. Place on lettuce-lined serving plates. Yield: 6 servings.

Note: Make sauce a day ahead of time for best flavor.

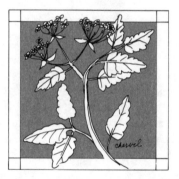

Crabmeat à la Winifred

Sweet crabmeat in a light sauce to serve in scallop shells or over hot French bread.

1 tablespoon butter
1 tablespoon instant-blending flour
1 (5.33-ounce) can evaporated milk,
   undiluted
¼ teaspoon dried green onion

¼ teaspoon minced parsley
¼ teaspoon salt
⅛ teaspoon mace
3 dashes hot sauce
1 cup lump or white crabmeat

Melt butter in heavy skillet over medium heat; add flour, stirring until smooth. Cook 1 minute; stirring constantly. Gradually add milk; cook over medium heat, stirring constantly, until thickened and bubbly. Add green onion, parsley, salt, mace, and hot sauce. Cook 3 or 4 minutes; add crabmeat and cook just until very hot. Spoon into scallop shells or serve over hot French bread. Yield: 2 servings. (This recipe may be doubled or tripled to serve 4 or 6 generously.)

Tomatoes Rellenos

The excellent dressing comes from a famous old New York restaurant.

8 medium-size firm tomatoes
1 cup finely chopped ham
1 medium onion, finely chopped

2 hard-cooked eggs, chopped
Rector's French Dressing

Cut a ¼-inch slice from the top of each tomato. Scoop out pulp, leaving shells intact. Set pulp aside. Invert tomatoes on paper towels to drain and set aside.

Combine tomato pulp, ham, onion, and eggs; spoon mixture into prepared tomato shells. Serve stuffed tomatoes with Rector's French Dressing. Yield: 8 servings.

Rector's French Dressing

1 teaspoon dry mustard
1 teaspoon paprika
¼ teaspoon salt
1 teaspoon freshly ground black
   pepper
⅛ teaspoon red pepper

¼ cup vinegar
1 cup olive or vegetable oil
6 drops Worcestershire sauce
1 whole clove garlic, finely
   chopped

Mix mustard, paprika, salt, and pepper in a small bowl. Whisk in vinegar, oil, Worcestershire sauce, and garlic. Yield: 1¼ cups.

Note: Delicious with crumbled blue cheese added.

Fresh Blueberry Pudding

Serve this with zesty Lemon Sauce or a dollop of ice cream.

1 pint fresh blueberries
1¼ cups sugar, divided
3 tablespoons lemon juice, strained
¼ cup plus 2 tablespoons butter,
   softened
1 teaspoon vanilla extract

1 egg
1¼ cups all-purpose flour
1 teaspoon baking powder
¼ teaspoon salt
½ cup milk
Lemon Sauce (page 269)

Combine blueberries, ¾ cup sugar, and lemon juice in a small saucepan over moderate heat until sugar dissolves and mixture simmers. Remove from heat and set aside to cool to lukewarm.

Cream butter, remaining ½ cup sugar, and vanilla on medium speed of electric mixer until light and fluffy. Add egg; beat until well blended. Combine flour, baking powder, and salt; add to creamed mixture alternately with milk, beginning and ending with flour mixture. Fold in lukewarm blueberry mixture. Pour into a greased and floured 9-inch pieplate and bake at 375° for 35 minutes or until cake tester inserted in center comes out clean. Serve warm with Lemon Sauce, if desired. Yield: 8 servings.

Tropical Flavor Luncheon

Appleade Fizz
Cheese Straws
Curried Chicken Salad
or
Island Pineapple and Tuna
Mango Bread
Avocado-Pecan Bread
Lime Chiffon Pie
or
Nectarine Pie

Serves 4

There is a note of surprise in this menu—a few unusual tastes. But the cook can relax, because the breads freeze well, the cheese straws keep several weeks, and the desserts can be chilled overnight. These are summer flavors, but the choice of a hot entrée also makes this meal perfect for those frigid winter days when you dream of being some place warm!

Appleade Fizz

This recipe makes one serving. Multiply it to serve as many as you wish. For a large group, stir all ingredients except club soda in a measuring cup or pitcher and refrigerate; strain over ice into glasses and add club soda.

¼ cup plus 2 tablespoons apple
   juice or cider
2 teaspoons lemon juice
2 teaspoons lime juice

2 teaspoons sugar
Crushed ice
Ice cubes
Club soda

Shake all ingredients except club soda with crushed ice and strain over ice cubes into highball glass. Fill with soda. Yield: 1 serving.

Adrienne Potter's Cheese Straws

2 (5-ounce) jars Old English
   Cheese, softened
½ cup margarine, softened
½ teaspoon salt

¼ to ½ teaspoon red pepper
Dash of Worcestershire sauce
1½ cups all-purpose flour

Combine cheese, margarine, salt, pepper, and Worcestershire sauce, stirring well. Gradually add flour, mixing well.

Roll dough to ⅛-inch thickness on a lightly floured surface; cut into 3- x ½-inch strips.

Place strips on ungreased cookie sheets. Bake at 350° for 12 minutes or until crisp. Place on wire racks to cool. Yield: 4 dozen.

Curried Chicken Salad

Turn leftover chicken or turkey into an unusual salad, and frame it with the pretty pale green of sliced kiwi fruit. Choose plump unwrinkled fruit and ripen at room temperature. It is ripe when it yields gently to pressure. Refrigerate in a plastic bag for 2 or 3 weeks, if desired. The taste of ripe kiwi is unique—like a combination of sweet strawberries and citrus.

2 cups diced, cooked chicken or turkey
½ cup toasted, slivered almonds (reserve 1 teaspoon for garnish)
½ cup raisins (reserve 1 teaspoon for garnish)
½ cup shredded coconut, (reserve 1 teaspoon for garnish)

1 (8-ounce) carton commercial sour cream
1 tablespoon lime juice
1 teaspoon curry powder or to taste
Dash of ground ginger
4 kiwi fruit, peeled and sliced
Lettuce leaves

Combine chicken, almonds, raisins, and coconut; set aside. Combine sour cream, lime juice, curry powder, and ginger. Add chicken mixture and toss well until all ingredients are coated. Arrange chicken salad and kiwi slices on lettuce-lined serving plates. Garnish with reserved almonds, raisins, and coconut. Yield: 4 servings.

Island Pineapple and Tuna

1 (13½-ounce) can pineapple chunks, drain and reserve syrup
¼ cup vinegar
¼ cup sugar
2 teaspoons soy sauce
½ cup water
2 tablespoons cornstarch

1 medium onion, cut into thin wedges
1 medium-size green pepper, cut into strips
1 (7-ounce) can tuna, drained
1 medium tomato, chopped
Hot cooked rice

Combine pineapple syrup, vinegar, sugar, and soy sauce in a large saucepan. Blend water and cornstarch; add to pineapple syrup mixture. Cook over medium heat until thickened, stirring constantly. Add pineapple and remaining ingredients, except rice. Cook, covered, until all ingredients are heated thoroughly. Serve over hot cooked rice. Yield: 4 servings.

Mango Bread

The rich flavor of ripe mango in a moist wholesome loaf.

¼ cup butter	1½ cups all-purpose flour
1 cup sugar	2 teaspoons baking powder
1 egg, lightly beaten	½ teaspoon salt
¼ cup wheat germ	½ teaspoon baking soda
1½ cups pureed mango (1	½ teaspoon cinnamon
large or 2 small)	1 teaspoon vanilla extract
2 tablespoons lime or lemon juice	1 cup chopped pecans or walnuts

Cream butter; gradually add sugar, beating well. Add beaten egg, wheat germ, pureed mango, and lime juice; mix until smooth.

Combine flour, baking powder, salt, soda, and cinnamon; add to creamed mixture, stirring just until dry ingredients are moistened. Stir in vanilla and nuts, if desired.

Pour batter into a greased 9- x 5- x 3-inch loafpan. Bake at 350° for 50 minutes or until a wooden pick inserted in center comes out clean. Cool in pan 10 minutes; remove from pan, and cool completely on a wire rack. Yield: 1 loaf.

Note: Keep Mango Bread in refrigerator for best taste.

Avocado-Pecan Bread

A rich bread with a nutty flavor, this also makes a great snack. Spread with seasoned cream or cottage cheese.

1 cup sugar	1 teaspoon lemon rind
2 cups all-purpose flour	1 teaspoon lemon juice
¼ teaspoon salt	½ teaspoon lemon extract
1 teaspoon baking soda	1 tablespoon vegetable oil
½ teaspoon baking powder	¾ cup chopped pecans
1 egg, lightly beaten	½ cup golden raisins (optional)
½ cup buttermilk	
1 cup mashed, ripe avocado (1	
large or 2 small)	

Sift sugar, flour, salt, soda, and baking powder into a large mixing bowl. Add egg, buttermilk, avocado, lemon rind, lemon juice, lemon extract, and oil; beat well, at medium speed of electric mixer. Fold pecans and raisins, if desired, into avocado mixture. Spoon into well-greased 9- x 5- x 3-inch loafpan and bake at 350° for 1 hour or until wooden pick inserted in center comes out clean. To prevent browning too quickly, place a pan of hot water on top rack of oven and remove after 40 minutes of baking. Cool in pan 10 minutes; remove from pan, and cool completely on a wire rack. Delicious served warm. Yield: 1 loaf.

Gift Breads: Clean, dry coffee cans make ideal baking containers for gift breads.

Lime Chiffon Pie

1 envelope unflavored gelatin
2 tablespoons cold water
4 eggs, separated
1 cup sugar, divided
¼ teaspoon salt
½ cup fresh lime juice
1 teaspoon grated lime rind

6 to 8 drops green food coloring
    (optional)
½ cup whipping cream, whipped
1 tablespoon sugar
½ teaspoon vanilla extract
1 baked (9-inch) pastry shell

Soften gelatin in cold water; set aside.

Beat egg yolks until thick and lemon colored. Combine yolks, ½ cup sugar, salt, and lime juice in a saucepan; stir until smooth. Cook over medium heat, stirring constantly, 5 minutes or until thickened. Remove from heat; add gelatin, lime rind, and food coloring, if desired. Stir well. Chill until slightly set.

Beat egg whites (at room temperature) until foamy; gradually add remaining ½ cup sugar, 1 tablespoon at a time, beating until stiff peaks form. Fold into chilled lime mixture. Set aside.

Beat whipping cream until soft peaks form. Gradually add 1 tablespoon sugar and vanilla, beating well. Fold the whipped cream into the lime mixture. Pour filling into pastry shell. Yield: one 9-inch pie.

Nectarine Pie

1 cup sugar, divided
2 tablespoons instant-blending
    flour
1 teaspoon ground cinnamon
8 medium-size ripe nectarines,
    peeled and sliced

1 unbaked (9-inch) pastry shell
2 eggs, beaten
1 tablespoon lemon juice
½ teaspoon almond extract
2 tablespoons butter or margarine

Combine ½ cup sugar, flour, and cinnamon in a medium mixing bowl, stirring well. Add nectarine slices, tossing to coat well.

Arrange nectarine slices in pastry shell. Combine eggs, remaining sugar, lemon juice, and almond extract in a small mixing bowl; mix well. Spoon evenly over fruit. Dot with butter.

Bake at 350° for 1 hour. Cool completely before cutting into wedges to serve. Yield: one 9-inch pie.

Pastry

1⅓ cups all-purpose flour
¼ teaspoon salt

½ cup shortening
3 tablespoons cold water

Combine flour and salt in a medium mixing bowl; cut in shortening with a pastry blender until mixture resembles coarse meal. Sprinkle water, 1 tablespoon at a time, over surface; stir with a fork until all ingredients are moistened. Shape dough into a ball; chill. Roll pastry to ⅛-inch thickness on a lightly floured surface. Fit into a 9-inch pieplate; trim off excess pastry along edges. Fold edges under and flute. Yield: one 9-inch pastry shell.

Italian-Style Luncheon

Artichoke-Crab Salad
Italian Cauliflower Frittata
Sausage Bread
Sliced Tomatoes with Fresh Basil
Biscuit Tortoni alla Mandora
or
Lemon Velvet Ice Cream

Serves 6 to 8

A very cosmopolitan luncheon, full of the fresh, light tastes of real Italian cooking. It would be appropriate to start with Campari, the refreshingly bitter Italian aperitif—splashed with soda, if you wish. If you have fresh basil, sprinkle some chopped leaves over a platter of sliced tomatoes to complement the menu and brighten the table.

Artichoke-Crab Salad

1 cup lump or flake crabmeat	2 (14-ounce) cans artichoke hearts,
1 cup diced celery	drained
¼ cup finely chopped dill pickle	1 cup commercial French dressing
¼ cup mayonnaise	Leaf lettuce
2 teaspoons lime juice	Mayonnaise
3 drops hot sauce	Paprika
Salt to taste	

Combine crabmeat, celery, pickle, mayonnaise, and lime juice; add hot sauce and salt to taste. Refrigerate crab mixture until ready to serve.

Marinate artichoke hearts in French dressing for at least an hour. Cut each artichoke heart (part way) and open like a flower. Place a scoopful of the crabmeat mixture and two artichoke hearts on leaf lettuce; top with a dollop of mayonnaise and sprinkle with paprika. Yield: 6 servings.

 Leftover Vegetable Idea: Marinate leftover vegetables (beets, carrots, beans, broccoli, cauliflower, corn, and brussel sprouts) in pourable salad dressings for relishes and salads.

Lou Malta's Italian Cauliflower Frittata

"Frittata" is the Italian term for omelet.

1 medium head cauliflower
2 tablespoons olive oil, divided
1¼ teaspoons salt, divided
8 eggs, lightly beaten

½ cup grated Parmesan cheese
¼ teaspoon pepper
1 tablespoon butter or margarine

Wash cauliflower; remove slight discolorations with a vegetable peeler. Trim stalk; remove core and outer leaves.

Place whole cauliflower, head side down, in a medium saucepan; add water to cover, 1 tablespoon olive oil, and 1 teaspoon salt. Place over medium heat; cover, and cook 15 minutes or until crisp-tender. Drain well, and let cool. Break into flowerets; set aside.

Combine eggs, cheese, remaining salt, and pepper in a large mixing bowl; beat well.

Heat remaining oil and butter in a 10-inch skillet over medium heat. Arrange cauliflower in skillet; pour in egg mixture. Cover, and cook over medium heat about 10 minutes or until egg mixture is set. Cut into wedges, and serve immediately. Yield: 8 servings.

Note: 1 medium bunch broccoli (about 1½ pounds) can be substituted for the cauliflower. Cook as above, just until crisp-tender. Break off flowerets; slice stems.

Miriam Mayo's Sausage Bread

1 pound mild or hot bulk pork
  sausage
½ cup finely chopped onion
½ cup (2 ounces) shredded Swiss
  cheese
¼ cup grated Parmesan cheese
2 tablespoons chopped fresh
  parsley

1 egg, lightly beaten
¼ teaspoon salt
2 (5.5-ounce) packages biscuit mix
⅔ cup milk
¼ cup mayonnaise
1 egg yolk, lightly beaten

Cook sausage and onion in a large skillet until sausage is browned and onion is tender; drain off drippings. Stir in cheese, parsley, beaten egg, and salt. Set aside.

Combine biscuit mix, milk, and mayonnaise in a small mixing bowl, stirring until dry ingredients are moistened. Spoon half of batter into a greased 9- x 5- x 3-inch loafpan. Spread sausage mixture evenly over batter. Spread remaining batter over sausage. Brush with egg yolk.

Bake at 400° for 30 minutes or until golden brown. Cool in pan 10 minutes; remove from pan to wire rack. Slice and serve hot. Yield: 1 loaf.

Biscuit Tortoni alla Mandora

An elegant frozen almond dessert that can be made days ahead of serving.

4 cups whipping cream
2 cups sifted powdered sugar
½ cup amaretto or other
   almond-flavored liqueur

2 egg whites
1⅓ cups slivered almonds,
   toasted

Beat whipping cream in a large mixing bowl at medium speed of an electric mixer until foamy; gradually add ½ cup powdered sugar and 2 tablespoons amaretto, beating until soft peaks form. Add remaining sugar and amaretto; beat well.

Beat egg whites (at room temperature) in a small mixing bowl until stiff peaks form. Gently fold into cream mixture.

Alternate layers of toasted almonds and cream mixture in 8 chilled parfait glasses, beginning and ending with toasted almonds. Cover glasses loosely with foil and freeze 3 hours; remove from freezer 30 minutes before serving. Yield: 8 servings.

Lemon Velvet Ice Cream

A marvelous and easy-to-make ice cream for a churn freezer only.

3 quarts half-and-half
4 cups sugar
1 tablespoon grated lemon rind

1⅓ cups fresh lemon juice
2 teaspoons lemon extract

Mix all ingredients in a large bowl; refrigerate overnight. Pour mixture into 5-quart ice cream freezer. Freeze according to manufacturer's directions. Serve directly from freezer or spoon into chilled plastic containers for later use. Yield: 5 quarts.

Page 45: *Gems of the Ocean Shrimp served over a fish-shaped rice mold highlights A Welcoming Luncheon (page 26) for a new friend or old. Easy Bellini wine coolers are made from fresh summer peaches. Chocolate-Raspberry Dessert can be made ahead.*

Page 46: *For this Classic Italian Dinner (page 55), brighten your dining table with red, green, and white—the colors of the Italian flag. Bracciolini—lean beef rolled around a savory stuffing and simmered in tomato sauce—is the star of the meal. Red Lettuce and Mushroom Salad and Savory Breadsticks are simple accompaniments. Light and tangy Lemon Sorbet is served with Ice Cream Wafers.*

Perfect Dinner Parties

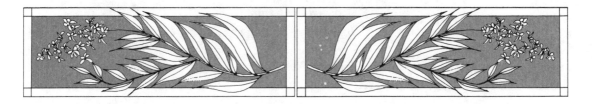

Harmony is the key to a perfect dinner party menu. And the key to harmony, oddly enough, is contrasts. The food should be both savory and sweet, bland and spicy, crunchy and smooth. Colors should be both bright and muted. Preparations should be paced so that if one dish requires last-minute attention, the foods that go with it can be ready in advance.

You can select any of the menus in this chapter according to the type of entrée most appropriate for the occasion and be confident that it will be highlighted by the side dishes. For example, if you would like to feature beef, you'll find the richness of steak and potatoes in the Beef Lover's Dinner enhanced by the intrigue of a curry-spiked soup and the delicacy of crêpes suzette.

Reason to Celebrate

Scallops with Watercress Sauce
Boeuf aux Champignons à la Crème
Squash Julienne
Topsy-Turvy Apple Pie

Serves 4

Make the Topsy-Turvy Apple Pie 1 to 2 days ahead; then the rest of this menu is easily accomplished the day of the dinner. Start by marinating the scallops in advance. Cut up the squash and refrigerate in a plastic bag. Up to 2 hours before serving, prepare the entrée, but keep the beef and sauce separate. Make the dressing for the scallops up to 1 hour ahead, and prepare lettuce and tomato to garnish plates. When guests arrive, boil water for noodles, steam squash, and reheat the entrée.

Wine Suggestion: Choose a light red wine, such as a Beaujolais or Zinfandel, to drink throughout this meal, or start with a dry, white wine, such as a Chenin Blanc or Sauvignon Blanc, and switch to a more robust California Burgundy or a Côtes du Rhône with the beef.

Scallops with Watercress Sauce

The scallops "cook" in the lime juice marinade; then the juice is blended with oil and fresh greens for an unusual seafood complement.

1 pound fresh bay scallops	2 teaspoons Dijon mustard
1 cup lime juice	¼ teaspoon salt
¼ cup chopped fresh parsley	Leaf lettuce
¼ cup chopped fresh watercress	Tomato wedges
⅔ cup vegetable oil	¼ cup sliced pitted ripe olives
⅔ cup olive oil	

Rinse scallops thoroughly in cold water; drain well. Combine scallops and lime juice in a large mixing bowl; cover and refrigerate overnight. Drain scallops; reserve ¼ cup lime juice. Set aside.

Position knife blade in food processor bowl; add parsley, watercress, and reserved lime juice. Process 20 seconds or until smooth.

With machine running, gradually add vegetable oil and olive oil through food chute. Add mustard and salt; process until smooth. Chill sauce thoroughly.

Spoon scallops onto a lettuce-lined serving dish. Garnish with tomato wedges; sprinkle olives over top of scallops. Serve chilled with watercress sauce. Yield: 4 servings.

Boeuf aux Champignons à la Crème

2 tablespoons butter or margarine,
  divided
1 tablespoon vegetable oil, divided
½ pound fresh mushrooms, sliced
4 green onions, chopped
¾ teaspoon salt, divided
¼ teaspoon white pepper, divided
1 (1-pound) flank steak, partially
  frozen

1 cup beef broth
¼ cup dry white vermouth
2 teaspoons cornstarch
1 cup whipping cream
Hot cooked noodles
Chopped fresh parsley

Combine 1 tablespoon butter and 1½ teaspoons oil in a small skillet. Place over medium heat, and add mushrooms; sauté until tender. Stir in green onion, ½ teaspoon salt, and ⅛ teaspoon white pepper; sauté an additional minute. Remove from heat, and set aside.

Slice flank steak across the grain into 4-inch strips. Combine remaining butter and oil in a large skillet. Place over medium-high heat; add meat, a few pieces at a time, and cook until desired degree of doneness. Drain on paper towels, and set aside.

Drain and discard pan drippings. Add beef broth and vermouth to skillet; continue to cook over medium-high heat until mixture is reduced to ⅓ cup.

Stir cornstarch into cream, mixing until well blended. Gradually add cornstarch mixture to broth mixture, beating well with a wire whisk. Bring to a boil, reduce heat, and simmer, beating constantly with whisk, until thickened. Stir in reserved sautéed mixture, beef, remaining salt and white pepper; continue cooking until thoroughly heated.

Spoon mixture over hot cooked noodles on a serving platter. Garnish with chopped parsley. Serve immediately. Yield: 4 servings.

Squash Julienne

1 pound yellow squash (3 medium)
1 pound zucchini (3 medium)
1½ tablespoons grated onion
½ teaspoon dried whole chervil

¼ teaspoon dried whole thyme
¼ teaspoon salt
¼ teaspoon freshly ground pepper
Pimiento strips (optional)

Wash squash and cut into 3- x ¼-inch strips. Arrange squash on steaming rack, and place over boiling water; cover and steam 5 to 7 minutes or until crisp-tender.

Combine steamed squash, grated onion, chervil, thyme, salt, and pepper in a serving dish; toss gently. Garnish with pimiento strips, if desired. Yield: 4 to 6 servings.

Topsy-Turvy Apple Pie

A marvelous variation of the French tarte tatin, *this pie is turned out onto a plate for serving—so the pecan halves arranged in the bottom of the pan come out on top!*

¼ cup plus 1 tablespoon butter or
    margarine, divided
½ cup pecan halves
½ cup light brown sugar
Pastry for 1 double-crust (9-inch)
    pie
8 medium-size apples, peeled,
    cored, and sliced

2 tablespoons lemon juice
1 tablespoon flour
1 cup sugar
½ cup dark brown sugar
1 teaspoon cinnamon
½ teaspoon nutmeg
1 teaspoon vanilla extract

Melt ¼ cup butter in a 9-inch deep-dish pieplate; tilt pieplate to coat sides. Place pecans on bottom of pieplate in a pattern, rounded side down. Pat light brown sugar evenly over pecans and butter. Cover with one pastry layer; set aside.

Place apples in a large mixing bowl. Add lemon juice, flour, sugar, dark brown sugar, cinnamon, nutmeg, and vanilla; mix well. Spoon mixture over pastry in pieplate; dot with remaining butter.

Fit top pastry over filling. Trim edge of top pastry, leaving a ½-inch overhang. Fold overhang under edges of bottom pastry, pressing firmly to seal; flute. Cut slits in top pastry to allow steam to escape. Moisten edges lightly with a little cold water and bake at 350° for 45 to 50 minutes. Cool 5 to 10 minutes on a wire rack; turn out on a large plate. Serve hot or cold. Yield: one 9-inch deep-dish pie.

Pastry

2⅔ cups all purpose flour, sifted
1 teaspoon salt

1 cup shortening
6 tablespoons ice water

Combine flour and salt in a mixing bowl; cut in shortening with a pastry blender until mixture resembles coarse meal. Sprinkle with water, one tablespoon at a time, and stir with a fork until dry ingredients are moistened. Shape dough into a ball; chill.

Roll half of pastry to ⅛-inch thickness on a lightly floured surface; roll dough to an 11-inch circle. Repeat procedure with remaining dough. Yield: pastry for one 9-inch deep-dish double-crust pie.

Fluted Mushroom Caps: Fluted mushroom caps are an appropriate garnish for the serving platter or individual plates. To flute the cap, hold each mushroom by the stem. Using a small paring knife with the blade held toward you, cut a thin strip from the top of the cap to the base. Turn mushroom to remove 5 or 6 more strips in a spiral pattern. Remove stem from fluted cap.

Beef Lover's Dinner

Curried Cream of Tomato Soup
Filet Mignon with Oysters
Stuffed Baked Potatoes
Garden Salad with Dill-Mustard Dressing
Crêpes Frangipane
or
Crêpes Suzette

Serves 6

You can get a long head start on this menu by refrigerating or freezing the crêpes, stuffed potatoes, and soup days or weeks ahead. The salad dressing will keep refrigerated up to a week; the salad can be refrigerated without the dressing for several hours. You'll have time now to give last-minute attention to the steaks and the assembly of the crêpes.

Wine Suggestion: This meal will flatter the most full-bodied red wine, such as a Cabernet Sauvignon or a Pinot Noir.

Curried Cream of Tomato Soup

¼ cup butter
1 large onion, minced
3 carrots, shredded
2 tablespoons chopped pitted ripe
    olives
1 tablespoon curry powder
1 (28-ounce) can tomatoes or 3
    cups chopped, seeded fresh
    tomatoes

3 tablespoons chopped parsley
2 (13¾-ounce) cans chicken broth,
    divided
¼ teaspoon ground allspice
¼ teaspoon ground cumin
1 cup half-and-half
Salt to taste
Croutons

Melt butter in large saucepan over medium heat. Add onion, carrots, and olives; cook 35 minutes, stirring occasionally. Sprinkle vegetables with curry powder; cook, stirring frequently, 5 minutes. Reduce heat to low; stir in tomatoes, parsley, 1 can chicken broth, allspice, and cumin. Simmer 30 minutes. Press mixture through food mill. Return soup to saucepan over low heat; stir in remaining can chicken broth and half-and-half. Add salt to taste. Serve hot, topped with croutons. Yield: 6 servings.

Filet Mignon with Oysters

An opulent combination—fit for a king or your best friends! You may want to buy a whole beef tenderloin and slice it into steaks yourself. Save the tips and cut up or grind for stroganoff, stir fry, or steak tartare.

2 (12-ounce) containers Standard oysters, undrained	1 tablespoon plus ½ teaspoon Worcestershire sauce, divided
2 tablespoons butter or margarine	3 drops hot sauce
2 tablespoons instant-blending flour	6 (1¼-inch-thick) beef tenderloin steaks (about 2½ pounds)
1 cup beef broth	Salt and pepper to taste
½ cup finely chopped mushrooms	Fluted mushroom caps
1½ teaspoons finely chopped chives	Fresh parsley sprigs

Drain oysters, reserving ½ cup liquor; set aside.

Melt butter in a large heavy skillet over low heat; add flour, stirring until smooth. Cook 1 minute, stirring constantly. Gradually add reserved oyster liquor and beef broth; cook over medium heat, stirring constantly, until thickened and bubbly. Reduce heat; stir in mushrooms, chives, ½ teaspoon Worcestershire sauce, and hot sauce. Simmer 10 minutes, stirring occasionally. Stir in oysters; simmer 2 minutes or until oyster edges curl. Keep warm until ready to serve.

Brush steaks with remaining 1 tablespoon Worcestershire sauce; sprinkle with salt and pepper to taste. Place steaks on a well-greased rack in a shallow roasting pan about 5 inches from heating element. Broil 8 minutes on each side or until desired degree of doneness. Remove steaks to individual warm serving plates. Spoon sauce and oysters over steaks to serve. Garnish with fluted mushroom caps and parsley sprigs. Yield: 6 servings.

Stuffed Baked Potatoes

A marvelous way to have frozen prepared potatoes on hand and ready for use.

5 pounds baking potatoes	1½ teaspoons salt
Vegetable oil	¼ teaspoon pepper
¾ cup butter or margarine	2 teaspoons freeze-dried chives
1 (13-ounce) can evaporated milk	Paprika

Rub potato skins with oil. Bake at 400° for 1 hour or until done.

Let potatoes cool to touch; cut in half lengthwise. Carefully scoop out pulp, leaving shells intact. Mash pulp and combine with butter, milk, salt, pepper, and chives in a large mixing bowl; mix well. Stuff shells with potato mixture; garnish with paprika. Place on baking sheets, and bake at 400° for 20 minutes or microwave for 5 minutes. Yield: 20 to 26 servings.

Note: Stuffed Baked Potatoes can be frozen before baking. Remove from freezer, thaw to room temperature, and bake as directed.

Garden Salad with Dill-Mustard Dressing

4 green onions, thinly sliced
1 small cucumber, peeled, seeded and diced
1 large tomato, diced
1 large green pepper, seeded and diced
1 carrot

3 radishes
1 small head romaine lettuce, torn into pieces
1 head Boston lettuce, torn into pieces
Dill-Mustard Dressing

Combine green onions, cucumber, tomato, and green pepper in large salad bowl. Shred carrot and radishes over vegetables; toss well. Add lettuce, and spoon on dressing. Toss before serving. Yield: 6 to 8 servings.

Dill-Mustard Dressing

2 tablespoons red wine vinegar
1 teaspoon Dijon mustard
2 tablespoons commercial sour cream
¼ cup vegetable oil

3 tablespoons olive oil
Salt to taste
2 tablespoons minced fresh dill or 2 teaspoons dried dill weed

Whisk vinegar and mustard in small bowl; whisk in sour cream and oils. Stir in salt and dill. Let stand 30 minutes for flavors to blend; stir well before serving. Yield: about ¾ cup.

Dessert Crêpes

⅓ cup all-purpose flour
1 tablespoon sugar
Dash of salt
1 egg

1 egg yolk
¾ cup milk
1 tablespoon butter, melted
1 tablespoon Grand Marnier

Combine all ingredients in container of an electric blender; process 1 minute. Scrape down sides of blender container with rubber spatula; process an additional 15 seconds. Refrigerate batter 1 hour. (This allows flour particles to swell and soften so that crêpes are light in texture.)

Coat the bottom of a 6-inch crêpe pan with oil; place pan over medium heat until oil is just hot, not smoking.

Pour 2 tablespoons batter into pan. Quickly tilt pan in all directions so that batter covers bottom of pan. Cook crêpe 1 minute.

Lift edge of crêpe to test for doneness. Crêpe is ready for flipping when it can be shaken loose from pan. Flip crêpe, and cook 30 seconds. (This side is rarely more than spotty brown and is the side on which the filling is placed.)

Place on paper towels to cool. Stack crêpes between layers of waxed paper to prevent sticking. Repeat procedure until all batter is used, stirring batter occasionally. Yield: 12 (6-inch) crêpes.

Note: Crêpes can be made ahead and frozen between layers of waxed paper.

Crêpes Frangipane

Pastry cream flavored with almonds and vanilla is still called frangipane, *after the Italian Marquis Frangipani who is said to have first blended the fragrances. Here, the luscious cream is baked in delicate crêpes.*

1 cup sugar	½ cup almonds, toasted and
2 eggs	ground
2 egg yolks	Melted butter
½ cup all-purpose flour	12 Dessert Crêpes (page 53)
1 cup hot milk, (about 125°)	Powdered sugar
3 tablespoons butter	Whipped cream
2 teaspoons vanilla extract	Unsweetened chocolate curls
½ teaspoon almond extract	

Beat sugar, eggs, and egg yolks in large bowl on high speed of electric mixer until they are pale yellow and form a ribbon when dropped from a spoon. Pour mixture into a medium saucepan.

Add flour and then hot milk. (The addition of flour lets you bring this to a boil. Without flour or cornstarch, eggs would curdle over heat.) Bring to a boil, stirring constantly. Remove from heat. Add 3 tablespoons butter, extracts, and almonds. (Recipe can be made to this point, covered, and refrigerated overnight. Bring to room temperature before proceeding.)

Place filling in crêpe and roll. Place in baking dish seam side down. Brush with melted butter and bake at 350° for 20 minutes. Top with powdered sugar, whipped cream, and unsweetened chocolate curls. Yield: 6 servings.

Crêpes Suzette

Keep a batch of Dessert Crêpes in the freezer, and you'll always be ready to serve this dramatic dessert.

⅓ cup butter	3 tablespoons Curaçao, Cointreau,
¼ cup sugar	or Triple Sec
½ cup orange marmalade	3 tablespoons Grand Marnier
1 tablespoon lemon rind	12 Dessert Crêpes (page 53)
1 tablespoon lemon juice	2 tablespoons sugar
⅓ cup orange juice	¼ cup brandy

Combine butter and sugar in a large skillet or chafing dish; cook over medium heat until mixture is lightly browned. Stir in marmalade, lemon rind and juice, orange juice, and liqueur; cook until bubbly. Dip both sides of crêpe in orange sauce; fold in half, and in quarters. Sprinkle with sugar. Repeat procedure with remaining crêpes, pushing folded crêpes to side of pan.

Place brandy in a small saucepan; heat just until warm. Pour over crêpes, and ignite with a long match. Allow flames to die down, and serve immediately. Yield: 6 servings.

Classic Italian Dinner

Antipasto Tray
Savory Breadsticks
Bracciolini
Veal Scallopini
Red Lettuce and Mushroom Salad
Lemon Sorbet
Ice Cream Wafers

Serves 8 to 12

The stars of the antipasto tray, Pickled Mushrooms and Spiced Olives, are keep-on-hand items. The Savory Breadsticks and Bracciolini sauce can be frozen ahead and the sorbet should be. Make the salad, arrange the Antipasto Tray, and boil the pasta while either entrée is cooking.

Wine Suggestion: Serve any of the excellent dry Italian red wines—Valpolicella or Bardolino for light taste, Chianti or Barolo for fuller flavor, or a Brunello for elegance.

Antipasto Tray

Prepare Pickled Mushrooms and Spiced Olives several days ahead.

Pickled Mushrooms, drained
Spiced Olives, drained
24 slices Provolone cheese

24 slices honeydew melon
24 slices prosciutto

Arrange all ingredients attractively on a large tray. Keep chilled until ready to serve. Yield: 8 to 12 servings.

Pickled Mushrooms

½ pound fresh mushrooms
1 teaspoon salt
½ cup olive oil
¼ cup white wine vinegar

1 tablespoon finely chopped onion
1 teaspoon dried green onion
2 cloves garlic, thinly sliced
6 whole peppercorns

Rinse mushrooms; pat dry and place in a saucepan. Sprinkle with salt and 2 tablespoons water; cover and cook over medium heat 12 minutes. Remove from heat; drain well.

Combine olive oil, vinegar, onion, and green onion; mix well. Add mushrooms, garlic, and peppercorns; stir well. Chill mushrooms 4 to 6 hours. Yield: about 2 cups.

Spiced Olives

Hildegarde Harrington, a renowned cook and teacher, created this especially for my Italian dinner.

1 (7.8-ounce) can pitted ripe olives, drained and rinsed
2 tablespoons olive oil
1 medium clove garlic, crushed

½ teaspoon red wine vinegar
½ teaspoon dried whole oregano
¼ teaspoon dried hot pepper flakes

Combine all ingredients in a quart jar. Cover and chill 2 days. (Shake jar several times each day.) Serve at room temperature. Yield: about 1 cup.

Savory Breadsticks

Great with soup, pasta, or salads.

4 cups bread flour, divided
¼ cup sugar
1½ teaspoons salt
1 package dry yeast
1¼ cups milk

¼ cup plus 1 tablespoon margarine, divided
2 teaspoons dried basil leaves
½ teaspoon celery seeds
¼ teaspoon poultry seasoning

Combine 1 cup flour, sugar, salt, and yeast in a large mixing bowl. Set aside.

Combine milk and 3 tablespoons margarine in a small saucepan; heat to 125°. Gradually add milk to dry ingredients, beating constantly at low speed of an electric mixer. Beat 2 minutes at medium speed, scraping sides of bowl occasionally. Add ¾ cup flour, basil, celery seeds, and poultry seasoning; beat at high speed 2 minutes. Stir in remaining flour as needed to make a soft dough.

Turn dough out onto a lightly floured surface, and knead 8 minutes or until smooth and elastic.

Place dough in a well-greased bowl, turning to grease top. Cover and let rise in a warm place (85°), free from drafts, 1 hour and 30 minutes.

Punch dough down, and turn out onto a lightly floured surface. Divide dough into 24 equal portions. Roll each portion into a 9-inch rope, and place on greased baking sheets. Cover and repeat rising procedure 1 hour or until doubled in bulk. Melt remaining 2 tablespoons margarine; brush tops of breadsticks. Bake at 400° for 8 to 10 minutes or until golden brown. Yield: 24 breadsticks.

Note: Breadsticks can be wrapped in aluminum foil and frozen. Unwrap and bake at 350° just until warm to re-crisp before serving.

Bracciolini

The recipe, from the Malta family, is easy to do but requires time.

2 pounds boneless round steak, cut
   ¼-inch thick
1 tablespoon shortening
1½ tablespoons butter or margarine
1 tablespoon olive oil
4 green onions, finely chopped
3 stalks celery, chopped
3 cloves garlic, minced
1 cup chopped fresh parsley
7 slices bread

1 cup water
3 hard-cooked eggs, chopped
1 egg, beaten
½ cup grated Parmesan cheese
¼ cup grated Romano cheese
1 teaspoon salt
¼ teaspoon pepper
Spaghetti Sauce
1 (16-ounce) package thin spaghetti

Trim and discard excess fat from steak; pound with a meat mallet to ⅛-inch thickness, and cut into 12 pieces. Melt shortening in a large skillet; brown steak on both sides. Remove from skillet and set aside, reserving pan drippings.

Add butter and 1 tablespoon olive oil to skillet. Sauté onion, celery, garlic, and parsley in butter mixture until tender. Remove from heat.

Place bread in colander; pour water over bread to thoroughly soak. Press out excess water. Add bread, eggs, cheese, salt, and pepper to vegetable mixture, stirring well. Place equal portions of mixture on each piece of steak. Roll up each piece jellyroll fashion; secure with wooden picks or string. Place rolls in Spaghetti Sauce. Simmer 1½ hours or until steak is tender.

Cook spaghetti according to package directions; drain, and place on large, warm platter. Spoon Spaghetti Sauce over spaghetti; place steak rolls over sauce. Yield: 12 servings.

Spaghetti Sauce

3 large onions, finely chopped
1 large green pepper, finely
   chopped
2 cloves garlic, minced
3 tablespoons olive oil
3 (15-ounce) cans tomato sauce
1 (12-ounce) can tomato paste
1 tablespoon sugar
1 teaspoon Italian seasoning
1 teaspoon Worcestershire sauce

½ teaspoon celery seeds
¼ teaspoon dried basil
⅛ teaspoon red pepper
3 bay leaves
2 teaspoons salt
1 medium potato, quartered
2 pounds Italian sausage
2¾ cups water
1 pound fresh mushrooms, sliced

Sauté onion, green pepper, and garlic in olive oil in a large Dutch oven until tender. Add tomato sauce, tomato paste, sugar, seasonings, and potato. Bring to a boil. Reduce heat; cover and simmer 30 minutes. Remove and discard potato.

Remove casing from sausage. Brown sausage in a large skillet, stirring to crumble. Drain off drippings; stir sausage into tomato sauce mixture. Add water; cover and simmer 45 minutes. Stir in mushrooms; cover and simmer 15 minutes. Yield: 12 servings.

Ann Lomax's Veal Scallopini

This is a lovely dish to serve guests when you don't have much time to cook. Quantities can be doubled or tripled, but sauté the veal in several batches so as not to overcrowd the pan.

4 veal scallops (cut ⅜-inch thick)
3 tablespoons all-purpose flour
4 tablespoons olive oil
2 cloves garlic, minced
1 (4-ounce) can mushroom buttons
2 (10½-ounce) cans beef-flavored bouillon

1 (6-ounce) can tomato paste
Salt and pepper to taste
½ cup Marsala wine
Hot cooked vermicelli
¼ cup grated Parmesan cheese
Chopped parsley (optional)

Flatten veal scallops to ¼-inch thickness, using a meat mallet or rolling pin. Dredge scallops in flour, coating well. Sauté scallops in olive oil in a large skillet 3 minutes on each side or until browned. Remove scallops, and set aside.

Sauté garlic and mushrooms in pan drippings. Remove garlic, and discard; remove mushrooms, and set aside.

Add beef-flavored bouillon, tomato paste, salt, and pepper to pan drippings; cook over low heat, stirring constantly, until thickened and bubbly. Return scallops and mushrooms to tomato mixture; cover and cook over low heat 25 minutes or until veal is tender. Add wine; serve veal and sauce over vermicelli. Sprinkle with Parmesan cheese. Garnish with chopped parsley, if desired. Yield: 4 servings.

Red Lettuce and Mushroom Salad

This simple salad will complement either entreé.

2 heads red lettuce, torn into
   bite-size pieces
2 cups sliced fresh mushrooms

⅔ cup vegetable oil
¼ cup dry vermouth
½ teaspoon salt

Combine lettuce and mushrooms in a large bowl. Set aside.

Combine oil, vermouth, and salt in a jar. Cover tightly and shake vigorously. Pour over salad; toss gently. Serve immediately. Yield: 12 servings.

 Al Dente: Keep in mind that you cook pasta only until it's tender and slightly firm to the bite—al dente. Overcooking makes it soft and mushy.

Betty Kruger's Lemon Sorbet

Deliciously refreshing! For the most attractive presentation, serve in hollowed-out lemon or orange halves or place small scoops on scored lemon or orange slices. To serve 12, double the recipe.

1 cup sugar	2 egg whites
1 cup water	Lemon slices (optional)
2 tablespoons grated lemon rind	Orange slices (optional)
2 cups lemon juice	

Combine sugar and water in a small saucepan; cook over low heat, stirring constantly, until sugar dissolves. Cool.

Combine sugar mixture, lemon rind, and juice; stir well. Pour mixture into freezer can of a 1-gallon hand-turned or electric freezer. Freeze according to manufacturer's instructions.

Beat egg whites (at room temperature) until stiff peaks form; fold into frozen mixture. Spoon mixture into a lightly greased 10- x 6- x 2-inch baking dish. Cover and freeze. Spoon individual servings on top of lemon or orange slices, if desired. Yield: 1 quart.

Ice Cream Wafers

These crisp, lemony cookies will keep in the freezer for months.

¼ cup butter, softened	½ teaspoon salt
¼ cup shortening	1 teaspoon lemon extract
½ cup sugar	½ teaspoon vanilla extract
¾ cup all-purpose flour	Pecan halves

Cream butter and shortening; gradually add sugar, beating well. Combine flour and salt; stir into creamed mixture. Add flavorings; stir well.

Drop batter by rounded teaspoonfuls 2 inches apart on lightly greased baking sheets. Gently press a pecan half into the center of each cookie. Bake at 350° for 8 minutes or until lightly browned. Cool 1 minute. Carefully remove to wire racks to cool completely. Store in airtight container up to 1 week. Yield: about 2½ dozen.

Italian Meatless Dinner

Roasted Pepper Vegetable Platter
Eggplant Parmigiana
Fettuccine Alfredo
Pesto Bread
Espresso Baked Custard

Serves 8

---

he vegetable platter, the bread, and the custard are all do-ahead, as is the sauce for the eggplant. Everything should be well in hand just before dinnertime, when you'll need to prepare the Fettuccine Alfredo and broil the eggplant. Wine Suggestion: Although there is no meat on this menu, a robust Italian red wine, such as a vintage Barolo or Chianti, would highlight the rich flavors.

Roasted Pepper Vegetable Platter

A temptingly bright arrangement of chilled, vinaigrette-dressed vegetables — it would look beautiful on a buffet.

4 large red peppers
3 cloves garlic, chopped
¼ cup olive oil
¼ cup vegetable oil
1 tablespoon plus 1 teaspoon red wine vinegar
½ teaspoon dried basil leaves
¼ teaspoon dried whole oregano
Pinch dried whole thyme
1 (10-ounce) package frozen, cut asparagus
1 ounce chopped almonds, toasted

1 teaspoon fresh lemon juice
1 small head cauliflower
¼ teaspoon ground coriander
Pinch ground mustard
Pinch ground nutmeg
Salt
1 small head romaine lettuce, torn into pieces
2 hard-cooked eggs, sliced
1 (2-ounce) can anchovies, rinsed and patted dry (optional)
Ripe olives

Place peppers on foil-lined broiler pan. Broil, turning often, until skin is blistered and charred on all sides. Wrap peppers in paper toweling and place in plastic bag until cool. Rub off skins under cold running water; remove cores and rinse out seeds. Cut peppers into thin strips; toss in small bowl with garlic and combined oils. Refrigerate, covered, at least overnight or up to 2 weeks.

Pour off oil from peppers into small bowl (there should be at least ¼ cup); stir in vinegar, basil, oregano, and thyme.

Cook asparagus in boiling water 1 minute; rinse immediately under cold water and drain well. Toss asparagus in small bowl with almonds, lemon juice, and half of oil mixture.

Wash cauliflower and break into flowerets. Cook cauliflower in boiling water until crisp-tender, 2 to 3 minutes; rinse immediately under cold water and drain well. Add coriander, mustard, and nutmeg to remaining oil mixture; spoon over cauliflower in bowl, add salt to taste, and toss well.

Arrange lettuce on large platter. Arrange cauliflower in strip in center of platter; arrange peppers on one side and asparagus on the other. Place egg slices around edges of platter; garnish with anchovies and olives. Refrigerate platter until ready to serve, up to 8 hours. Yield: 8 servings.

Note: If red peppers are not available, use green peppers. Substitute 8 ounces cherry tomatoes, cut into halves, or 1 large tomato, cut into thin wedges, for the asparagus to maintain color balance of platter.

Eggplant Parmigiana

2 medium eggplant
4 cups milk
1 cup chopped onion
1 large clove garlic, minced
1 cup plus 2 tablespoons butter or margarine, melted and divided
2 tablespoons olive oil
½ cup chopped ham (optional)
1 (14½-ounce) can whole tomatoes, undrained
1 (10¾-ounce) can tomato puree
1¼ cups water
2 teaspoons Worcestershire sauce

1 teaspoon sugar
1½ teaspoons salt, divided
½ teaspoon pepper
2 teaspoons dried whole basil
¼ teaspoon dried whole thyme
½ cup chopped fresh parsley
1 cup self-rising flour
½ cup vegetable oil
2 cups (8 ounces) shredded mozzarella cheese
½ cup (2 ounces) grated Parmesan cheese

Peel eggplant, and cut into ½-inch slices. Place eggplant slices in a medium bowl, and add milk. Cover and refrigerate 2 hours.

Sauté onion and garlic in 2 tablespoons butter and olive oil in a large skillet until tender. Add ham, if desired, and cook over low heat 15 minutes. Add whole tomatoes, tomato puree, water, Worcestershire sauce, sugar, ½ teaspoon salt, pepper, basil, thyme, and parsley; stir gently until well blended. Bring to a boil. Reduce heat; cover and simmer 1 hour and 30 minutes.

Drain eggplant slices. Combine flour and remaining salt; dip eggplant slices into flour mixture. Fry eggplant slices in vegetable oil and remaining 1 cup butter over medium-high heat until golden brown, turning once. Drain on paper towels. Recipe can be prepared to this point up to 2 hours ahead.

Place fried eggplant slices on a baking sheet. Top each slice with 2 tablespoons tomato sauce mixture, mozzarella cheese, and Parmesan cheese. Broil until cheese melts. Transfer to a warm platter and serve immediately. Yield: 8 servings.

Fettuccine Alfredo

2 quarts water
1 tablespoon salt
1 tablespoon vegetable oil
1 (12-ounce) package fettuccine
¼ cup butter

½ cup whipping cream, divided
½ cup (2 ounces) grated Parmesan
   cheese
⅛ teaspoon pepper

Combine water, salt, and oil in a large Dutch oven; bring to a boil. Slowly add fettuccine; cook, uncovered, 12 minutes or until fettuccine is tender but firm. Drain well.

Melt butter in a small saucepan over low heat. Add ¼ cup whipping cream; cook over low heat, stirring constantly, until thickened. Pour mixture over fettuccine; toss gently. Add remaining ingredients; toss gently. Serve immediately. Yield: 8 servings.

Pesto Bread

¼ cup unsalted butter, softened
1 tablespoon vegetable oil
2 tablespoons sugar
3 eggs
1 cup milk
1 cup all-purpose flour
1 cup whole wheat flour

1 tablespoon baking powder
1½ teaspoons salt
1 cup coarsely ground almonds
2 teaspoons dried basil leaves
2 teaspoons parsley flakes
1 teaspoon garlic powder

Combine butter, oil, and sugar; beat well. Combine eggs and milk; beat well. Add egg mixture to butter mixture, mixing well.

Combine flour, baking powder, and salt; add to batter, beating well. Stir in almonds, basil, parsley, and garlic. Spoon batter into a well-greased 8½- x 4½- x 3-inch loafpan. Bake at 350° for 55 minutes or until a wooden pick inserted in center comes out clean. Remove loaf from pan, and cool on a wire rack. Yield: 1 loaf.

Espresso Baked Custard

1 quart milk
¼ cup whipping cream or
   undiluted evaporated milk
3 tablespoons plus 1 teaspoon
   espresso instant coffee

6 eggs
⅔ cup sugar
1 tablespoon vanilla extract
Additional whipping cream,
   whipped (optional)

Scald milk, cream, and coffee in a saucepan; coffee will completely dissolve. Set aside.

Combine eggs and sugar in a large mixing bowl; beat well. Continue beating with a wire whisk, and gradually pour in hot coffee mixture in a slow, thin stream. Add vanilla, and strain into twelve 6-ounce custard cups.

Set custard cups in a pan; pour hot water into pan to a depth of 1 inch. Bake at 325° for 35 minutes or until a knife inserted in center of custard comes out clean. Remove custard cups from water; cool. Chill, if desired. Garnish with a dollop of whipped cream, if desired. Yield: 12 servings.

Old Winston-Salem Dinner

Blue Danube Cocktails
Cold Peach Soup
Wiener Schnitzel
Rotkohl (Red Cabbage)
Hot German Potato Salad
Gingerbread with Lemon Sauce

Serves 8

The easy, delicious recipes in this menu can all be prepared the day of the dinner, although you can make the soup and refrigerate or freeze it almost anytime. Cook the red cabbage, start the potato salad, and bake the gingerbread early in the day, if you wish. The Wiener Schnitzel should be prepared at least 1 hour before cooking. Sauté the schnitzel and finish the potato salad just before serving.

Wine Suggestion: A medium-dry German Reisling would match the food beautifully, but beer would also be appropriate.

Blue Danube Cocktails

A delightful apéritif. You'll need two bottles of Liebfraumilch to serve eight guests.

**1 tablespoon (½ ounce) Petite
Bleuzette (blueberry liqueur)**

¼ cup (4 ounces) Liebfraumilch

Pour blueberry liqueur into the bottom of a white wine glass; slowly add Liebfraumilch. Do not stir. Yield: 1 serving.

Cold Peach Soup

**6 cups peeled, diced peaches, or 2
(29-ounce) cans peach halves in
heavy syrup**
**2 (8-ounce) cartons commercial
sour cream**

**2 tablespoons Triple Sec or other
orange-flavored liqueur**
2 tablespoons lemon juice
2 teaspoons almond extract
¼ teaspoon salt

Combine all ingredients in container of an electric blender; process 3 minutes, or until smooth. Pour into bowl or pitcher. Cover and chill at least 3 hours. Yield: 6 cups.

Wiener Schnitzel à la Winifred

This favorite recipe tastes best if you prepare and season the veal at least 1 hour before cooking.

2 pounds veal cutlets, cut ¼-inch thick
1 tablespoon salt, divided
¼ teaspoon white pepper
2 eggs, beaten
½ cup milk
2 tablespoons vegetable oil

1½ cups all-purpose flour
3 cups soft breadcrumbs
½ cup butter or margarine
1 lemon, thinly sliced
¼ cup capers
¼ cup lemon juice

Flatten cutlets to ⅛-inch thickness, using a meat mallet or rolling pin. Cut into serving-size pieces. Sprinkle with 2 teaspoons salt and white pepper.

Combine eggs, milk, oil, and remaining salt in a shallow bowl; mix well. Dredge cutlets in flour and dip in egg mixture. Dredge in breadcrumbs, coating well. Chill cutlets at least 1 hour so coating will adhere to veal.

Sauté cutlets in butter in a large skillet about 3 minutes on each side or until browned. Drain well on paper towels. Transfer to serving platter and garnish with lemon slices and capers. Pour lemon juice over top before serving. Yield: 8 servings.

Rotkohl (Red Cabbage)

As sturdy as it is delicious, this red cabbage dish can be prepared early in the day and reheated just before serving.

2 medium apples, cored and thinly sliced
2 small onions, thinly sliced
¼ cup butter or margarine
2 medium-size red cabbage, cleaned and shredded
½ cup vinegar

1 cup Burgundy or other dry red wine
¼ cup plus 2 tablespoons apple jelly
⅛ teaspoon ground cloves
2 tablespoons all-purpose flour

Sauté apple and onion slices in butter in a large Dutch oven until tender. Add remaining ingredients, except flour; stir well. Cook, covered, over medium heat 15 minutes or until cabbage is tender. Remove ¼ cup liquid from pan; add flour, stirring until a smooth paste is formed. Add paste to cabbage; stir well. Cook, uncovered, 5 minutes or until slightly thickened. Yield: 8 servings.

Hot German Potato Salad

You can prepare the potatoes and onion mixture hours in advance, but don't toss them with the warm dressing until you're ready to serve. The flavors are fabulous!

3 pounds red potatoes
10 slices bacon
¾ cup minced onion
½ cup minced green onion
¼ cup minced celery
2 teaspoons all-purpose flour
1 tablespoon plus 2 teaspoons
   sugar

2 teaspoons salt
¼ teaspoon pepper
1 tablespoon plus 1 teaspoon
   prepared mustard
½ cup vinegar
¾ cup water

Scrub potatoes; cook in boiling water 30 minutes or until tender. Drain, and cool slightly. Peel potatoes; cut into ½-inch cubes. Set aside.

Cook bacon in a large skillet until crisp; remove bacon, reserving 2 tablespoons drippings in skillet. Crumble bacon, and set aside. Sauté onion, green onion, and celery in reserved bacon drippings until tender; set aside.

Combine flour, sugar, salt, pepper, and mustard in a medium saucepan; add vinegar and water. Cook 10 minutes over medium heat, or until slightly thickened.

Combine potatoes and onion mixture in a large mixing bowl; top with vinegar mixture, tossing gently. Sprinkle with crumbled bacon. Serve immediately. Yield: 8 to 10 servings.

Gingerbread with Lemon Sauce

Very light and very rich.

1 cup butter or margarine, softened
1 cup sugar
1 cup molasses
3 eggs
3 cups all-purpose flour
1½ teaspoons baking soda
½ teaspoon salt

1½ teaspoons ground ginger
1 teaspoon ground cinnamon
½ teaspoon ground cloves
1 (8-ounce) carton commercial sour
   cream
Lemon Sauce (page 269)

Cream butter, add sugar and molasses, beating well. Add eggs, one at a time, beating well after each addition. Combine flour, baking soda, salt, ginger, cinnamon, and cloves; add to creamed mixture, beating well. Stir in sour cream.

Pour batter into a greased and floured 13- x 9- x 2-inch baking pan. Bake at 350° for 55 minutes or until a wooden pick inserted in center comes out clean. Cool in the pan before cutting into 2-inch squares. Top each serving with Lemon Sauce, if desired. Yield: 2 dozen (2-inch) squares.

 To Peel Peaches: Hold each on a long-handled fork and dip in boiling water about 10 seconds; then rinse under cold water. The skin will loosen enough for you to pull it off with your fingers.

Lamb Curry Dinner

Israeli Eggplant Salad
Lamb Curry
Exotic Cabbage
Nectarine Chutney
Orange Floating Island
Pecan Thins

Serves 6

The Israeli Eggplant Salad, Lamb Curry, and the dessert can be made the day before. The cookies will keep for weeks. If you don't have a jar or two of homemade chutney on hand, you can quickly do a batch of Nectarine Chutney in the food processor or use a favorite purchased brand. Because everything, including the rice and cabbage, can be done ahead, this is a good menu to come home to after a show or other evening activity. If you are making the rice and cabbage ahead, undercook them slightly, so that they don't become dried out or limp while standing.

Beverage Suggestion: Beer is the traditional brew served with curry, but an inexpensive red wine would go well too. Serve a spiced tea, such as apple or mint, with dessert.

Israeli Eggplant Salad

Colorful and piquant, this eggplant salad may be served as a first course, side dish, dip, or snack. Cut rounds of pita bread into wedges and serve warm from the oven with the salad.

1 large or 2 medium eggplant
⅛ to ¼ cup lemon juice
¼ cup green pepper, finely chopped
¼ cup parsley, finely chopped
2 green onions, finely chopped
¼ cup finely chopped dill pickle
¼ teaspoon garlic powder

2 tablespoons olive oil
¼ teaspoon freshly ground black pepper
1 tablespoon mayonnaise
1 tomato, cut into wedges
Iceberg lettuce
Pita bread

Place whole unpeeled eggplant on squares of aluminum foil. Roast in oven at 400° for 40 minutes, turning occasionally so eggplant will be tender on all sides. Eggplant is done when the peel looks charred all over and the flesh feels soft.

Rinse roasted eggplant, and peel. Scoop out pulp into a bowl; add lemon juice. Mash pulp with a wooden spoon and let cool. Add green pepper, parsley, green onion, dill pickle, garlic powder, olive oil, pepper, and mayonnaise. Stir well, and chill until served. Serve on individual plates and garnish with tomato wedges. Yield: 6 servings.

Note: This mixture may be used to fill pita bread for sandwiches, or serve small wedges of pita bread with the salad.

Lamb Curry

This curry will taste even better if made 1 day ahead, refrigerated, and, reheated before serving. Set out at least one chutney and several other condiments to add intrigue.

2 pounds ground lamb	1 teaspoon Worcestershire sauce
2 ribs celery, finely chopped	½ teaspoon salt
1 medium onion, peeled and finely chopped	1 teaspoon seasoned salt
1 medium apple, peeled and finely chopped	¼ teaspoon garlic salt
	2 tablespoons all-purpose flour
3 tablespoons butter	2 cups chicken bouillon, heated
1 tablespoon plus 1 teaspoon curry powder	Additional bouillon or milk
	1½ cups cooked regular rice
	Condiments

Cook lamb in a large skillet over medium heat until browned, stirring to crumble meat. Set aside.

Sauté celery, onion, and apple in butter in a large skillet 7 minutes. Add curry powder, Worcestershire sauce, salt, seasoned salt, and flour; blend well. Cook 2 minutes, stirring constantly. Add heated bouillon, bring to a boil, stirring constantly. Add lamb and continue simmering 12 to 15 minutes. If mixture becomes too thick, thin with bouillon or milk to desired consistency. Serve with cooked rice and condiments. Yield: 6 servings.

Note: Finely chopped leftover lamb may be substituted for ground lamb. Omit the first step of instructions.

Condiments to Serve with Lamb

Apple, fig, mango, nectarine, orange, or peach chutney	Ground peanuts
Watermelon pickle or preserves	Sliced candied ginger
Grated coconut	Sliced bananas
	Golden raisins

Exotic Cabbage

I sampled this first in Barbados, although its origin is East Indian. It would also be great served with barbecued beef or pork.

1 medium onion, finely chopped
½ cup grated coconut
¾ teaspoon mustard seeds
1 teaspoon turmeric
½ cup butter or margarine

1 large cabbage, cleaned and
   shredded
1 teaspoon salt
1 teaspoon pepper

Sauté onion, coconut, mustard seeds, and turmeric in butter in a medium Dutch oven 2 minutes. Add cabbage, salt, and pepper; stir well. Cover and cook 15 minutes, stirring occasionally. Serve warm. Yield: 8 servings.

Nectarine Chutney

A zesty chutney that goes beautifully with lamb and is especially good with Indian curry dishes. This will keep for several months if tightly covered and refrigerated or almost indefinitely if processed in sterilized jars.

4 pounds ripe nectarines, washed,
   quartered and seed removed
2 large onions, peeled and
   quartered
2 large green peppers, seeded and
   quartered
1 fresh green chili pepper, washed
   or 1 (3-oz.) can green chili
   peppers, seeded

3 cloves garlic
½ cup ginger, cut into pieces
2½ teaspoons salt
3½ cups brown sugar
2½ cups cider vinegar
2 cups white raisins
½ teaspoon cayenne or 1 teaspoon
   hot sauce (optional for very hot
   curry)

Position slicing disc in food processor bowl; fill feed tube with nectarine quarters, standing them upright. Process, using moderate pressure on pusher. Place nectarines in large Dutch oven. With knife blade in place, add onions, green peppers, chili pepper, garlic, ginger and salt to processor bowl. Process, turning off and on rapidly, until finely chopped, about 10 to 15 seconds.

Combine chopped ingredients, nectarines, brown sugar, vinegar, and raisins. Cook uncovered over low heat, stirring frequently for about 2 hours to make a thick rich chutney. If you desire a very hot chutney, add ½ teaspoon cayenne pepper or 1 teaspoon hot sauce. Pour mixture into sterilized jars, leaving ½-inch headspace. Cover at once with metal lids and screw bands tight. Process in boiling-water bath 10 minutes. Yield: 11 half-pints.

 To Speed Ripening of Fruit: Place unripe fruit in a plastic bag along with a ripe apple, or a similar piece of ripe fruit. Ripe fruit gives off a natural gas which speeds up the ripening of the other fruit.

Ida Belle Young's Orange Floating Island

A light dessert with the refreshing taste of chilled oranges.

4 large oranges, peeled and
    sectioned
1¼ cups plus 2 tablespoons sugar,
    divided
2 cups milk

3 egg yolks
1 tablespoon plus 2 teaspoons
    cornstarch
3 egg whites
½ teaspoon vanilla extract

Place orange sections in a large, ovenproof bowl, and sprinkle with 1 cup sugar; chill.

Combine egg yolks, milk, and cornstarch in top of a double boiler. Cook, stirring constantly, until mixture is thickened. Remove from heat; cover and chill.

Pour chilled mixture over chilled orange sections; set aside.

Beat egg whites (at room temperature) until soft peaks form. Gradually add ¼ cup plus 2 tablespoons sugar, 1 tablespoon at a time, until stiff peaks form. Stir in ½ teaspoon vanilla. Spoon meringue over top of custard, spreading to cover custard completely. Bake at 325° for 15 minutes or until meringue is golden brown. Cool on wire racks. Serve cold. Yield: 6 to 8 servings.

Pecan Thins

Crisp wafers to accompany any light dessert.

1 cup butter or margarine, softened
1 cup sugar
1 cup firmly packed dark brown
    sugar
1 egg

1 tablespoon vanilla extract
3 cups all-purpose flour
½ teaspoon baking powder
½ teaspoon baking soda
1½ cups finely chopped pecans

Cream butter in a large mixing bowl; gradually add sugar, beating well. Add egg and vanilla; beat until well blended.

Combine flour, baking powder, and soda in a medium mixing bowl. Gradually add to creamed mixture, beating well after each addition. Stir in pecans.

Divide dough in half; shape each half into a roll 1½ inches in diameter. Wrap in waxed paper, and chill 3 hours or until firm. Cut dough into ¼-inch-thick slices; place 2 inches apart on lightly greased cookie sheets. Bake at 350° for 12 minutes or until lightly browned. Cool on wire racks. Place in airtight containers. These will keep for several weeks. Yield: about 8 dozen.

Spring Lamb Dinner

Cream of Artichoke Soup
Lamb Stuffed with Apricots and Wild Rice
Carrots Lyonnaise
Eggplant Patties
Hot Rolls
Grand Marnier Soufflé

Serves 6

This is a menu of delicate tastes and impressive dishes, but it's not hard to accomplish. Make the soup and marinate the lamb up to 2 days ahead. While the lamb is in the oven, prepare the carrots and eggplant patties. The carrots will reheat well, and the eggplant can be kept warm until serving time. The timing for the soufflé is less tricky than you might think. You can make the custard base before dinner; then beat the egg whites and put the soufflé in the oven after the entrée has been served and while the coffee is brewing.

Wine Suggestion: A California Petite Sirah or Merlot red wine would match the range of subtle tastes in this menu.

Cream of Artichoke Soup

2 large artichokes, cleaned and boiled	1 teaspoon dried minced onion
½ cup finely chopped green onion	¼ teaspoon hot sauce
½ cup finely chopped carrots	⅛ teaspoon pepper
1 stalk celery, finely chopped	⅛ teaspoon ground thyme
¼ cup butter or margarine, melted	1 bay leaf
3 (10¾-ounce) cans chicken broth	1 cup whipping cream
	2 egg yolks, beaten

Pull away the leaf section of each cooked artichoke, starting from the outside and working toward the center. Scrape the base of each leaf section with a knife; reserve pulp and set aside. Discard leaves.

Scrape out the fuzzy thistle center (choke) with a spoon, leaving the heart. Trim rough edges from bottom of heart. Chop heart and set aside.

Sauté green onion, carrots, and celery in butter 10 minutes. Add chicken broth, minced onion, hot sauce, pepper, thyme, and bay leaf; bring to a boil. Reduce heat; simmer 15 minutes. Add reserved artichoke pulp and chopped heart; simmer an additional 10 minutes. (Recipe can be prepared to this point and refrigerated up to 2 days or frozen. Reheat over low heat before proceeding with recipe.)

Combine whipping cream and egg yolks; beat with a wire whisk until smooth. Add whipping cream mixture to hot soup, stirring constantly. Yield: about 1½ quarts.

Lamb Stuffed with Apricots and Wild Rice

Marinate the lamb at least 1 day to mellow its flavor. Then match the robust taste with an aromatic stuffing.

1 (7- to 8-pound) leg of lamb, bone removed
1 cup red wine
½ cup Worcestershire sauce
2 teaspoons lemon-pepper seasoning, divided
1 (6-ounce) package dried apricots, finely chopped

1 cup apple brandy
1 cup chopped onion
¼ cup chopped fresh basil or 4 teaspoons dried basil leaves
2 teaspoons salt, divided
1 (6-ounce) package long grain and wild rice, cooked according to package directions

Marinate lamb in wine, Worcestershire sauce, and 1 teaspoon lemon-pepper seasoning in a large container in the refrigerator for at least 24 hours.

Marinate apricots in brandy for 24 hours.

Remove lamb from marinade; reserve marinade for basting.

Combine remaining lemon-pepper seasoning, marinated apricots, onion, basil, salt, and cooked rice in a large bowl; blend well. Stuff lamb with rice mixture, packing lightly to allow stuffing to expand during cooking. Secure opening with skewers or string. Place lamb on rack in a shallow roasting pan, stuffed side up. Bake at 325° for 40 minutes per pound. Pour some of reserved marinade over roast and baste three to four times during cooking.

Remove skewer or string; slice and serve. Yield: 10 to 12 servings.

Carrots Lyonnaise

This preparation brings out the sweetness of carrots—making them a great match for the fruit-stuffed lamb or pork or poultry.

1 pound carrots, scraped and shredded
1¾ cups chicken broth, divided
3 medium onions, sliced
¼ cup butter or margarine

Pinch of sugar
1 tablespoon all-purpose flour
¼ teaspoon salt
⅛ teaspoon white pepper
Dash of freshly grated nutmeg

Combine carrots and 1 cup chicken broth in saucepan. Cover and cook 10 minutes.

Sauté onion in butter in a large skillet. Add sugar; cover and cook 15 minutes, stirring occasionally. Add flour, stirring until onion is coated. Cook 1 minute, stirring constantly. Gradually add salt, pepper, and remaining chicken broth; bring to a boil. Add carrots and dash of nutmeg; simmer, uncovered, 10 minutes. Yield: 6 to 8 servings.

Eggplant Patties

These crisp patties can be placed on a baking sheet and held in a warm oven up to 2 hours.

1 medium eggplant, peeled	2 teaspoons butter, melted
1 onion, minced	1 cup breadcrumbs
2 eggs, well beaten	Vegetable oil
1 cup milk	

Finely chop eggplant. Add remaining ingredients except oil, and mix well. Drop mixture by tablespoonfuls into deep hot oil (375°). Cook 2 to 4 minutes or until golden brown. Drain on paper towels. Yield: 6 to 8 patties.

Grand Marnier Soufflé

Heavenly, and easy to do.

1 tablespoon butter or margarine, softened	5 eggs, separated
¾ cup plus 2 tablespoons sugar, divided	1 teaspoon vanilla extract
	¼ teaspoon salt
2 tablespoons unsalted butter	¼ teaspoon cream of tartar
2 tablespoons all-purpose flour	¼ cup Grand Marnier
¾ cup whipping cream, divided	Sifted powdered sugar

Grease a 2-quart soufflé dish with butter; sprinkle with 1 tablespoon sugar. Chill.

Melt butter over low heat in a heavy saucepan. Add flour, stirring until smooth. Cook 1 minute, stirring constantly. Add ½ cup whipping cream and ¾ cup sugar; stir until smooth. Remove from heat; set aside. Combine remaining cream and egg yolks, beating well.

Add yolk mixture to sugar mixture; cook over medium heat 1 minute, stirring constantly. Stir in vanilla, and set aside. (Recipe can be prepared to this point 2 hours ahead and held at room temperature.)

Beat egg whites (at room temperature), salt, and cream of tartar until foamy. Gradually add remaining sugar, beating until stiff peaks form. Gently fold egg whites into egg yolk mixture; pour into prepared soufflé dish. Pour Grand Marnier over soufflé mixture and stir to distribute evenly throughout mixture. Bake at 375° for 30 minutes or until golden brown. Sprinkle with powdered sugar, and serve immediately. Yield: 6 to 8 servings.

Festive Chicken Dinner

Parmesan Canapés
Chicken Casserole
Sweet Potato Pone
Green Beans with Almonds
Asphodel Bread
Blueberry Jam Cake
or
Strawberry Cake

Serves 8

Make the strawberry cake at least 1 day ahead, and pace the bread and sweet potato pone any way you wish. Both are easy enough to do the day of the dinner, but the bread can be frozen in advance and the pone will keep in the refrigerator for several days. Put the Parmesan Canapés in the oven when the doorbell rings—and don't forget them because they brown quickly! Cook the green beans after guests have arrived, while the chicken finishes baking.

Wine Suggestion: Any not-too-dry white wine, such as French Vouvray, or a rosé would be fine. A glass of champagne would be delightful with the strawberry cake!

Parmesan Canapés

Good with cocktails or a glass of wine.

½ cup mayonnaise
¼ cup grated Parmesan cheese
2 tablespoons dried minced onion

3 tablespoons (1½ ounces) beer
4 slices whole wheat bread

Combine mayonnaise, Parmesan cheese, minced onion, and beer. Mix well.

Remove crust from bread, and slice into four triangles. Spread filling on each triangle. Bake at 375° until puffed and brown. (Watch carefully to prevent burning.) Yield: 16 canapés.

Variations: For herbed canapés add 1 teaspoon dried dill weed or celery seed.

To make spicy canapés, add ⅛ teaspoon red pepper and 1 teaspoon cumin.

To make blue cheese canapés substitute 2 tablespoons crumbled blue cheese for half of the Parmesan cheese.

Evelyn Wills's Chicken Casserole

4 chicken breasts, halved
¼ cup butter or margarine
¼ cup vegetable oil
1 pound fresh mushrooms
¾ cup all-purpose flour
1 cup dry white wine
2 cups chicken stock

½ cup half-and-half
Salt and pepper to taste
½ teaspoon tarragon
2 (14-ounce) cans artichoke hearts, drained
6 green onions, chopped
Chopped fresh parsley

Brown chicken in butter and oil in a large skillet. Remove chicken; place in casserole and set aside. Reserve drippings in skillet.

Sauté mushrooms in skillet until tender. Stir in flour, wine, and chicken stock; cook, stirring constantly, until sauce thickens. Stir in half-and-half, salt, pepper, and tarragon. Pour sauce over chicken in casserole and bake, uncovered, at 350° for 1 hour. (Recipe can be prepared to this point several hours ahead.)

Remove casserole from oven; place artichoke hearts between pieces of chicken. Sprinkle with chopped green onion; bake an additional 5 minutes or until artichokes are heated through. Sprinkle parsley over top; serve immediately. Yield: 8 servings.

Bitty Creekmore's Sweet Potato Pone

A sweet side dish for chicken, ham, or pork roast.

4 cups peeled and shredded sweet potatoes
Rind of 1 orange, grated
1½ cups sugar
½ teaspoon salt
¾ cup butter or margarine, softened

1 cup milk
2 eggs, lightly beaten
1 teaspoon cinnamon
¼ teaspoon nutmeg
1 teaspoon vanilla extract (optional)

Combine sweet potatoes and orange rind in a large mixing bowl; mix well. Add sugar, salt, butter, milk, eggs, cinnamon, nutmeg, and vanilla, if desired; blend thoroughly. Spoon mixture into a greased 8-inch square baking dish. Bake at 325° for 1 hour and 30 minutes. Serve hot or cold. Yield: 10 to 12 servings.

Asphodel Bread

A shortcut to freshly baked bread.

2 packages dry yeast
2 cups warm milk (105° to 115°)
5 cups biscuit mix
¼ cup sugar

½ teaspoon salt
4 large eggs
¼ teaspoon cream of tartar

Dissolve yeast in warm milk; let stand 5 minutes or until bubbly.

Sift together biscuit mix, sugar, and salt into a large mixing bowl; set aside.

Combine eggs and cream of tartar in a small mixing bowl; beat slightly. Add yeast mixture, beating well. Stir egg mixture into reserved dry ingredients, mixing well. (Dough will be very sticky.)

Cover, and let rise in a warm place (85°), free from drafts, 1 hour or until doubled in bulk. Stir mixture down; pour into 2 greased 8½- x 4½- x 3-inch loafpans. Repeat rising procedure.

Bake at 350° for 20 minutes or until golden brown. Remove from pans immediately; slice, and serve very warm. Yield: 2 loaves.

Blueberry Jam Cake

1 cup butter or margarine, softened	1 teaspoon ground cloves
2 cups sifted sugar	1 cup milk
4 large eggs	1 teaspoon lemon extract
3 cups all-purpose flour	1 teaspoon grated lemon rind
1 tablespoon baking powder	1 cup blueberry jam
⅛ teaspoon salt	Seven Minute Frosting
1 teaspoon ground cinnamon	

Cream butter; gradually add sugar, beating with an electric mixer until light and fluffy. Add 2 eggs, one at a time, beating well after each addition. Beat mixture at high speed of electric mixer for 4 minutes. Add 2 remaining eggs, one at a time, beating well after each addition.

Sift together flour, baking powder, salt, cinnamon, and cloves. Add flour mixture to creamed mixture alternately with milk, beginning and ending with flour mixture. Beat well. Add lemon extract, rind, and jam; mix well. Spoon batter into 3 greased and floured 9-inch round cakepans. Bake at 350° for 25 minutes or until cake tests done. Cool in pans 10 minutes. Remove from pans and let cool completely before frosting with Seven Minute Frosting. Yield: one 3-layer cake.

Seven Minute Frosting

3 egg whites (at room temperature)	¼ cup plus 1 tablespoon cold water
¼ teaspoon cream of tartar	1½ teaspoons light corn syrup
1½ cups sifted sugar	1 teaspoon vanilla extract

Place all ingredients except vanilla in top of a double boiler over boiling water. Beat at high speed of an electric mixer 7 minutes or until stiff peaks form. Remove from heat; add vanilla. Spread frosting on cake. Yield: frosting for one 3-layer cake.

 Frosting a Cake: To keep the plate neat while frosting a cake, place three or four strips of waxed paper over the edges. Position the cake on the plate, and fill and frost it; then carefully pull out the waxed paper strips.

Marie Rose's Strawberry Cake

1 (18.5-ounce) package deluxe
  white cake mix
2 egg whites
1⅓ cups water

1 teaspoon vanilla extract
Custard Filling
Glazed Strawberries and Topping

Combine cake mix, egg whites (at room temperature), water, and vanilla in a large mixing bowl. Blend until moistened. Beat at high speed of an electric mixer 2 minutes; reduce speed to medium, and beat 1 minute.

Pour batter into two greased, floured, and waxed paper-lined 9-inch round cakepans. Bake at 350° for 20 to 25 minutes or until cake tests done. Cool in pan 15 minutes; remove and let cool completely on wire racks. Yield: one 2-layer cake.

To assemble cake: Place one cake layer on crystal platter or cake stand. Spoon chilled set Custard Filling over cake layer. Cover custard layer with 1 cup sliced strawberries; reserve remaining strawberries and juice to use as sauce. Place second cake layer on top. Frost top and sides of cake with flavored whipped cream.

Arrange 8 glazed strawberries in a circle around top edge of cake. Cut remaining 12 glazed strawberries in half, and stand up around bottom edge of cake. Refrigerate until served.

Slice cake and serve with strawberries and juice Yield: 20 servings.

Custard Filling

1 envelope unflavored gelatin
2 cups milk, divided
3 egg yolks
1 egg
2 tablespoons instant-blending
  flour

¾ cup sugar
⅛ teaspoon salt
1 teaspoon vanilla extract
1 tablespoon strawberry liqueur
  (optional)

Dissolve gelatin in ¼ cup cold milk; set aside.

Combine egg yolks and whole egg; beat lightly. Add flour, sugar, and salt to beaten egg and yolks; mix well.

Place remaining milk in top of a double boiler, and heat until warm; slowly add egg mixture. Cook over boiling water, stirring constantly, 20 minutes or until mixture begins to coat a metal spoon. Add dissolved gelatin mixture to egg mixture; cook 10 minutes or until the mixture thickens. Remove from heat and cool to room temperature; add vanilla and liqueur, if desired. Chill custard until set. Yield: about 2 cups.

Glazed Strawberries and Topping

3 pints large, ripe strawberries,
  washed and drained
1 (10-ounce) jar red currant jelly
1 cup sugar

¼ cup plus 2 tablespoons sifted
  powdered sugar
2 tablespoons Grand Marnier
2 cups whipping cream, whipped

Slice off stem end of strawberries. Select 20 berries uniform in size. Place currant jelly in a small saucepan and melt over low heat. Dip strawberries in melted jelly and place on a platter. Slice remaining strawberries in a glass bowl, and cover with 1 cup sugar.

Fold powdered sugar and Grand Marnier into whipped cream. Yield: about 3 cups.

A Small Dinner Party

Shrimp Sauté
Cornish Hens with Soy Sauce
Spicy Rice
Asparagus Casserole
Oriental Salad with Ginger Dressing
Luscious Raspberry Cream

Serves 4

An enticing meal for a small group. You can double the shrimp, Cornish hen, and rice recipes to expand the menu for eight. Either way, careful timing will yield best flavors. Make the dessert and assemble the Asparagus Casserole 1 day ahead. Start the rice up to 3 hours ahead; finish it while the hens are baking. The salad dressing can be made and refrigerated up to 5 days ahead, and the salad can be made the morning of the dinner; combine the two just before serving. The shrimp can be reheated, but they'll taste better if you sauté them just before serving.

Wine Suggestion: Serve any simple white or red wine with this meal—ranging from a California Chenin Blanc to a French Brouilly. The assertive tastes of the food would overwhelm a more complex wine.

Shrimp Sauté

A fast first course served with French bread. This recipe also serves two as a main course with rice.

2 tablespoons butter	⅛ teaspoon black pepper
2 cups small shrimp, peeled and deveined	⅛ teaspoon mace
½ teaspoon chopped garlic	2 teaspoons chopped parsley
¼ teaspoon salt	Toasted French bread

Melt butter in large heavy skillet over medium heat; add all ingredients except parsley. Cook about 10 minutes; add parsley. Serve with toasted French bread. Yield: 4 servings.

Shrimp Tip: Use kitchen shears to cut shells from shrimp, to snip parsley, to trim pastry shells, and to cut many other foods.

Cornish Hens with Soy Sauce

Two Cornish hens will feed four people amply with the rest of this menu, but you may wish to double the recipe if appetites are hearty.

2 (1- to 1½-pounds) Cornish hens	⅛ teaspoon pepper
3 tablespoons butter or margarine, softened	¼ cup soy sauce
	Hot cooked rice (optional)
¼ teaspoon lemon-pepper seasoning	Radish flowers (optional)

Remove giblets from hens; reserve for other uses. Rinse hens with cold water, and pat dry; truss. Rub butter over surface of each hen; sprinkle with lemon-pepper seasoning and pepper. Brush generously with soy sauce.

Place hens in a prepared large oven cooking bag; secure with tie provided. Place hens in a roasting pan and make six ½-inch slits in the oven cooking bag. Bake at 400° for 45 minutes. Remove from bag. Transfer hens to a bed of hot cooked rice, if desired, or Spicy Rice on a serving platter. Garnish with radish flowers, if desired. Yield: 4 servings.

Note: Double the ingredients and use another bag to serve 8.

Spicy Rice

1 large tomato, peeled, seeded, and quartered	⅛ teaspoon ground cloves
1 teaspoon salt	⅛ teaspoon coriander
1 medium onion, chopped	⅛ teaspoon ground ginger
1½ cloves garlic, minced	⅛ teaspoon pepper
2½ tablespoons vegetable oil	1 cup uncooked regular rice
	1½ cups hot water

Place tomato and salt in container of electric blender; process at high speed 5 seconds or until tomato is pureed. Set aside.

Sauté onion and garlic in oil in a large skillet until onion is tender. Stir in cloves, coriander, ginger, pepper, and rice; cook over medium heat, stirring constantly, until rice is lightly browned. (Recipe can be prepared to this point several hours in advance.) Stir in reserved tomato and water. Bring to a boil. Reduce heat; cover, and simmer 20 minutes or until rice is tender. Serve hot. Yield: 4 servings.

Beauty Luckett's Asparagus Casserole

2 eggs, lightly beaten	1 cup (4 ounces) shredded sharp Cheddar cheese
1 cup milk	
1 cup coarsely crushed crackers	⅛ teaspoon hot sauce
1 (10½-ounce) can green cut asparagus spears, undrained	Paprika

Combine eggs and milk in a medium mixing bowl, beating well. Stir in crackers, asparagus, cheese, and hot sauce. Pour mixture into a greased 1-quart casserole. Sprinkle with paprika. Bake at 375° for 45 minutes or until puffed and browned. Serve immediately. Yield: 4 servings.

Note: Casserole may be prepared ahead of time, and refrigerated until ready to bake.

Oriental Salad with Ginger Dressing

4 ounces fresh or frozen and thawed
    snow peas, ends trimmed
¼ cup rice vinegar
1 teaspoon finely grated gingerroot
2 tablespoons plus 1 teaspoon
    vegetable oil
2 teaspoons sesame oil

1 small red onion, peeled and
    thinly sliced
1 small cucumber, scored and
    thinly sliced
8 cherry tomatoes
½ teaspoon salt
⅛ teaspoon pepper

If using fresh snow peas, cook in boiling water 1 minute. Drain; rinse under cold water, and pat dry.

Combine vinegar and gingerroot in a small mixing bowl. Gradually add oils, beating constantly with a wire whisk. Set aside.

Combine snow peas, onion, cucumber, and tomatoes in a salad bowl; sprinkle with salt and pepper. Pour dressing over vegetables; toss lightly. Chill 1 hour. Serve on salad plates. Yield: 4 servings.

Luscious Raspberry Cream

2 (10-ounce) packages frozen
    raspberries, thawed
1 envelope plus 2 teaspoons
    unflavored gelatin
¾ cup sugar

1 teaspoon raspberry liqueur
2 teaspoons lemon juice
1 (13-ounce) can evaporated milk
3 tablespoons powdered sugar
1 cup whipping cream, whipped

Drain raspberries, reserving juice. Set aside.

Combine raspberry juice and enough water to equal 2 cups in a medium saucepan over medium heat. Add gelatin and sugar to liquid; bring to a boil. Strain and cool to room temperature. Add raspberry liqueur and lemon juice. Stir in milk; set aside.

Fold powdered sugar into whipped cream. Stir sweetened whipped cream and raspberries into cooled mixture. Pour into a large glass bowl, and chill until set. Yield: 8 servings.

Fall Dinner

Butternut Squash Soup
Smothered Quail
Double Mushroom Brown Rice
Braised Kale
or
Green Bean Casserole
Apricot Salad
Hot Rolls
Black Russian Cake
or
Mocha Dacquoise

Serves 8

The lush flavors of this dinner are those of sturdy autumn fare. The soup, salad, casserole, and desserts can all be made at least 1 day ahead. The Smothered Quail, Double Mushroom Brown Rice, and Braised Kale can all be held a few hours and reheated.

Wine Suggestion: A California Gamay Beaujolais or an Alsatian Gewurztraminer will hold its own with the spectrum of fall flavors.

Butternut Squash Soup

The velvety texture of cooked butternut squash gives this soup a natural richness.

1 (2- to 2½-pound) butternut
    squash
¼ cup butter
2 medium onions, minced
1 large tart apple, cored, chopped
1 large pear, cored, chopped
1 stalk celery, minced
¼ teaspoon ground cinnamon
¼ teaspoon ground mace
¼ teaspoon ground mustard

2 (14-ounce) cans chicken broth,
    divided
½ cup white wine
1 tablespoon apple brandy
    (optional)
Salt and pepper
Freshly grated nutmeg
Toasted chopped black walnuts or
    pecans (optional)

Place squash on baking sheet; prick skin in several places with tines of fork. Bake at 400° for 50 to 60 minutes or until completely tender. Let stand until cool enough to handle.

Melt butter in large, heavy saucepan over medium-low heat; add onion, apple, and pear. Cook, stirring occasionally, 40 minutes.

Cut squash in half lengthwise; remove and discard seeds. Scoop squash from rind and add to saucepan, mashing to mix into onion mixture. Add celery and spices. Stir in one can chicken broth; heat to boiling. Reduce heat; simmer 15 minutes. Transfer to food processor or blender (in two batches, if necessary); puree until smooth. Return to saucepan; stir in remaining 1 can chicken broth, white wine, apple brandy, if desired, and salt and pepper to taste. Heat until hot. Spoon into individual bowls; garnish with generous grating of nutmeg and chopped nuts, if desired. Yield: 8 cups.

Note: The soup can be refrigerated up to 2 days or frozen up to 3 months.

Smothered Quail

An easy and delicious way to serve quail.

8 quail, dressed	3 tablespoons all-purpose flour
1 teaspoon salt	2 beef-flavored bouillon cubes
½ teaspoon black pepper	2 cups boiling water
5 tablespoons butter	½ cup sherry
1 tablespoon vegetable oil	1 teaspoon dried green onion

Sprinkle quail with salt and pepper. Brown quail in a large heavy skillet in butter and oil over medium high heat. Remove quail to an oblong baking dish. Whisk flour into butter and blend well. Dissolve bouillon cubes in boiling water; gradually add bouillon, sherry, and dried green onion to butter mixture. Cook over medium heat, stirring constantly until mixture is thickened. Salt to taste. Pour over quail. Cover baking dish with foil and bake at 350° for 1 hour or until quail is tender. Yield: 8 servings.

Double Mushroom Brown Rice

2 ounces dried mushrooms	1 pound fresh mushrooms, sliced
1 cup Burgundy or other dry, red wine	Salt and pepper
	2 (14-ounce) cans beef broth
¼ cup butter	2 cups uncooked brown rice

Soak dried mushrooms in wine in small bowl 30 minutes. Remove any hard cores from dried mushrooms and discard. Tear mushrooms into pieces; return to wine. Set aside.

Melt 2 tablespoons butter in medium skillet over medium heat; add half of fresh mushrooms and toss to coat. Increase heat to high; sauté mushrooms just until softened. Sprinkle with salt and pepper to taste; spoon into bowl and reserve. Repeat with remaining butter and fresh mushrooms; set aside.

Combine broth and wine-soaked mushrooms in a large saucepan; bring to boil. Stir in rice. Cook, covered, over low heat until rice is tender and all liquid is absorbed, 40 to 50 minutes. Stir in sautéed mushrooms. Yield: 8 servings.

Note: Recipe can be made up to 8 hours in advance and reheated over low heat.

Braised Kale

Collard or turnip greens can be prepared the same way.

4 slices bacon
1 large onion, minced
2 pounds kale, stems removed and
　　leaves torn into pieces
1 cup chicken broth

1 (8-ounce) carton commercial sour
　　cream
2 teaspoons Dijon mustard
¼ teaspoon freshly ground pepper

Cook bacon in large skillet until crisp; remove, drain, crumble, and reserve. Add onion to bacon drippings in skillet; cook over medium heat 5 minutes. Stir in kale and chicken broth. If all of the kale will not fit into the skillet, wait a few minutes before adding remainder; the kale will cook down quickly. Cook, covered, stirring occasionally, until kale is tender, about 45 minutes. (Recipe can be made to this point several hours in advance.) Stir in sour cream, mustard, pepper, and reserved bacon; simmer, uncovered, 3 minutes. Yield: 8 servings.

Allan Cheney's Green Bean Casserole

3 (16-ounce) cans French-style
　　green beans
1 (10¾-ounce) can of cream of
　　mushroom soup, undiluted
1 (8-ounce) carton sour cream
1 cup (4 ounces) shredded sharp
　　Cheddar cheese, divided

1 teaspoon garlic salt
¼ teaspoon hot sauce
½ cup cracker crumbs
2 tablespoons butter or margarine,
　　melted

Drain green beans well. Transfer to a 1-½-quart casserole; set aside.

Combine soup, sour cream, ½ cup shredded cheese, garlic salt, and hot sauce; mix until well blended. Pour over beans; sprinkle with remaining cheese and cracker crumbs, and pour butter evenly over top. Bake at 350° for 30 minutes. Serve hot. Yield: 8 servings.

Elizabeth Cheney's Apricot Salad

A delightful and refreshing salad to serve with any meal.

1 (16-ounce) can apricots, pitted
   and diced
1 (8-ounce) can crushed pineapple
1 (3-ounce) package apricot gelatin
1 teaspoon unflavored gelatin

1 tablespoon lemon juice
1 tablespoon apple brandy
Lettuce
Mayonnaise

Drain fruits and reserve juices. Add enough water to fruit juice to make 1½ cups liquid. Heat juice in small saucepan. Dissolve gelatin in heated juices. Allow to cool. Add apricots, pineapple, lemon juice, and brandy. Pour into lightly greased 1-quart casserole or six 6-ounce individual molds. Chill until set. Unmold and serve on lettuce leaves. Top with a dollop of mayonnaise. Yield: 6 servings.

Note: Grease salad molds with mayonnaise for easier removal of a congealed salad.

Emmett's Black Russian Cake

An easy cake with a distinctive flavor.

1 (18.5-ounce) package yellow cake
   mix
1 (4.5-ounce) package instant
   chocolate pudding
2 teaspoons cinnamon
2 teaspoons instant coffee

4 large eggs
¾ cup water
¾ cup vegetable oil
¼ cup vodka
¼ cup Tia Maria or crème de cacao
Milk Chocolate Frosting

Combine all ingredients except frosting in a large mixing bowl. Blend for 1 minute with electric mixer at low speed; beat at high speed for 2 minutes. (If hand mixing, beat vigorously 300 strokes.) Spoon into greased and floured Bundt pan. Bake at 350° for 45 minutes or until cake tester inserted in cake comes out clean. Cool at least 10 minutes in pan; turn out on wire rack and cool. Ice with Milk Chocolate Frosting. This cake freezes well. Yield: 18 to 20 servings.

Milk Chocolate Frosting

½ (14.3-ounce) package milk
   chocolate frosting mix (about
   1½ cups)
2 tablespoons hot water
2 tablespoons butter, softened
1 tablespoon brandy

1 tablespoon Cointreau, Grand
   Marnier, or other
   orange-flavored liqueur
¼ teaspoon almond extract
2 tablespoons powdered sugar

Combine all ingredients in a small mixing bowl; beat 1 minute at low speed of electric mixer; scraping bowl constantly. Turn to high speed and beat 1 minute, scraping occasionally until frosting is smooth and creamy. Stir in a few more drops water until mixture reaches desired spreading consistency. Yield: frosting for 1 Bundt cake.

Mocha Dacquoise

This is a classic French dessert of meringue discs sandwiched with buttercream. It's time-consuming, but the result is worth the effort. The nut meringue layers can be made several days ahead and stored at room temperature. The finished cake should be refrigerated several hours or overnight.

6 large egg whites	⅛ teaspoon almond extract
¼ teaspoon cream of tartar	1½ cups ground walnuts
¼ teaspoon salt	2 tablespoons cornstarch
1½ cups sugar	Mocha Butter Cream
1 teaspoon vanilla extract	8 walnut halves

Combine egg whites (at room temperature), cream of tartar, and salt in a large mixing bowl; beat until frothy. Add sugar, 1 tablespoon at a time, beating until stiff peaks form and sugar dissolves. Add flavorings, beating well.

Combine ground walnuts and cornstarch in a small mixing bowl; mix well. Gently fold walnut mixture into the meringue. Spoon meringue mixture into a pastry bag fitted with a ⅜-inch tip.

Line three baking sheets with parchment paper. Draw one 8-inch circle on each sheet. Starting at center of each circle, pipe meringue in a flat spiral fashion using a circular motion to fill in each complete circle. Bake at 275° for 1 hour. Turn oven off, and allow meringue to cool in oven 2 hours. (Do not open oven door.) Carefully remove meringue rounds from parchment paper. (Use immediately, or store in an airtight container.)

Place one baked meringue layer on a serving plate. Spread one-third of Mocha Butter Cream evenly over meringue layer. Repeat procedure with second meringue layer. Top with remaining meringue layer. Spoon remaining one-third Mocha Butter Cream into a pastry bag fitted with a star tip. Pipe rosettes around outer edge of meringue layers; pipe 8 rosettes on top. Place a walnut half on top of each rosette.

Chill 3 hours. Slice into wedges, and serve on individual dessert plates. Yield: 8 to 10 servings.

Mocha Butter Cream

6 egg yolks	¼ cup instant coffee granules
2½ cups sifted powdered sugar	1 tablespoon hot water
1½ cups milk, scalded	2 tablespoons Cognac
1 cup unsalted butter, softened	

Combine egg yolks and sugar in a large heavy saucepan; beat well. Gradually add milk, stirring constantly. Cook over medium heat, stirring constantly with a metal spoon, until mixture thickens and coats the spoon. Remove from heat. Set custard aside, and cool to room temperature.

Transfer custard to a large mixing bowl. Add butter, beating until fluffy. Combine coffee, water, and Cognac in a small mixing bowl; add to custard, beating well. Chill. Yield: about 4 cups.

Note: Sift ¼ cup cocoa with the sugar and substitute 2 tablespoons crème de cocoa for the Cognac for a more deeply flavored butter cream.

Seafood Casserole Dinner

Salad Alma
Seafood Supreme
Saffron Rice
Broccoli Parmesan
Lemon Meringue Pie
or
Chocolate Pie with Brown Sugar Meringue

Serves 8

The luxury of this meal belies its ease of preparation. Make the casserole the day before, if you wish. Bake the pie, make the salad dressing, and cut up the citrus for the salad hours ahead. Cook the saffron rice and broccoli, and arrange the salads while the casserole is baking.

Wine Suggestion: Don't serve any wine with the salad — the citrus would spoil the taste. A rich California Chardonnay would go beautifully with the seafood.

Salad Alma

1 head romaine lettuce
2 large grapefruit, peeled and
  sectioned
2 large oranges, peeled and
  sectioned
2 large ripe avocados, peeled,
  seeded, and sliced
Pimiento strips
Vinaigrette Sauce

Arrange lettuce leaves on a large salad platter; arrange grapefruit, orange, and avocado over lettuce. Garnish with pimiento. Serve with Vinaigrette Sauce. Yield: 8 servings.

Note: To peel and section citrus, first cut a slice from each end. Then stand the fruit upright and cut straight down on all sides to remove peel and white membrane. Holding fruit in your hand, separate sections from membrane with a paring knife.

Vinaigrette Sauce

¼ cup plus 2 tablespoons olive oil
¼ cup white wine vinegar
2 tablespoons chopped hard-cooked
  egg
2 teaspoons salt
¼ teaspoon pepper
2 teaspoons capers
2 teaspoons chopped chives
2 teaspoons chopped fresh parsley
2 teaspoons dried whole tarragon

Combine all ingredients, and mix well. Yield: about ½ cup.

Seafood Supreme

Delightfully seasoned seafood creation designed either for a casserole or individual servings in scallop shells. It freezes well and may be reheated. You may use 1½ pounds shrimp and ½ pound crabmeat.

¼ cup plus 2 tablespoons butter or margarine
½ pound fresh mushrooms, cleaned and sliced
1 tablespoon instant-blending flour
1½ cups half-and-half or undiluted evaporated milk, warmed
1 tablespoon dried green onion
¼ teaspoon mace

1 tablespoon minced parsley
½ teaspoon salt
¾ to 1 tablespoon hot sauce
2 egg yolks, beaten
½ cup mayonnaise
1 pound lump crabmeat
1 pound large shrimp, cooked, peeled, and deveined
3 tablespoons breadcrumbs

Sauté mushrooms in 2 tablespoons butter in a large skillet; remove from skillet and set aside.

Melt ¼ cup butter in a large skillet; blend in flour slowly with a wire whisk. Slowly stir in warm half-and-half, dried green onion, mace, parsley, salt, and hot sauce; cook, stirring constantly, until thickened. Add a small amount of thickened sauce to beaten egg yolks, and return to sauce. Cook for a few minutes longer; taste and correct seasonings. Remove from heat.

Fold in mayonnaise; add mushrooms, crabmeat, and shrimp. Pour into a buttered 2½-quart casserole or 8 scallop shells. (Recipe can be made to this point and refrigerated overnight.) Sprinkle breadcrumbs over top. Bake at 350° for 15 to 20 minutes or until mixture is bubbling hot. Yield: 8 to 10 servings or 8 individual scallop shells.

Note: This recipe can be doubled easily.

Broccoli Parmesan

2½ pounds fresh broccoli, cleaned and cooked
½ teaspoon salt
Dash of pepper

2 tablespoons butter or melted margarine
¾ cup grated Parmesan cheese

Arrange broccoli in a serving dish. Season with salt and pepper. Pour melted butter over broccoli, and sprinkle with Parmesan cheese. Place under broiler for 2 minutes or until cheese is golden brown. Yield: about 8 servings.

Lemon Meringue Pie

A wonderful lemony flavor with a breath-taking meringue.

2 cups plus 2 tablespoons sugar,
   divided
¼ cup plus 2 teaspoons cornstarch
¼ teaspoon salt
½ cup plus 1 tablespoon fresh
   lemon juice
½ cup cold water

5 eggs, separated
1¼ cups hot water
¼ cup butter or margarine, melted
1 tablespoon grated lemon rind
1 baked (9-inch) pastry shell
½ teaspoon cream of tartar
½ teaspoon vanilla extract

Combine 1½ cups sugar, cornstarch, and salt in a non-aluminum saucepan; set aside.

Combine lemon juice, cold water, and egg yolks, stirring until well combined. Add egg yolk mixture, hot water, and butter to sugar mixture, stirring well. Bring to a boil; cook over high heat, stirring constantly, 1 minute. Remove from heat and stir in lemon rind. Pour mixture into pastry shell.

Beat egg whites (at room temperature) until foamy; add cream of tartar and beat until soft peaks form. Gradually add remaining sugar, 2 tablespoons at a time, beating until stiff peaks form and sugar dissolves. Add vanilla; beat well. Spread meringue over hot filling, sealing to edge of pastry. Bake at 325° for 12 to 15 minutes or until golden brown. Cool to room temperature. Yield: one 9-inch pie.

Chocolate Pie with Brown Sugar Meringue

An unusual meringue tops this delectable confection.

1¼ cup plus 1 tablespoon firmly
   packed brown sugar, divided
⅓ cup instant-blending flour
2 (1-ounce) squares unsweetened
   chocolate
2 cups milk, scalded

3 eggs, separated
1 tablespoon water
¼ teaspoon salt, divided
2 tablespoons butter or margarine
1½ teaspoons vanilla extract
1 baked (9-inch) pastry shell

Combine 1 cup brown sugar and flour in a small mixing bowl; mix well, and set aside.

Place chocolate in top of a double boiler; cook over simmering water until melted. Stir in milk and sugar mixture. Cook over boiling water, stirring constantly, until mixture thickens. Cover, and continue cooking 5 minutes, stirring once.

Beat egg yolks in a small mixing bowl until thick and lemon colored; add water and ⅛ teaspoon salt, mixing well. Gradually stir about one-fourth hot mixture into yolks; add to remaining hot mixture in top of double boiler. Add butter, and cook 1 minute, stirring constantly. Remove from heat, and cool. Stir in vanilla. Pour filling into pastry shell.

Beat egg whites (at room temperature) and remaining salt in a medium mixing bowl until soft peaks form. Sift remaining brown sugar; add 1 tablespoon at a time to meringue, beating until stiff peaks form. Spread meringue over filling, sealing to edge of pastry. Bake at 325° for 15 minutes or until meringue is lightly browned. Cool completely before cutting into wedges to serve. Yield: one 9-inch pie.

Elegant Fish Dinner

Shrimp-Stuffed Artichokes
Poisson au Beurre Blanc
Rice Pilaf
Green Beans with Raspberry Vinegar
Food Processor Petits Pains
Nectarine Dessert Pizza

Serves 6

---

*T*he dessert pizza can be refrigerated overnight, and the bread can be baked 1 day ahead or frozen for longer storage. The artichokes, rice, and green beans can be started several hours ahead. These preparations will free you to sauté the fish and finish the green beans just before serving.

Wine Suggestion: The best choice with the fish would be a French white wine from the Loire valley, such as a Sancerre or Quincy. Use the same wine in the Beurre Blanc, which originated in the Loire Valley as a way to sauce the area's abundant fresh fish.

Shrimp-Stuffed Artichokes

A zesty Cajun recipe.

6 artichokes
1 tablespoon plus 1 teaspoon salt, divided
¼ cup butter or margarine
¼ cup plus 1 tablespoon olive oil, divided
1 large onion, finely chopped
6 green onions, finely chopped
4 stalks celery, finely chopped
2 tablespoons tomato paste or catsup
2 cups water

2 tablespoons finely chopped parsley
5 cloves garlic, finely chopped
¼ teaspoon ground thyme
2 bay leaves
1 pound medium shrimp, cooked, peeled, deveined, and chopped
2 cups seasoned, dry breadcrumbs
⅛ teaspoon freshly ground black pepper
¼ teaspoon hot sauce
½ cup grated Parmesan cheese

Wash artichokes by plunging up and down in cold water. Cut off stem end; cut off about 1-inch straight across top. Discard loose bottom leaves. Trim away one-fourth of each outer leaf with scissors. Spread leaves apart; pull out center leaves, and cut away fuzzy thistle center (choke) with a paring knife; discard choke. Soak artichokes in cold water to cover for 30 minutes. Drain.

Place artichokes in 2 inches of fresh water and 1 tablespoon salt in a large Dutch oven. Bring to a boil; reduce heat, cover, and simmer 45 minutes. Drain well, and set aside.

Combine butter and 3 tablespoons olive oil in a large skillet; place over medium heat to melt butter. Add onion and celery; sauté 5 minutes or until tender. Stir in tomato paste or catsup and water; bring to a boil, and add parsley, garlic, thyme, and bay leaves. Reduce heat, and simmer, uncovered, until mixture is reduced by half.

Remove from heat, and remove bay leaves. Transfer mixture to a large mixing bowl, and add shrimp, breadcrumbs, remaining salt, pepper, hot sauce, and cheese. Mix well.

Carefully fill centers of artichokes with stuffing mixture. Gently separate leaves; add stuffing mixture. Transfer stuffed artichokes to a 13- x 9- x 2-inch baking dish; pour about ½ inch water in bottom. (Recipe can be prepared to this point, covered and refrigerated until ready to bake.) Drizzle remaining olive oil evenly over tops of artichokes. Cover with aluminum foil and bake at 350° for 20 minutes. Serve hot. Yield: 6 servings.

Poisson au Beurre Blanc

An easy and delightful way to serve fish. The Beurre Blanc will hold up to 1 hour if you place the saucepan in a large pan of warm water.

3 tablespoons all-purpose flour
½ teaspoon salt
⅛ teaspoon white pepper
⅛ teaspoon ground mace
6 trout or flounder fillets, fresh or
   frozen, thawed

¼ cup butter
1 tablespoon vegetable oil
Beurre Blanc (page 90)
Chopped parsley

Put flour, salt, white pepper, and mace into brown paper bag; shake each fillet in bag separately. Melt butter with oil over medium high heat; sauté the fillets lightly in the hot butter, without crowding, until lightly browned on one side. Turn with spatula and cook second side until lightly browned and fish flakes when prodded with a fork. Transfer to a warm serving dish. Top with room temperature Beurre Blanc and garnish with chopped parsley. Serve immediately. Yield: 6 servings.

Beurre Blanc

2 minced shallots
½ cup white wine
2 teaspoons white wine vinegar

½ cup butter, softened
Salt and white pepper to taste

Combine shallots, wine, and vinegar in a small saucepan over medium high heat. Cook until mixture reduces to 3 tablespoons. Whisk in the butter, tablespoon by tablespoon, over low heat, until the sauce thickens. Add salt and pepper to taste. This is a room temperature sauce. Serve over hot foods. Yield: about ½ cup.

Rice Pilaf

1½ cups uncooked regular rice
¼ cup butter or margarine, divided
¼ cup finely minced onion
½ cup finely chopped green pepper
3 cups chicken or beef stock

Salt and pepper to taste
Bouquet garni (parsley, bay leaf,
   and thyme placed in
   cheesecloth bag and tied with
   string)

Sauté rice in 2 tablespoons butter in a heavy skillet 3 minutes or until each grain is well coated and translucent. Add remaining butter, onion, and green pepper. Cook 5 to 7 minutes or until vegetables are tender but not browned. (Recipe can be prepared to this point several hours in advance. Reheat rice over low heat before adding boiling stock.)

Bring stock to a boil in a saucepan; add salt and pepper. Pour boiling stock over rice mixture. Add bouquet garni; cover and cook over low heat 20 to 25 minutes or until rice is tender and most of the liquid has been absorbed. Remove and discard bouquet garni before serving. Yield: 4 to 6 servings.

Note: Leftover cooked chicken, beef, pork, lamb, ham, shrimp, lobster, or flaked fish may be added to cooked rice mixture. Add ¾ cup of leftover meat or fish to rice mixture; cover and cook until added ingredients are thoroughly heated and all liquid has been absorbed.

Green Beans with Raspberry Vinegar

2 slices bacon
1 medium onion, thinly sliced
1½ pounds fresh green beans,
   cooked in boiling water until
   crisp-tender

2 tablespoons raspberry vinegar
½ teaspoon salt
⅛ teaspoon pepper

Cook bacon in a medium skillet over low heat until crisp. Drain bacon on paper towels; reserve drippings in skillet. Crumble bacon; set aside.

Add sliced onion to bacon drippings; cover and cook over low heat 10 minutes or until tender. (Recipe can be prepared to this point several hours ahead. Cook beans just before adding to onion.) Add beans, vinegar, salt, and pepper to onion, stirring well. Cook over medium heat 10 minutes. Sprinkle crumbled bacon over beans to serve. Yield: 6 servings.

Food Processor Petits Pains

The name simply means "little breads" in French, but the whole wheat flour and honey give these rolls a special richness.

1 package dry yeast
1 teaspoon sugar
1 cup warm water (105° to 115°)
1½ cups whole wheat flour
1½ cups all-purpose flour

1 teaspoon salt
2 tablespoons honey
2 tablespoons cornmeal
1 egg, beaten
1 tablespoon water

Dissolve yeast and sugar in warm water; stir well, and let stand 5 minutes.

Position knife blade in food processor bowl; add flour, salt, honey, and yeast mixture. Process quickly 3 to 4 times. Stop processor and scrape sides of bowl. Process continuously 5 to 10 seconds or until dough forms a soft ball.

Place dough in a greased bowl, turning to grease top. Cover and let rise in a warm place (85°), free from drafts, 1 hour or until doubled in bulk.

Punch dough down; shape into 16 balls. Sprinkle a well-greased baking sheet with cornmeal. Place balls on baking sheets; cover and let rise in a warm place (85°), free from drafts, 30 minutes or until doubled in bulk. Combine egg and water; stir well. Brush tops of rolls with egg mixture. Bake at 375° for 20 minutes. Yield: 16 rolls.

Elly Launius's Nectarine Dessert Pizza

An extremely attractive way to bake a fresh fruit tart.

½ cup butter or margarine
¼ cup sifted powdered sugar
1 cup sifted all-purpose flour
2 tablespoons cornstarch
2 tablespoons sugar
¼ teaspoon ground mace
⅔ cup orange juice

½ cup currant jelly
Red food coloring (optional)
6 fresh nectarines, peaches or
    pears, peeled, pitted, and thinly
    sliced
Whipped cream (optional)

Cream together butter and powdered sugar. Blend in flour to make a soft dough. Pat evenly on bottom and sides of a 12-inch pizza pan or on a small baking sheet; prick dough with a fork. Bake at 350° for 15 to 20 minutes.

Combine cornstarch, 2 tablespoons sugar, and mace in a small saucepan. Stir in orange juice and jelly. Cook 2 minutes, stirring constantly, until thickened and bubbly. Cool slightly. Stir in food coloring, if desired.

Arrange nectarine slices in baked pastry shell, starting a circle around outside and working into center. Spoon currant glaze over nectarines. Chill. Garnish with whipped cream, if desired. Cut into wedges or squares. Yield: 10 to 12 servings.

To Freshen Bread: Freshen dry, crusty rolls or French bread by sprinkling with a few drops of water, wrapping in aluminum foil, and reheating at 350° about 10 minutes.

Luscious Pork Dinner

Crab Dip
Vegetable Relishes
Glazed Pork Loin Roast
Broccoli Surprise
Spiced Peach Salad
Spoonbread
Caramel Nut Pound Cake

Serves 8

Schedule your timing around the Spoonbread, which should be eaten hot from the oven. Make the dip, salad, and cake 1 day ahead. Arrange the broccoli up to 2 hours ahead, undercooking the broccoli slightly; bake it just before serving. The pork roast can be finished 1 hour before serving and lightly covered with aluminum foil to retain heat.

Wine Suggestion: A California Blanc de Pinot Noir or white Zinfandel would be fun with this dinner, but choose the more traditional red versions of these wines if you wish.

Bob Lyon's Crab Dip

1 (8-ounce) package cream cheese, softened
6 to 8 ounces fresh or frozen crabmeat
1 tablespoon minced onion
¼ cup mayonnaise
¼ cup seafood cocktail sauce
Dash of Worcestershire sauce
Assorted crackers

Combine all ingredients in a medium mixing bowl; mix well. Refrigerate for several hours to allow flavors to blend. Serve with assorted crackers. Yield: about 2 cups.

Glazed Pork Loin Roast

1 small onion, sliced
¼ cup sliced celery
¼ cup sliced carrots
1 (3-pound) pork loin roast, boned, rolled, and tied
Salt and pepper
1 small bay leaf, crumbled
½ cup pineapple juice
¼ cup soy sauce
¼ cup apricot jam
1 teaspoon cornstarch

Arrange vegetables in a lightly greased roasting pan. Season roast with salt and pepper; place roast over vegetables, fat side up, and sprinkle bay leaf over top.

Insert meat thermometer horizontally into one end of roast. Bake at 325° for 45 minutes or until browned; turn roast over, and bake 30 minutes to brown bottom side. Turn roast over again, and drain off drippings.

Combine pineapple juice and soy sauce; pour over roast, and bake 15 to 25 minutes or until meat thermometer registers 170°.

Remove roast from oven. Place roast and vegetables on serving platter; cover with foil. Reserve pan drippings. Combine jam and cornstarch; add to drippings. Cook over medium heat until slightly thickened, stirring constantly with a whisk or wooden spoon. Spoon glaze over roast; let stand 10 minutes before slicing. Yield: 8 to 10 servings.

Broccoli Surprise

3 (10-ounce) packages frozen
   broccoli spears, thawed
½ cup butter or margarine

½ cup golden raisins
¼ cup sliced almonds
2 tablespoons lemon juice

Cook broccoli according to package directions. Drain broccoli well, and arrange in a buttered 10- x 6- x 2-inch baking dish. Set aside.

Melt butter in a small skillet over low heat. Add raisins, and cook, stirring frequently, 2 minutes or until raisins plump. Remove from heat; stir in almonds and lemon juice. Pour raisin mixture over broccoli in baking dish.

Bake, uncovered, at 375° for 10 minutes or until thoroughly heated. Yield: 8 servings.

Dorothy Whitney's Spiced Peach Salad

1 (29-ounce) can peach halves,
   undrained
¼ cup vinegar
1 teaspoon whole cloves
1 (3-inch) stick cinnamon

1 (3-ounce) package
   orange-flavored gelatin
1 (8-ounce) carton commercial sour
   cream
Lettuce leaves

Drain peach halves, reserving syrup. Set peach halves aside.

Combine reserved syrup, vinegar, cloves, and cinnamon in a large saucepan. Bring to a boil. Add peaches, and cook over low heat 10 minutes. Remove peach halves from spiced syrup, and distribute peach halves equally among eight lightly oiled 6-ounce custard cups.

Strain spiced syrup into a 1-quart glass measure; discard cloves and stick cinnamon. Add enough boiling water to spiced syrup to yield 2 cups. Combine hot syrup and orange gelatin in a medium mixing bowl, stirring to dissolve; set aside to cool 20 minutes. Stir in sour cream.

Pour gelatin mixture evenly over peach halves in custard cups; chill until firm. Unmold on lettuce leaves to serve. Yield: 8 servings.

Spoonbread

3 cups milk, divided
1 cup cornmeal
2 tablespoons plus 1 teaspoon
   butter or margarine, softened

2¼ teaspoons baking powder
¾ teaspoon salt
4 large eggs, separated

Pour 1 cup milk over cornmeal in a medium mixing bowl. Scald remaining milk in a heavy saucepan over medium heat. Let milk cool until it registers 150° on candy thermometer. Add cornmeal mixture, and cook over medium heat 10 minutes, stirring constantly. (Mixture will be very thick.) Remove from heat, and add butter, baking powder, and salt; stir until butter melts.

Beat egg yolks in a small mixing bowl until thick and lemon colored. Add yolks to cornmeal mixture, mixing well. Beat egg whites (at room temperature) in a small mixing bowl until stiff peaks form. Gently fold into cornmeal mixture. Pour mixture into a lightly greased 2-quart casserole. Bake at 375° for 50 minutes. Serve immediately. Yield: 8 servings.

Caramel Nut Pound Cake

½ cup butter, softened
½ cup margarine or shortening
1 (16-ounce) package light brown
   sugar
5 large eggs
3 cups all-purpose flour

1 teaspoon baking powder
½ teaspoon salt
¾ cup milk
1 tablespoon vanilla extract
1½ cups finely chopped nuts

Cream butter and margarine; gradually add sugar, beating at medium speed of electric mixer until light and fluffy. Add eggs, one at a time, beating well after each addition. Combine flour, baking powder, and salt; add to creamed mixture alternately with milk, beginning and ending with flour. Mix just until blended after each addition. Stir in vanilla and nuts. Pour batter into a greased and floured 10-inch tube pan. Bake at 325° for 1 hour and 20 minutes or until a wooden pick inserted in center comes out clean. Cool cake in pan 10 to 15 minutes; remove from pan and cool completely. Yield: one 10-inch cake.

Page 95: *Serve Cold Peach Soup in chilled pewter mugs to begin this Old Winston-Salem German Dinner (page 63). Guests will rave about the Wiener Schnitzel, Rotkohl (Red Cabbage), Hot German Potato Salad, and Gingerbread with Lemon Sauce.*

Page 96: *Chocolate Roulage (page 115) is the perfect ending to Easter Dinner. The tender chocolate cake is rolled around a whipped cream filling lightly flavored with rum and peppermint candy. Chocolate-dipped strawberries make an elegant garnish.*

Holidays and Celebrations

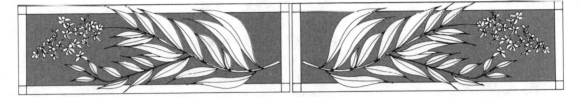

*I*f you look forward to old-fashioned holidays, you'll love the Cheney family favorites included in the Christmas and Easter dinners, and the Big Fourth of July Barbecue. You'll also find special Southern traditions honored in the New Year's Day Halftime, which features a great way to serve black-eyed peas.

But the menus in this chapter also suggest fresh ways to celebrate. During winter's gloomiest days, you can plan a Chinese New Year's party. For Valentine's Day, share a romantic dinner for two. Treat young ghosts and goblins to a Halloween party, complete with Witch's Brew. Set aside a Yuletide evening for an informal Tree-Trimming Supper. If you crave a break from turkey, try Thanksgiving with a Difference. For any occasion that is meaningful to you, whether it's a welcome-home party or an engagement to announce, turn to the all-purpose menu designed for A Special Birthday or Anniversary.

New Year's Day Halftime

Bloody Marys
Shrimp Roll-Ups
Black-Eyed Pea Loaf with Creole Sauce
Snappy Coleslaw
Buttermilk Cornbread
German Chocolate Cake

Serves 12

Ease gently into the New Year with a menu that can be ready for serving whenever football fans are ready for a break. The cake can be baked up to 2 days in advance and refrigerated; let stand at room temperature before serving. Black-Eyed Pea Loaf, Creole Sauce, and Snappy Coleslaw can be made 1 day ahead and refrigerated. Bake Shrimp Roll-Ups before guests arrive and reheat just before serving. The Bloody Mary mix can be refrigerated in a covered jar, without the vodka, for up to a week; stir vodka into the serving pitcher or individual glasses.

Bloody Marys

1 (46-ounce) can tomato juice
½ cup fresh lime juice
¼ cup plus 1 tablespoon
    Worcestershire sauce
1 tablespoon salt

1 teaspoon sugar
1 teaspoon hot sauce
1½ to 2 cups vodka
Ice cubes
Lime slices

Combine first 6 ingredients, mixing well; pour in vodka. Serve in individual glasses over ice cubes. Garnish each serving with a lime slice. Yield: 12 servings.

 To Juice Citrus: A lemon (or other citrus fruit) heated in hot water for 2 minutes or microwaved for 30 seconds will yield more juice than an unheated one.

Shrimp Roll-Ups

½ cup plus 1 tablespoon finely
   chopped green pepper
¼ cup plus 2 tablespoons minced
   onion
¼ cup plus 2 tablespoons butter or
   margarine, divided

1½ teaspoons onion salt
2 pounds jumbo shrimp, peeled,
   deveined, and butterflied
18 slices bacon, cut in half

Sauté green pepper and onion in 1 tablespoon butter until tender. Drain well, and set aside. Sprinkle onion salt in the opening of each shrimp; top with reserved green pepper and onion mixture. Dot with remaining butter. Close each shrimp, and wrap with a half slice of bacon; secure with a wooden pick. (Recipe can be prepared to this point and refrigerated several hours in advance.)

Place shrimp in a lightly greased 15- x 10- x 1-inch baking dish. Cover, and bake at 450° for 20 minutes. Uncover and bake an additional 5 minutes or until bacon is crisp. Drain well on paper towels. Serve immediately. Yield: 12 appetizer servings.

Black-Eyed Pea Loaf with Creole Sauce

According to Southern lore, if you eat black-eyed peas on New Year's Day, you will have good luck all the year through.

1½ cups dried black-eyed peas
1 cup chopped ham
1 hot red pepper, seeded
2 teaspoons salt
¼ teaspoon pepper
2 cups cracker crumbs
⅔ cup chopped onion
1 cup chopped green pepper

2 stalks celery, chopped
2 eggs, beaten
¼ cup catsup
2 teaspoons steak sauce
2 cups (8 ounces) shredded sharp
   Cheddar cheese
Creole Sauce (page 100)

Sort and wash peas; place in a large saucepan. Cover with water; soak overnight. Drain.

Combine peas, ham, hot pepper, and water to cover in a large saucepan. Bring to a boil; cover, reduce heat, and simmer 35 minutes or until tender. Drain, reserving 1 cup liquid. Remove and discard pepper.

Combine peas, 1 cup reserved liquid, and remaining ingredients; stir until well blended. Spoon mixture into a greased 9- x 5- x 3-inch loafpan. Bake at 350° for 45 minutes or until firm. Cool in pan 10 minutes. (Recipe can be refrigerated overnight at this point; cover and reheat at 350° for 20 minutes before serving.) Invert loaf onto a serving platter. Serve with Creole Sauce. Yield: one 9-inch loaf.

Creole Sauce

½ cup chopped green pepper
3 tablespoons chopped onion
2 tablespoons butter or margarine
1 (2-ounce) can sliced mushrooms,
  undrained
1 cup tomato juice
½ cup catsup

1 tablespoon Worcestershire sauce
¼ teaspoon hot sauce
1 tablespoon cornstarch
2 tablespoons cold water
¼ teaspoon salt
¼ teaspoon dried whole thyme

Sauté green pepper and onion in butter in a medium saucepan over low heat until tender. Add mushrooms with liquid, tomato juice, catsup, Worcestershire sauce, and hot sauce; stir well.

Dissolve cornstarch in water, stirring until well blended. Add salt and thyme. Stir cornstarch mixture into sauce. Bring to a boil; reduce heat and cook 1 minute or until thickened, stirring constantly. Yield: 2 cups.

Snappy Coleslaw

1 cup cider vinegar
2 tablespoons butter or margarine
½ cup sugar
½ teaspoon salt

½ teaspoon dry mustard
½ teaspoon celery seeds
1 large cabbage, shredded

Combine vinegar and butter in a small saucepan; bring to a boil and remove from heat. Add sugar, salt, mustard, and celery seeds; stir until well blended. Set aside to cool.

Pour dressing over cabbage, and refrigerate until ready to serve. Yield: 12 servings.

Marguerite Melvin's Buttermilk Cornbread

2 cups cornmeal
⅔ cup all-purpose flour
2 teaspoons sugar
2 teaspoons baking powder
1 teaspoon baking soda

1 teaspoon salt
2½ cups buttermilk
3 eggs, lightly beaten
¼ cup bacon drippings,
  melted

Sift together cornmeal, flour, sugar, baking powder, soda, and salt; stir well. Combine buttermilk, eggs, and bacon drippings; add to dry indredients, stirring just until moistened.

Pour batter into a greased 10-inch cast-iron skillet. Bake at 400° for 30 minutes or until lightly browned. Yield: 12 servings.

Ruth Cheney's German Chocolate Cake

1 cup butter, softened	1 cup buttermilk
2 cups sugar	1 (4-ounce) package sweet baking
4 eggs, separated	chocolate, melted
2½ cups all-purpose flour	2 teaspoons vanilla extract
¼ teaspoon salt	Frosting
1 teaspoon baking soda	

Cream butter; gradually add sugar, beating until light and fluffy. Add egg yolks, one at a time, beating well after each addition.

Combine flour and salt; set aside. Dissolve soda in buttermilk; add to creamed mixture alternately with flour mixture, beginning and ending with flour mixture. Add melted chocolate and vanilla; stir well. Beat egg whites (at room temperature) until stiff peaks form; fold into batter.

Pour batter into two greased and wax paper-lined 9-inch round cakepans. Bake at 325° for 30 minutes or until a wooden pick inserted in center comes out clean. Cool in pans 10 minutes; remove from pans, and cool completely.

Spread frosting between layers and on top and sides of cake. Yield: one 9-inch layer cake.

Frosting

½ cup plus 2 tablespoons butter or	1 teaspoon vanilla extract
margarine, softened	4½ cups sifted powdered sugar
2 tablespoons strong coffee	1 tablespoon plus 2 teaspoons
1 tablespoon plus 2 teaspoons	cocoa
Kahlua or other coffee-flavored	1 cup chopped pecans
liqueur	

Combine first 4 ingredients in a large mixing bowl; beat well. Add powdered sugar and cocoa; beat until light and fluffy. Stir in chopped pecans. Yield: enough frosting for one 2-layer cake.

For Chocolate Cakes: Dust pans for chocolate cakes with cocoa instead of flour to keep the outside of the cake from being white when it is removed from the pan.

Chinese New Year's Dinner

Chinese Mushroom Soup
Shrimp Toast
Sweet-and-Sour Pork Ribs
Chinese Cooked Rice
Stir-Fried Broccoli with Walnuts
Fruit in Plum Wine
Sesame Seed Wafers
or
Date-Filled Wontons

Serves 8

A few weeks after the excitement of our New Year's has begun to fade, Chinese people mark the beginning of the lunar calendar with several days of visiting and feasting. It is customary to begin preparing well in advance. Make the Sesame Seed Wafers up to 3 weeks ahead and the Date-Filled Wontons up to 1 week ahead; store in airtight containers at room temperature.

Beverage Suggestion: Chilled Chinese plum wine is a pleasant apéritif for those who like a mildly sweet beverage. Rice wine or a dry sherry is equally appropriate with the appetizer. With the meal, serve Chinese beer or a light, fruity red wine.

Chinese Mushroom Soup

Chinese ham is salty, very tasty, and similar to Smithfield ham. Smithfield or other Virginia ham will work well in this recipe.

3 (10¾-ounce) cans chicken broth
1 tablespoon cornstarch
½ cup diced cooked ham
1 teaspoon dried green onion
1 (8-ounce) can bamboo shoots, sliced
¾ cup frozen English peas

½ pound fresh mushrooms, sliced
3 tablespoons Sauterne or other dry white wine, divided
1 teaspoon soy sauce
⅛ teaspoon pepper
2 egg whites, lightly beaten

Combine first 4 ingredients in a small Dutch oven; bring to a boil. Reduce heat; simmer 5 minutes, stirring occasionally. Add bamboo shoots and peas; continue cooking 4 minutes.

Add mushrooms; cook an additional 2 minutes. Stir in 2 tablespoons wine, soy sauce, and pepper. Bring mixture to a boil. (Soup can be refrigerated at this point; reheat over low heat and complete the recipe at serving time.) Add egg whites and remaining white wine. Serve immediately. Yield: about 7 cups.

Shrimp Toast

An easy make-ahead recipe.

1 egg
1½ teaspoons cornstarch
1 teaspoon dried parsley flakes
1 teaspoon vermouth
½ teaspoon salt
½ pound fresh small shrimp, uncooked, peeled, and deveined

5 whole water chestnuts, chopped
5 slices bread, toasted
¼ cup plus 2 tablespoons vegetable oil

Combine egg, cornstarch, parsley, vermouth, and salt in medium mixing bowl; mix well. Finely chop shrimp. Stir in shrimp and water chestnuts.

Remove crust from toasted bread slices; cut into 20 triangles. Spread 1 tablespoon shrimp mixture on each triangle. Heat oil in medium skillet and fry triangles until shrimp mixture becomes golden brown. Drain on paper towels and serve immediately. Yield: 8 servings.

Note: Shrimp Toast can be made up to the point of frying 2 hours before serving. Place on a baking sheet, cover with plastic wrap, and refrigerate; fry just before serving.

Sweet-and-Sour Pork Ribs

Meaty pork ribs take on a savory Oriental flavor—the sauce adds bright color and a crunchy texture.

2 (20-ounce) cans pineapple chunks
¼ cup plus 2 tablespoons soy sauce
4½ to 5 pounds country-style pork ribs or backbones
1 teaspoon garlic powder

2 teaspoons ground coriander
2 (6-ounce) packages Chinese pea pods, thawed and drained
1 tablespoon finely chopped crystallized ginger

Drain pineapple chunks, reserving pineapple juice; set pineapple chunks aside. Combine soy sauce and reserved pineapple juice; set aside.

Place ribs in two well-greased 12- x 8- x 2-inch baking pans. Pour soy sauce mixture evenly over ribs. Sprinkle with garlic powder and coriander. Bake, uncovered, at 325° for 1½ hours or until tender, basting every 20 minutes. Remove ribs to a warm serving platter, reserving pan juices.

Pour pan juices into a large saucepan. Cook over medium heat 10 minutes or until liquid is reduced to 1 cup. Add reserved pineapple chunks and pea pods; cook over medium heat 5 minutes or until pea pods are crisp-tender. Pour sauce over ribs and sprinkle with crystallized ginger. Yield: 8 servings.

Chinese Cooked Rice

This is the traditional Chinese method for cooking rice. It yields fluffy, separate grains.

4 cups water
2 cups uncooked regular rice

2 teaspoons salt

Bring water to a boil in a heavy saucepan; add rice and salt, stirring well. Cook over medium heat 13 minutes or until water has evaporated. Cover and reduce heat to low; continue cooking 20 minutes. Serve hot as a side dish. Yield: 8 servings.

Stir-Fried Broccoli with Walnuts

2 (1-pound) bunches broccoli
2 tablespoons vegetable oil
2 cloves garlic, minced
1 teaspoon minced gingerroot
½ cup walnut pieces

1 large red pepper, cut into thin strips
2 tablespoons soy sauce
1 tablespoon sesame oil

Trim and peel broccoli stems. Cut off flowerets; slice stems. Pour vegetable oil into a wok over high heat, turning wok to coat evenly. Add garlic and gingerroot; stir-fry 1 minute. Add broccoli stems; stir-fry 1 minute. Add walnuts; stir-fry until slightly toasted, about 2 minutes. Add broccoli flowerets and red pepper; stir-fry until broccoli turns bright green. Combine soy sauce and sesame oil; stir into vegetables. Stir-fry 2 or 3 minutes or until vegetables are crisp-tender. Yield: 8 servings.

Fruit in Plum Wine

3 (11-ounce) cans Mandarin oranges, drained
1 pound red seedless grapes

2 medium bananas, sliced
3 kiwi fruit, peeled and sliced
1 cup plum wine

Combine all ingredients in a large bowl. Cover and refrigerate overnight. Drain before serving in individual compotes. Yield: 8 servings.

Sesame Seed Wafers

Butter or margarine
All-purpose flour
1 (2.6-ounce) jar sesame seeds
¼ cup plus 2 tablespoons butter or
   margarine, softened
1 cup firmly packed dark brown
   sugar

1 egg, beaten
½ cup all-purpose flour
¼ teaspoon baking powder
⅛ teaspoon salt
1 teaspoon vanilla extract

Grease baking sheets with butter and dust with flour; set aside.

Pour sesame seeds into an ungreased heavy skillet; cook over low heat 5 minutes or until golden brown, stirring constantly. Cool, and set aside.

Cream butter; gradually add sugar, beating well. Add egg; beat well. Combine flour, baking powder, and salt; add to creamed mixture, mixing well. Stir in vanilla, and reserved sesame seeds; mix well.

Drop dough by teaspoonfuls, at least 2 inches apart, onto prepared baking sheets. Bake at 350° for 8 minutes. Cool 1 minute; carefully remove to wire racks to cool completely. Yield: 4½ dozen.

Date-Filled Wontons

1 (8-ounce) package pitted dates,
   finely chopped
½ cup walnuts, chopped
2 teaspoons grated orange rind

Wonton wrappers
Oil for deep frying
Sifted powdered sugar

Combine dates, walnuts, and orange rind. Mix to form a ball. Pinch off small amounts and roll into cylinders about 1½ inches long.

To assemble, place a cylinder of filling in center of each wonton. Fold top corner of wonton over filling. Fold left and right corners over filling. Lightly brush exposed corner of wonton with water. Tightly roll the filled end of wonton toward the exposed corner, and gently press to seal.

Heat 1½ inches of oil to 375° in wok or large skillet. Deep fry wontons for 2 to 3 minutes or until golden brown and crisp. Drain and roll in powdered sugar. Yield: 36 wontons.

Party Decorations: Red signifies good luck in Chinese lore, so you may want to choose your tablecloth and napkins accordingly. The many lovely, inexpensive baskets imported from China can suggest other decorations. Fill small baskets with candies and wrap them in red cellophane for guests to take home, since the Chinese greet New Year's visitors with little gifts. Or fill a large basket with red tissue-wrapped tangerines or mandarin oranges, another Chinese good luck token.

Romantic Valentine's Dinner

Champagne
Coeur à la Crème
Rack of Lamb for Two
Potato Soufflé
Bibb Lettuce Salad with Tarragon Dressing
Poached Pears with Chocolate Sauce

Serves 2

This is a Valentine for the two of you to share, both in the kitchen and at the table. The Coeur à la Crème must be made in advance. The rest of the cooking will go quickly if you join forces in the kitchen. Start by boiling the potatoes for the individual soufflés and poaching the pears; then prepare the soufflés, the lamb, and the salad. Enjoy the entrée before returning to the kitchen to make the chocolate sauce for the poached pear dessert.

Wine Suggestion: You can sip a vintage Bordeaux red wine or a brut champagne throughout this meal. If you'd like to change wines with the courses, consider buying a split of champagne and a half bottle of red wine.

Coeur à la Crème

This savory appetizer was inspired by the classic French heart-shaped dessert cheese. Red caviar adds a deluxe holiday accent.

1 cup low-fat cottage cheese	**1 slice onion**
4 ounces Neufchâtel cheese	**1 teaspoon lemon juice**
1 tablespoon commercial sour	**Salmon caviar**
cream	**Toasted pumpernickel rounds**

Combine all ingredients except caviar and pumpernickel in a food processor or blender; process until smooth. Line coeur à la crème mold with wet cheesecloth. Spread cheese mixture evenly in mold. Fold over ends of cheesecloth to cover cheese completely. Place mold on a pieplate so that the cheese can drain. Chill overnight. Unmold on a platter to serve. Garnish with caviar. Serve with pumpernickel. Yield: 1½ cups.

Rack of Lamb for Two

1 tablespoon vegetable oil
¼ teaspoon salt
¼ teaspoon pepper
¼ teaspoon dried whole oregano
⅛ teaspoon garlic powder

1 (1½- to 2-pound) rack of lamb
¼ cup chopped fresh parsley
½ cup Burgundy or other dry red
  wine
¼ cup butter

Combine oil, salt, pepper, oregano, and garlic powder; brush on lamb. Place lamb, bone ends up, in a shallow roasting pan. Insert meat thermometer, if desired.

Bake, uncovered, at 400° until desired degree of doneness: about 35 minutes or 140° (rare); about 55 minutes or 160° (medium); about 1 hour and 10 minutes or 170° (well done).

Transfer lamb to a warm serving platter, reserving pan drippings. Sprinkle with parsley. Let lamb stand 10 minutes before slicing.

Add wine to pan drippings in roasting pan. Cook over low heat, stirring with a wooden spoon to loosen browned crumbs. Add butter; simmer 4 to 5 minutes, stirring occasionally. Serve sauce with lamb. Yield: 2 servings.

Potato Soufflé

1¼ cups hot mashed potatoes
¼ cup whipping cream
1 egg, separated
1 tablespoon all-purpose flour
⅛ teaspoon baking powder
½ teaspoon salt

⅛ teaspoon white pepper
⅛ teaspoon minced green onion
⅛ teaspoon paprika
¼ cup (1 ounce) shredded sharp
  Cheddar cheese

Combine hot potatoes, whipping cream, egg yolk, flour, baking powder, salt, pepper, green onion, and paprika in a medium mixing bowl; mix well. Gently fold in cheese; set aside.

Beat egg white (at room temperature) in a small mixing bowl, beating until stiff peaks form; gently fold into potato mixture. Spoon mixture into two greased 10-ounce custard cups. Bake at 325° for 35 minutes. Serve warm. Yield: 2 servings.

Note: Recipe can be made in advance and reheated in oven.

Coeur à la Crème Mold: The traditional French coeur à la crème mold is a heart-shaped ceramic dish with holes in the bottom to allow the cheese to drain. You can substitute a basket, a small colander, or even a round dairy carton with holes punched in the bottom to allow for drainage. **Dessert:** Omit the slice of onion if using as a dessert. Surround with fresh strawberries and serve with Raspberry Sauce (page 246).

Bibb Lettuce Salad with Tarragon Dressing

1 tablespoon fresh lemon juice
1 teaspoon tarragon leaves
2 tablespoons vegetable oil
1 tablespoon plus 1 teaspoon
   mayonnaise
Salt

1 head Bibb lettuce or ½ head
   Boston lettuce
1 small tomato, cut into thin
   wedges
¼ small cucumber, scored, seeded,
   and sliced

Place lemon juice and tarragon in a small bowl; let stand 10 minutes. Gradually add oil, mayonnaise, and salt to taste, stirring with a whisk until blended.

Arrange lettuce, tomato, and cucumber on two serving plates. Spoon dressing over salad. Yield: 2 servings.

Poached Pears with Chocolate Sauce

2 ripe pears
2 teaspoons sugar
¼ teaspoon ground cinnamon
Sauterne or other sweet white wine

Sweetened whipped cream
   (optional)
Chocolate Sauce

Peel pears; core from bottom end, leaving stem intact. Slice ¼ inch from bottom of each pear to make a flat base.

Place pears in a small saucepan; sprinkle with sugar and cinnamon. Add wine to cover pears; bring to a boil. Reduce heat and simmer, uncovered, 10 minutes or until tender. Remove from heat; cool to room temperature.

Remove each pear to an individual serving dish, using a slotted spoon; pipe or dollop sweetened whipped cream around the base of each pear, if desired. Spoon warm Chocolate Sauce over each pear. Serve immediately. Yield: 2 servings.

Chocolate Sauce

1 (1-ounce) square unsweetened
   chocolate, broken into pieces
2 teaspoons butter or margarine

¼ cup plus 2 tablespoons sifted
   powdered sugar
2 tablespoons whipping cream

Combine chocolate and butter in the top of a double boiler; place over simmering water, stirring constantly, until chocolate and butter melt. Gradually add powdered sugar, beating with a wire whisk until smooth; add whipping cream, beating with a wire whisk until well blended. Remove from heat. Yield: ½ cup.

Mardi Gras Brunch

Chicken Liver Pâté
Eggs Benedict
Bananas Foster
Teche Pralines
Café au Lait

Serves 8

A brunch of French Quarter classics will put everyone in the mood to let the good times roll! Get ready up to 3 weeks in advance by making Teche Pralines. Chicken Liver Pâté should be made at least 1 day ahead to allow flavors to blend; it can be refrigerated up to 1 week. Bananas Foster can be prepared up to the point of heating the rum 1 or 2 hours ahead; leave them at room temperature and flambé with rum just before serving. Assemble the other ingredients for Eggs Benedict on serving plates and place in a warm oven while you're poaching the eggs.

Beverage Suggestion: Mimosas go well with Eggs Benedict. Combine 1 quart of orange juice and 2 (25.4-ounce) bottles of champagne in a large pitcher or punch bowl. Do not stir. This makes about 2 quarts—enough for 8 servings.

Chicken Liver Pâté

This Cognac-flavored pâté must be prepared ahead of time and may be refrigerated up to a week.

1 cup butter or margarine, divided	⅛ teaspoon pepper
1 tablespoon chopped onion	½ teaspoon hot sauce
½ bay leaf	2 tablespoons Cognac
⅛ teaspoon ground thyme	Parsley (optional)
1 pound chicken livers	Crackers
1 teaspoon salt	

Melt 2 tablespoons butter in a large skillet; add onion, bay leaf, thyme, and chicken livers, and cook 8 minutes, stirring often. Remove and discard bay leaf. Combine chicken liver mixture and remaining butter in a food processor bowl or blender; process until smooth. Add salt, pepper, hot sauce, and Cognac; process until mixture is well blended.

Spoon mixture into a lightly oiled 7½- x 3- x 2-inch loafpan; cover and chill 8 hours or overnight. Remove from refrigerator 15 to 30 minutes before serving. Garnish with parsley, if desired. Serve with crackers. Yield: about 2 cups.

Eggs Benedict

It is easiest to serve this three-part dish if you prepare the buttered rusks and ham first, then make the Hollandaise, and poach the eggs last. But the eggs may be poached in advance and held in the refrigerator.

8 eggs
8 Holland rusks, lightly buttered,
    or 4 English muffins, halved
    and buttered

8 slices ham, cut into 3-inch
    rounds
Blender Hollandaise Sauce

Fill a large non-aluminum saucepan with 1½ inches water; bring to a boil. Reduce heat to simmer. (Do not allow water to boil.) Break eggs, one at a time, into a custard cup. Hold lip of cup near water; gently slip egg into water. Simmer until eggs reach desired degree of doneness. Remove egg with a slotted spoon; drain well.

Place 1 ham slice on each Holland rusk. Top each with a poached egg, and cover with Blender Hollandaise Sauce. Serve immediately. Yield: 8 servings.

Blender Hollandaise Sauce

½ cup butter or margarine
2 egg yolks
2 tablespoons lemon juice

½ teaspoon salt
¼ teaspoon hot sauce

Melt butter in a heavy saucepan over medium heat. Combine egg yolks, lemon juice, salt, and hot sauce in container of an electric blender; set on high speed, and process 3 seconds.

Turn blender to low speed; add butter to yolk mixture in a slow, steady stream. Turn blender back to high, and process until thick. Place blender container in bowl of warm water to keep sauce warm up to 30 minutes. Yield: about ¾ cup.

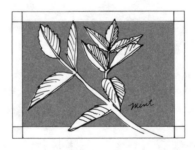

Bananas Foster

6 ripe bananas, peeled, sliced
    lengthwise and quartered
1 tablespoon lemon juice
¾ cup butter
1½ cups firmly packed dark brown
    sugar

1½ teaspoons ground cinnamon
¼ cup banana-flavored liqueur
½ cup dark rum
Vanilla ice cream

Place bananas in a large bowl, sprinkle with lemon juice; set aside.

Melt butter in a chafing dish or small skillet. Add sugar and cinnamon; cook over medium heat until bubbly. Add bananas; heat 3 to 4 minutes, basting constantly with syrup. Pour banana-flavored liqueur over bananas, stirring well.

Place rum in a small long-handled pan; heat just until warm. Remove from heat; ignite and pour over bananas. Baste bananas with sauce until flames die down. Serve immediately over ice cream. Yield: 8 servings.

Teche Pralines

A great favorite in New Orleans and around Louisiana.

1¼ cups sugar	½ cup whipping cream
¾ cup dark brown sugar, firmly packed	¼ cup butter
⅛ teaspoon soda	2½ cups pecan halves (English walnuts may be substituted)
⅛ teaspoon salt	1 teaspoon vanilla extract

Combine sugar, soda, salt and whipping cream in a large heavy saucepan. Cook over medium heat 5 minutes, stirring frequently. Scrape bottom of pan; add butter and pecans and continue cooking about 5 minutes or until candy reaches soft ball stage or 234° on a candy thermometer. Remove from heat, and add vanilla; cool slightly.

Beat until mixture begins to thicken; quickly drop by tablespoonfuls on buttered waxed paper or buttered marble slab. (For a smaller party praline use a rounded teaspoon.) Store in an airtight container at room temperature. Yield: about 24 pralines.

Café au Lait

1 tablespoon drip or finely ground coffee	1 cup milk
1 cup boiling water	Sugar (optional)

Place coffee grounds in basket of a French drip coffee pot. Pour boiling water, a few tablespoons at a time, over coffee grounds. Continue process until all water has dripped through grounds.

Bring milk to a boil. To serve, pour ½ cup coffee and ½ cup milk in a serving cup. Add sugar, if desired, stirring well. Serve immediately. Yield: 2 cups.

Candy Thermometers: Check the accuracy of meat, candy, or deep-fat thermometers by placing in boiling water. If thermometer reads 212°, it is accurate; if not, add or subtract number of degrees above or below 212° when using the thermometer in future recipes.

Easter Dinner

Asparagus Soup
Spring Lamb with Artichokes and Roasted Potatoes
Carrots Grand Marnier
Spring Greens with Creamy Herb Dressing
Hot Biscuits
Chocolate Roulage

Serves 8

The fresh ingredients that signal springtime provide exquisite flavors for this Easter meal. Make Carrots Grand Marnier, Asparagus Soup, and Chocolate Roulage up to 1 day ahead and refrigerate. Peel potatoes and prepare salad greens the morning of the dinner and refrigerate. Don't trim the artichokes until you're ready to cook them, as the cut edges tend to discolor.

Wine Suggestion: Use a good-quality Chardonnay wine, either French, California, or Italian, to make the soup; then serve the same wine with the soup. The lamb is worthy of the subtle bouquet of a good French Bordeaux red wine but can also be enjoyed with a lighter Beaujolais or Zinfandel.

Asparagus Soup

2½ pounds fresh asparagus spears, steamed until tender
½ teaspoon salt
1¼ cups Chardonnay or other dry white wine
2 teaspoons dried tarragon, divided
⅛ teaspoon pepper
¼ cup butter or margarine
¼ cup all-purpose flour
3½ cups chicken broth
2½ cups milk
Fresh parsley sprigs

Position knife blade in food processor bowl; add asparagus. Process 5 seconds. Stop processor, and scrape sides of bowl with a rubber spatula. Process 5 additional seconds or until asparagus is pureed. Set aside. (Asparagus may be pureed in a blender.)

Combine wine, 1 teaspoon tarragon, and pepper in a small saucepan. Bring to a boil; reduce heat, and simmer, uncovered, 20 minutes or until wine is reduced to ¼ cup. Strain and set aside.

Melt butter in a large Dutch oven; add flour, stirring until smooth. Cook over medium heat 1 minute, stirring constantly. Gradually add chicken broth; cook, stirring constantly, until mixture is well blended.

Combine remaining tarragon, reduced wine mixture, broth mixture, asparagus puree, and milk. Bring to a boil; reduce heat and simmer, uncovered, 20 minutes. Serve soup hot, and garnish each serving with parsley. Yield: about 2 quarts.

Spring Lamb with Artichokes and Roasted Potatoes

1 (7-pound) leg of lamb, shank bone removed	¼ teaspoon pepper
	2 cloves garlic, sliced
¼ cup butter or margarine, softened	24 new potatoes, peeled
	4 large artichokes
¾ cup lemon juice, divided	¼ cup all-purpose flour
2 tablespoons dried whole oregano	2 tablespoons salt
1 teaspoon salt	Lamb Gravy

Remove the fell (tissue-like covering) from lamb with a sharp knife. Place lamb, fat side up, in a well-greased roasting pan. Rub surface of lamb with butter, ¼ cup lemon juice, oregano, salt, and pepper. Make several small slits on outside of lamb, and stuff each slit with garlic. Add ½ cup boiling water to pan and bake at 500° for 15 minutes; reduce heat to 350°. Continue baking until desired degree of doneness: about 1 hour and 40 minutes or 140° (rare); about 2 hours or 160° (medium); about 2½ hours or 170° (well done). Add extra boiling water throughout baking to yield about 2½ cups pan drippings.

Arrange peeled potatoes around lamb in roasting pan during last hour of baking time. Baste potatoes frequently with pan drippings.

Trim base of artichokes, leaving about a 1-inch stem. Remove all tough outer leaves. Cut off about 1 inch of the tops. Cut each artichoke in half; scraping away the fuzzy center. Rub cut portions with 2 tablespoons of lemon juice to prevent browning. Place halves in a large Dutch oven; cover with water. Add remaining lemon juice, flour, and salt; stir well. Bring to a boil. Reduce heat and simmer, uncovered, 10 to 12 minutes. Drain well.

Transfer lamb and potatoes to a warm serving platter; reserve drippings in pan. Place artichokes, bottom side up, in roasting pan. Bake at 350° until thoroughly heated, basting often. Remove artichokes from pan, reserving drippings in pan for Lamb Gravy. Arrange artichokes on platter with lamb and potatoes. Yield: 8 servings.

Lamb Gravy

1 cup Burgundy or other dry red wine	1 teaspoon dried whole oregano
	2 tablespoons butter or margarine, softened
1 teaspoon dried whole rosemary, crushed	1 tablespoon brandy

Pour excess fat off drippings in roasting pan. Add red wine to deglaze roasting pan, and stir to loosen particles on bottom of pan. Place roasting pan on stovetop, and bring gravy to a boil. Reduce heat to medium; stir in rosemary and oregano. Cook, stirring constantly to loosen particles from bottom of pan, about 8 minutes or until gravy reduces to syrup.

Remove from heat; add butter and brandy, stirring until well blended. Yield: about 1 cup gravy.

Carrots Grand Marnier

For a pretty party effect serve in scalloped orange shells. Carrots may be prepared ahead and reheated.

2 pounds carrots, cleaned and cut
    into ½-inch thick slices
½ teaspoon salt
¼ cup plus 2 tablespoons butter
1 cup sugar

1 (12-ounce) jar orange marmalade
¾ cup Grand Marnier, divided
4 medium oranges, halved with
    pulp and pith removed
Nutmeg

Combine carrots, water to cover, and salt in a small Dutch oven. Cover and cook over medium heat 25 minutes. Drain and set aside.

Melt butter in a large skillet over medium heat. Add sugar and marmalade and simmer about 10 minutes or until sugar is melted. Stir in carrots and ½ cup Grand Marnier. Simmer, uncovered, about 30 minutes or until carrots are shiny and candied. Add remaining Grand Marnier. Sprinkle with nutmeg and serve in hollowed orange shells. Yield: 8 servings.

Spring Greens with Creamy Herb Dressing

½ small red onion, thinly sliced
4 ounces mushrooms, thinly sliced
1 large stalk celery, thinly sliced
1 cup frozen green peas, thawed
Salt and pepper to taste
1 head Boston lettuce, torn into
    pieces

1 head red leaf lettuce, torn into
    pieces
1 bunch watercress, torn into
    pieces
Creamy Herb Dressing

Toss red onion, mushrooms, celery, peas, salt, and pepper in a large salad bowl. Add lettuce and watercress. Spoon on dressing; toss well. Yield: 8 servings.

Creamy Herb Dressing

1 tablespoon dry sherry
1 egg yolk
2 teaspoons apple cider vinegar
1 teaspoon Dijon mustard
½ teaspoon salt
1 cup vegetable oil
¼ cup olive or walnut oil

2 tablespoons heavy cream
2 tablespoons minced green onion
    or snipped chives
1 tablespoon minced parsley
1 teaspoon dried dillweed
1 teaspoon celery seed

Combine sherry, egg yolk, vinegar, mustard, salt, and ¼ cup vegetable oil in a small bowl, stirring with a wire whisk until blended. Beat in additional vegetable oil, 1 teaspoon at a time, until mixture thickens; stir in olive oil and cream. Stir in green onion and herbs. Refrigerate until serving time. Yield: about 1¾ cups.

Note: Dressing can be made and refrigerated in a covered container up to 5 days in advance.

Chocolate Roulage

Chocolate at its best, with a marvelous filling of whipped cream lightly flavored with rum and peppermint candy. Spoon on the Rich Chocolate Sauce at your own risk!

Vegetable oil	**3 tablespoons cocoa**
5 eggs, separated	**½ teaspoon baking powder**
1 teaspoon vanilla extract	**Powdered sugar**
½ teaspoon salt	**Whipped Cream Filling**
¼ teaspoon cream of tartar	**Rich Chocolate Sauce**
1 cup sifted powdered sugar	**Fresh strawberries (optional)**
½ cup all-purpose flour	

Grease a 15- x 10- x 1-inch jellyroll pan with vegetable oil, and line with waxed paper. Grease waxed paper with vegetable oil; set aside.

Beat egg yolks in a small mixing bowl until light and lemon colored; stir in vanilla, and set aside.

Beat egg whites (at room temperature) in a large mixing bowl until foamy. Add salt and cream of tartar and continue beating until soft peaks form. Gradually add 1 cup powdered sugar, beating until stiff peaks form. Fold egg yolk mixture into egg white mixture. Sift together flour, cocoa, and baking powder; gently fold into egg mixture. Spread batter evenly in prepared pan. Bake at 350° for 10 to 12 minutes.

Sift powdered sugar in a 15- x 10-inch rectangle on a linen towel. When cake is done, immediately loosen from sides of pan, and turn out onto sugar. Peel off waxed paper. Starting at narrow end, roll up cake and towel together; cool on a wire rack, seam side down.

Unroll cake and remove towel. Spread cake with Whipped Cream Filling; reroll. Place on serving plate, seam side down. Cover and chill. Spoon ½ cup Rich Chocolate Sauce over the roulage. Slice and serve with the remaining sauce. Garnish with fresh strawberries, if desired. Yield: 8 to 10 servings.

Whipped Cream Filling

1 cup whipping cream	**2 tablespoons cold water**
¼ cup sifted powdered sugar	**3 tablespoons crushed peppermint**
1 tablespoon dark rum	**candy**
1 teaspoon plain gelatin	

Beat whipping cream until foamy; gradually add powdered sugar and rum. Dissolve gelatin in cold water in a small saucepan over low heat. Let cool, but not harden. Slowly add gelatin to whipped cream, and beat well. Fold in crushed candy. Yield: about 2½ cups.

Rich Chocolate Sauce

¾ cup sugar	**1 (5.33-ounce) can evaporated milk**
3 tablespoons cocoa	**2 tablespoons butter**
⅛ teaspoon salt	**1 teaspoon vanilla extract**
2 tablespoons water	

Combine sugar, cocoa, salt, water, and milk in a medium saucepan. Bring to a boil and boil 3 to 4 minutes. Remove from heat, and stir in butter and vanilla. Serve over Chocolate Roulage. Yield: about 1½ cups.

Mother's Day Brunch

Champagne Crêpes
Fresh Asparagus with Lemon Butter Sauce
Cantaloupe, Celery, and Grape Salad
Strawberry Angel Pies

Serves 8

A simple but elegant brunch invites all generations to enjoy each other's company in a relaxed way. If you would like to divide preparations among siblings, have one person bring the salad and another the dessert. You can freeze the crêpes, stacked between sheets of waxed paper and wrapped in aluminum foil, for 2 months; thaw overnight in the refrigerator. Store meringues for strawberry angel pies up to 1 week in an airtight container. Assemble crêpes without sauce and refrigerate until guests arrive. Steam asparagus while crêpes are baking.

Champagne Crêpes

2 eggs, lightly beaten
1 pound crabmeat
1 medium onion, finely chopped
1 whole pimiento, chopped
1 cup soft breadcrumbs
1 cup mayonnaise
2 tablespoons Worcestershire sauce

½ teaspoon hot sauce
1 teaspoon dry mustard
½ teaspoon salt
¼ teaspoon white pepper
Basic Crêpes
Champagne Sauce

Combine eggs, crabmeat, onion, pimiento, and breadcrumbs in a medium mixing bowl; mix well and set aside. Combine mayonnaise, Worcestershire sauce, hot sauce, dry mustard, salt, and pepper in a small mixing bowl; mix well. Stir into crabmeat mixture.

Spread a heaping ¼ cup crabmeat-mayonnaise mixture in center of each crêpe; roll up, and place seam side down in two buttered 13- x 9- x 2-inch baking dishes. Spread half of Champagne Sauce (about 1¼ cups) over crêpes in each baking dish. Bake at 350° for 15 to 20 minutes. Place two crêpes on each serving plate. Serve hot. Yield: 8 servings.

Basic Crêpes

1 cup plus 2 tablespoons
    all-purpose flour
1½ cups milk
3 eggs

1 tablespoon butter or margarine,
    melted
⅛ teaspoon salt
Vegetable oil

Combine all ingredients except vegetable oil in the container of an electric blender; process until smooth. Refrigerate batter 1 to 2 hours.

Brush bottom of an 8-inch crêpe pan or skillet with oil; place pan over medium heat until oil is just hot, not smoking.

Pour 3 tablespoons batter into pan; quickly tilt pan in all directions so batter covers bottom of pan in a thin film. Cook about 1 minute.

Lift edge of crêpe to test for doneness. Crêpe is ready for flipping when it can be shaken loose from pan. Flip crêpe, and cook about 30 seconds. (This side is rarely more than spotty brown and is the side on which the filling is placed.) Place on paper towels to cool. Stack crêpes between layers of waxed paper to prevent sticking. Repeat procedure until all batter is used, stirring batter occasionally. Yield: 16 crêpes.

Note: Crêpes can be stacked between layers of waxed paper, wrapped in foil, and frozen for several months.

Champagne Sauce

¼ cup plus 1 tablespoon butter or
   margarine, divided
3 tablespoons all-purpose flour
2 cups milk
¼ teaspoon salt
⅛ teaspoon white pepper

⅛ teaspoon ground nutmeg
2 egg yolks
2 tablespoons whipping cream
¼ cup (1 ounce) shredded Swiss
   cheese
3 tablespoons champagne

Melt 3 tablespoons butter in a heavy saucepan over low heat; add flour, stirring until smooth. Cook 1 minute, stirring constantly. Gradually add milk; cook over medium heat, stirring constantly, until mixture is thickened and bubbly. Stir in salt, pepper, and nutmeg. Remove from heat.

Beat egg yolks in a small mixing bowl until thick and lemon colored; add cream, mixing well.

Add yolk mixture to sauce; cook over medium heat, stirring constantly, until thickened. Add remaining butter, cheese, and champagne; cook, stirring constantly, until cheese melts. Yield: about 2½ cups.

Fresh Asparagus with Lemon Butter Sauce

2 pounds fresh asparagus
½ teaspoon salt
¼ cup fresh lemon juice, strained

¼ cup butter, melted
¼ teaspoon Worcestershire sauce

Snap off tough ends of asparagus. Remove scales using a knife or vegetable peeler. Gently tie asparagus together in a bundle. Place in rapidly boiling salted water. Cover and quickly return to a boil; reduce heat and cook 12 to 15 minutes. Carefully remove bundle from cooking water. Cut and remove string. Transfer to serving dish.

Combine lemon juice, butter, and Worcestershire sauce in a small saucepan; cook over medium heat until thoroughly heated. Spoon over asparagus. Serve immediately. Yield: 8 servings.

Cantaloupe, Celery, and Grape Salad

This refreshing salad can be made a day ahead.

½ cup red currant jelly
¾ cup vegetable oil
¼ cup tarragon wine vinegar
1 tablespoon finely chopped chives
1 teaspoon poppy seeds
½ teaspoon salt

¼ teaspoon freshly ground black
  pepper
3 cups cantaloupe cubes
2 cups white seedless grapes,
  halved
3 celery hearts, thinly sliced

Place jelly in a small saucepan; cook over low heat until melted. Remove from heat, and cool. Stir in oil, vinegar, chives, poppy seeds, salt, and pepper; mix until well blended. Cover, and chill.

Combine cantaloupe, grapes, and sliced celery in a large bowl; toss lightly to mix. Cover, and chill.

Stir oil and vinegar mixture when ready to serve, and pour over fruit mixture; toss lightly to coat well. Spoon into individual serving bowls. Yield: 8 servings.

Strawberry Angel Pies

3 egg whites
1 teaspoon cold water
1 teaspoon vinegar
1½ teaspoons vanilla extract,
  divided
½ teaspoon baking powder
⅛ teaspoon salt
1 cup plus 3 tablespoons sugar,
  divided

1 cup whole strawberries
2 tablespoons lemon juice
1 cup whipping cream
2 tablespoons sifted powdered
  sugar
Sliced strawberries (optional)

Combine egg whites (at room temperature), water, vinegar, 1 teaspoon vanilla, baking powder, and salt in a large mixing bowl; beat until frothy. Gradually add 1 cup sugar, 1 tablespoon at a time, beating until stiff peaks form. (Do not underbeat the mixture.)

Spoon the meringue into 8 equal portions on baking sheets lined with unglazed brown paper. (Do not use recycled paper.) Shape meringues into circles about 4 inches in diameter using back of spoon; shape each circle into a shell (sides should be about 1 inch high). Bake at 250° for 1 hour. Cool away from drafts. Carefully remove from brown paper, and transfer to individual serving plates. Set aside.

Combine whole strawberries, remaining 3 tablespoons sugar, and lemon juice in container of electric blender; process until smooth.

Beat whipping cream in a medium mixing bowl until foamy; gradually add powdered sugar, beating until soft peaks form. Fold in strawberry puree and remaining vanilla. Cover and refrigerate until thoroughly chilled (about 1 hour).

Mound strawberry filling evenly into meringue cups. Garnish each serving with sliced strawberries, if desired. Yield: 8 servings.

Note: Angel Pies should be assembled one day before serving, covered, and refrigerated overnight. Meringues will become creamy and permeated with fruit flavor.

A Special Birthday or Anniversary

Easy Canapés
or
Salmon Mousse
Spiced Beef Tenderloin
Roasted Potatoes
Pearl Onions
Broccoli and Cauliflower Scallop
Super Popovers
Mixed Greens with French Dressing Deluxe
Italian Cream Cake

Serves 8

A dinner of family favorites will make the day memorable for someone you love. If chocolate is their first choice, you might want to serve Emmett's Black Russian Cake (page 83) or Ruth Cheney's German Chocolate Cake (page 101) instead of the prize-winning Italian Cream Cake. Either way, make the cake, the salad dressing, and the popover batter, and marinate the Spiced Beef Tenderloin 1 day ahead; refrigerate everything. The morning of the dinner, make the Salmon Mousse; clean and cut up all vegetables and salad greens and refrigerate in plastic bags. Let the roast stand, loosely covered with aluminum foil, while you bake the Super Popovers and Broccoli and Cauliflower Scallop.

Wine Suggestion: A full-bodied red wine, such as a California Cabernet Sauvignon or a French Burgundy, would match the richness of the beef.

Easy Canapés

16 plain crackers	Sliced pimiento (optional)
1 tablespoon butter, softened	Red pepper strips (optional)
2 hard-cooked eggs, thinly sliced	Ripe olives (optional)
1 (2-ounce) can anchovies	Parsley sprigs (optional)

Spread plain crackers with softened butter. Place a slice of hard-cooked egg on each. Rinse flat anchovies under cold water and pat dry. Curl anchovies into spirals and place one on each egg slice. Arrange slices of pimiento, red pepper, or ripe olives, and parsley sprigs around anchovies to resemble flowers. Yield: 8 servings.

Salmon Mousse

1 envelope (1 tablespoon)
   unflavored gelatin
2 tablespoons lemon juice
2 tablespoons chopped onion
2 teaspoons dried green onion
½ cup boiling water
1 cup mayonnaise, divided
⅛ teaspoon white pepper
¼ teaspoon hot sauce
⅛ teaspoon paprika
¾ teaspoon salt

1 teaspoon Worcestershire sauce
1 teaspoon fresh or dried dillweed
1 (15½-ounce) can pink salmon,
   drained, skin and bones
   removed
1 cup whipping cream
1 tablespoon chopped dill pickle
Lettuce
Parsley or dill sprigs
Cherry tomatoes

Process first 5 ingredients in blender or food processor for 30 seconds. Add ½ cup mayonnaise, white pepper, hot sauce, paprika, salt, Worcestershire sauce, dillweed, and salmon; process for 30 seconds. Pour cream slowly into processor tube ⅓ cup at a time with processor on. Process until well blended. Pour mixture into well-oiled 4-cup mold or loafpan. Chill for several hours until set. Place in hot water 15 to 20 seconds to remove mold. Turn out onto platter. Mix ½ cup mayonnaise and chopped dill pickle; serve with Salmon Mousse. Garnish with lettuce, parsley, and cherry tomatoes. Yield: 8 servings.

Spiced Beef Tenderloin

4½ to 5 pound beef tenderloin,
   choice or prime beef
1 cup Marsala wine
½ cup Pickapeppa sauce

½ cup Worcestershire sauce
5 to 6 slices bacon
Boiled pearl onions
Tomato roses (optional)

Place meat in large glass or stainless steel bowl; set aside. Combine wine, Pickapeppa and Worcestershire sauce until well blended; pour over meat. Cover and refrigerate overnight; turn at least six times.

Wrap roast in bacon and place in an open roasting pan. Insert meat thermometer to half the depth of the meat. Bake 10 minutes at 475°; lower heat to 325°. Bake 15 to 18 minutes per pound for very rare meat, 140° on meat thermometer; for a medium roast allow 22 to 25 minutes per pound, 160°; for a well-done roast allow 27 to 30 minutes per pound, 170°. Allow the longer period of cooking for a large roast, the shorter period for a small roast. Garnish the roast with boiled pearl onions and tomato roses, if desired. Yield: 8 servings.

To Make Tomato Roses: Use large, firm tomatoes. Working from the bottom of the tomato, peel half the skin in a continuous strip about ¾ inch wide; then peel the rest of the skin in a second strip. Curl the first strip loosely into a rose shape; roll the second strip tightly and place it inside the first. Tomato pulp may be frozen in a plastic bag for other uses.

Broccoli and Cauliflower Scallop

1 pound fresh broccoli, cleaned
    and cooked
1 medium head cauliflower,
    cleaned and cooked
1 (3-ounce) can sliced mushrooms
1½ cups milk

¼ cup butter or margarine, divided
3 tablespoons all-purpose flour
1 cup (4 ounces) shredded sharp
    Cheddar cheese
1 cup herb-seasoned bread stuffing
    mix

Place broccoli and cauliflower in alternate rows in a 12- x 8- x 2-inch baking dish. Drain mushrooms; set aside. Combine mushroom liquid with milk.

Melt 3 tablespoons butter in a heavy saucepan over low heat; add flour, stirring with a wire whisk until smooth. Cook 1 minute, stirring constantly. Gradually add milk mixture; cook over medium heat, stirring constantly until thickened and bubbly. Add cheese; stir until cheese melts. Add mushrooms. Spoon sauce over broccoli and cauliflower. Combine remaining 1 tablespoon butter and stuffing mix. Sprinkle over casserole. Bake at 400° for 10 minutes. Yield: 8 servings.

Super Popovers

A marvelous quickie that takes about 5 minutes to make and an hour to bake. The popover batter may be made ahead and stored in a covered pitcher in the refrigerator. To increase quantities, double or triple the ingredients except the salt. Increase the salt to ¾ teaspoon for double, 1 teaspoon for triple.

3 eggs
1 cup milk
3 tablespoons butter, melted

1 cup sifted all-purpose flour
½ teaspoon salt
2 tablespoons vegetable oil

Beat eggs (at room temperature) with a wire whisk until frothy. Combine milk and butter. Stir in flour and salt; add to eggs alternately with milk mixture. Batter should be light but not foamy. Strain if it becomes lumpy. Generously oil popover pans or custard cups (4-to 6-ounce size). Fill each to within ½ inch of top. Arrange individual cups on cookie sheet for easier handling. Bake at 400° for 55 minutes to 1 hour or until dark brown on top. Cut two small slits in the top of each popover as soon as they are done to release steam; bake 5 minutes longer. Place on wire rack and cut around edges of popover with a small sharp knife. Serve hot but do not cover tops; this would cause sogginess. Yield: 6 (4-ounce) popovers; 4 (6-ounce) popovers.

Note: If batter is made ahead of time, stir with long-handled spoon before pouring into cups. Leftover popovers may be reheated at 350° about 10 minutes before serving.

Mixed Greens with French Dressing Deluxe

2 cups vegetable oil
½ cup wine vinegar
½ cup powdered sugar
2¼ teaspoons paprika
1½ teaspoons dry mustard
2½ teaspoons salt

¼ cup lemon juice
½ cup orange juice
1½ teaspoons Worcestershire sauce
½ clove garlic or ⅛ teaspoon garlic
    powder
Mixed greens

Thoroughly mix oil and vinegar in a deep narrow bowl. Combine dry ingredients and add to oil mixture; beat well. Add fruit juices and seasonings and beat until thoroughly blended. Keep refrigerated. Allow to reach room temperature, and stir well before using. Spoon over mixed greens at serving time. Yield: about 1 quart.

Italian Cream Cake

½ cup butter, softened
½ cup shortening
2 cups sugar, sifted
5 eggs, separated
2 cups all-purpose flour
1 teaspoon baking soda
¼ teaspoon salt

1 cup buttermilk
1 teaspoon vanilla extract
1 (3½-ounce) can flaked coconut
1½ cups chopped pecans or
    walnuts, divided
Italian Cream Icing

Cream butter and shortening; gradually add sugar, beating well. Add egg yolks, one at a time, beating well after each addition.

Combine flour, soda, and salt; add to creamed mixture alternately with buttermilk, beginning and ending with flour mixture. Mix well after each addition. Stir in vanilla, coconut, and 1 cup chopped nuts.

Beat egg whites (at room temperature) until stiff peaks form. Gently fold into batter.

Pour batter into 3 greased and floured 9-inch round cakepans. Bake at 325° for 35 minutes or until a wooden pick inserted in center comes out clean. Cool in pans 10 minutes; remove layers from pans, and let cool completely.

Spread frosting on top and sides of cake; sprinkle with remaining ½ cup chopped nuts. Yield: one 3-layer cake.

Note: Cake should be refrigerated if not eaten the day it is made.

Italian Cream Icing

1 (8-ounce) package cream cheese,
    softened
¼ cup plus 2 tablespoons butter,
    softened
1 (16-ounce) package powdered
    sugar, sifted

1 teaspoon vanilla extract
1 tablespoon brandy or 2
    tablespoons crème d'almond

Beat cream cheese and butter until smooth; add powdered sugar and beat until fluffy. Add flavorings. Yield: frosting for one (9-inch) 3-layer cake.

Big Fourth of July Barbecue

Olive and Cheese Dip
Barbecued Beef Short Ribs
Barbecued Pork Roast
Pesto Potato Salad
Coleslaw
Pickles and Sliced Tomatoes
Fresh Blueberry Ice Cream
Lemon Criss-Cross Cookies
Chocolate Sheet Cake

Serves 20

Everyone looks forward to the tantalizing smells of a big barbecue, and the joys of being outdoors. The large quantities of food make it appropriate to start preparations a week in advance. The cake, cookies, barbecue sauce, and ice cream will all hold for up to a week. The meats can be precooked up to 2 days ahead and refrigerated or frozen for longer storage. Make the potato salad and coleslaw up to 1 day in advance.

You'll need at least six 6-packs of beer and three gallons of lemonade for 20 people. Keep them cool in an ice chest to avoid overcrowding the refrigerator. It's a good idea to keep a jug of cold water handy, too. To serve 10, prepare only 1 meat recipe, cut the salad recipes in half, and bake either the cake or the cookies.

Olive and Cheese Dip

⅛ teaspoon garlic powder
1 (8-ounce) package cream cheese, softened
1 (4-ounce) jar pimiento-stuffed olives, well drained
3 hard-cooked eggs, chopped

2 tablespoons mayonnaise
1 teaspoon Worcestershire sauce
4 dashes hot sauce
½ teaspoon salt
Assorted crackers
Assorted chips

Sprinkle garlic powder over softened cream cheese. Finely chop olives in food processor, using steel blade. Combine cream cheese and chopped olives; process until creamy. Add eggs, mayonnaise, Worcestershire sauce, hot sauce, and salt; process until well blended. Serve with assorted crackers and chips. Yield: 1¾ cups.

Barbecued Beef Short Ribs

Simmer beef ribs until tender; then transfer to the grill for that smoky flavor.

10 pounds beef short ribs, cut into
    5-inch pieces
1 cup vinegar
1 cup catsup
1 (4-ounce) bottle liquid smoke
2 tablespoons Worcestershire sauce
1 teaspoon hot sauce
¼ cup plus 1 tablespoon lemon
    juice

1 tablespoon grated lemon rind
2 tablespoons prepared horseradish
3 tablespoons prepared mustard
¾ cup sugar
1 teaspoon celery salt
1 teaspoon garlic salt
1 teaspoon onion salt
1 tablespoon paprika
5 bay leaves

Combine ribs and salted water to cover in a large Dutch oven. Bring to a boil. Reduce heat; cover, and simmer 1 hour. Drain.

Combine remaining ingredients in a heavy saucepan. Bring to a boil. Remove from heat, and set aside.

Place ribs on grill over slow coals. Grill 10 minutes, turning as needed. Brush ribs with sauce and cook an additional 20 minutes, basting and turning frequently. Serve remaining sauce with ribs. Yield: 10 servings.

Barbecued Pork Roast

Slow baking makes this pork roast tender enough to melt in your mouth.

1 (5- to 6-pound) pork roast
1½ cups bottled hickory-flavored
    barbecue sauce

½ cup bottled hot barbecue sauce
Hamburger buns

Wrap roast in heavy aluminum foil; place in a shallow baking dish. Bake at 325° for 6 hours. Remove and discard all fat and bone from roast; chop meat, and set aside.

Combine remaining ingredients except buns in a small mixing bowl; add to meat. Serve warm on buns. Yield: 10 servings.

Pesto Potato Salad

Pesto Sauce makes a deliciously different potato salad.

8 pounds small red potatoes
2 teaspoons salt
1 cup white wine
¼ cup olive oil

2 cups mayonnaise
Pesto Sauce
¼ cup chopped fresh parsley

Scrub potatoes; cook in boiling salted water 25 minutes or until tender. Drain, and cool slightly. Peel potatoes, and cut into ¼-inch-thick slices.

Place potatoes in a large bowl. Sprinkle with salt, wine, and olive oil; toss lightly. Combine mayonnaise and Pesto Sauce. Pour over potatoes; toss lightly. Chill thoroughly. Sprinkle with parsley before serving. Yield: 20 servings.

Pesto Sauce

1 cup fresh basil leaves, packed
    tightly, or 2 teaspoons dried
    whole basil
½ cup olive oil
3 cloves garlic, minced

¼ cup pine nuts
1 teaspoon salt
¼ teaspoon pepper
1 cup freshly grated Romano
    cheese

Combine basil, olive oil, garlic, nuts, salt, and pepper in container of electric blender; process until smooth. Add cheese; process until smooth and creamy. Yield: 1½ cups.

Note: Keep a batch of this in the freezer from one basil harvest to the next, or refrigerate up to 2 weeks. But don't add the cheese until you're ready to use.

Coleslaw

2 large onions
4 small heads cabbage, shredded
2 cups sugar, divided
2 cups vinegar

1 cup vegetable oil
2 tablespoons salt
2 teaspoons celery seed
2 teaspoons mustard seed

Peel onions, and cut into ¼-inch slices. Separate into rings. Combine onion rings and cabbage in a large mixing bowl; toss gently to mix. Set aside.

Combine ¼ cup sugar, vinegar, vegetable oil, celery seed, and mustard seed in a small saucepan. Pour remaining sugar over cabbage mixture. Bring vinegar mixture to a boil; remove from heat, and immediately pour over cabbage. Stir gently to coat. Chill overnight. Yield: 20 servings.

Fresh Blueberry Ice Cream

This luscious ice cream keeps well in the freezer.

4 cups fresh blueberries
3½ cups sugar, divided
3 tablespoons lemon juice
4 eggs

2 tablespoons cherry-flavored
    brandy
1 tablespoon vanilla extract
4 cups whipping cream

Combine blueberries, 1 cup sugar, and lemon juice in the container of an electric blender; process until pureed. Set aside.

Beat eggs until thick and lemon colored. Gradually add remaining 2½ cups sugar, beating constantly. Add brandy, vanilla, and pureed blueberries; continue beating until well blended.

Pour mixture into freezer can of a 1 gallon hand-turned or electric freezer. Add whipping cream and freeze according to manufacturer's instructions. Let ripen 2 hours before serving. Yield: about 1 gallon.

Lemon Criss-Cross Cookies

½ cup butter or margarine,
   softened
¾ cup sugar
1 egg
1½ teaspoons lemon extract
1¾ cups all-purpose flour

¾ teaspoon cream of tartar
¾ teaspoon baking soda
¼ teaspoon salt
1 cup golden raisins
1 tablespoon wheat germ

Cream butter; gradually add sugar, beating well. Add egg and lemon extract; beat well.
Sift together flour, cream of tartar, baking soda, and salt in a small mixing bowl.
Gradually add flour mixture to creamed mixture, mixing well. Stir in raisins and wheat germ. Shape into 1-inch balls; place 2 inches apart on ungreased cookie sheets. Dip a fork in flour, and flatten cookies to ¼-inch thickness in a crisscross pattern. Bake at 400° for 8 minutes or until lightly browned. Remove to wire racks to cool. Yield: about 4 dozen.

Lorene Covington's Chocolate Sheet Cake

The iced cake will stay moist for a week if left in the pan and sealed tightly with foil.

2 cups sifted all-purpose flour
2 cups sugar
¼ cup plus 1½ teaspoons cocoa
½ teaspoon salt
1 cup water
1 cup butter or margarine

2 eggs
1 teaspoon baking soda
½ cup buttermilk
1 teaspoon vanilla extract
Chocolate Pecan Icing

Sift together flour, sugar, cocoa, and salt in a large mixing bowl; set aside.
Combine water and butter in a heavy saucepan; bring to a boil. Remove from heat, and pour into dry ingredients, beating constantly. Add eggs, one at a time, beating well after each addition. Dissolve soda in buttermilk; add buttermilk mixture and vanilla to chocolate mixture, beating well. Pour batter into a greased and floured 15- x 10- x 1-inch jellyroll pan. Bake at 325° for 30 minutes or until a wooden pick inserted in center comes out clean. Spread Chocolate Pecan Icing over warm cake. Cool and cut into 1½-inch squares. Yield: 4 dozen squares.

Chocolate Pecan Icing

½ cup butter or margarine
¼ cup plus 2 tablespoons milk
¼ cup cocoa
1 (16-ounce) package powdered
   sugar, sifted

1 teaspoon vanilla extract
1½ cups chopped pecans

Combine butter, milk, and cocoa in a heavy saucepan; bring to a boil. Remove from heat. Stir in powdered sugar, vanilla, and pecans. Spread hot icing over cake. Yield: enough for one 15- x 10-inch cake.

Halloween Party
for Children

Witch's Brew
or
Halloween Julep
Carrot and Olive Toppers
Franks with Catsup Sauce
Chips
Chocolate Chip Crunch
Halloween Cakes in a Cup
Popcorn Balls

Serves 15

Conjure up the magic of the day with a hot cider Witch's Brew, cakes baked in ice cream cones, and chocolate candies so easy to make that they seem like sleight of hand. Everything but the hot dogs can be made ahead.

All recipes can be increased by half or doubled to feed a larger crowd. For very young children, you may want to serve hot dogs without the Catsup Sauce.

Witch's Brew

3 quarts sweet apple cider
3 (2-inch) cinnamon sticks
10 whole cloves

Combine all ingredients in large saucepan; bring to a boil. Reduce heat, and simmer 10 minutes. Strain mixture, discarding spices; pour into cups. Serve hot. Yield: 3 quarts.

Halloween Julep

This recipe makes 6 servings. To serve 15, make 3 batches.

1 (6-ounce) can frozen orange juice
   concentrate
1 cup water
1 cup milk
½ cup sugar
1 teaspoon vanilla extract
12 ice cubes, crushed

Combine all ingredients in container of electric blender; process until mixture is smooth and thick. Yield: 1 quart.

Carrot and Olive Toppers

6 small to medium carrots, washed and scraped

1 (6-ounce) can large ripe pitted olives, drained

Cut carrots in half; then cut into small sticks 1½- to 2-inches in length. Place in bowl with olives and cover with water. Refrigerate overnight. Cut olives in half and pull carrot stick through, allowing the olive topper to be close to the top of the stick. Yield: 30 appetizers.

Franks with Catsup Sauce

¼ cup plus 2 tablespoons vinegar
3 tablespoons all-purpose flour
2 medium onions, finely chopped
1½ cups catsup
3 tablespoons Worcestershire sauce

2 tablespoons dark brown sugar
1½ teaspoons dry mustard
1 teaspoon paprika
24 frankfurters
24 hot dog buns

Blend vinegar and flour; add next 6 ingredients, mixing well. Dip each frankfurter into sauce, and place in a greased roasting pan. Pour remaining sauce over frankfurters. Cover and bake at 350° for 1 hour. Serve in warm buns. Yield: 24 servings.

Chocolate Chip Crunch

A good afternoon snack—takes about 15 minutes from start to finish.

1 (6-ounce) package semisweet chocolate morsels

1½ cups crushed corn chips

Place chocolate morsels in top of double boiler; bring water to a boil. Reduce heat to low; cook until chocolate melts, stirring occasionally. Remove from heat; stir in corn chips. Drop by teaspoonfuls onto waxed paper. Chill. Candy can be refrigerated in a covered container up to 1 week. Yield: 2 dozen.

Party Decorations: Start with simple decorations—black and orange balloons that the children can take home later, crêpe paper streamers, and a hollowed-out pumpkin big enough to hold a punch bowl of Witch's Brew. Then let the children create some Halloween art to carry the theme further. You can tape or tack long sheets of white paper or orange poster board on the walls and provide enough crayons, felt-tip pens, or tempera paint for each guest to draw an answer to the question, "What does a goblin look like?" If you cover the table with butcher paper or hand out sheets of orange construction paper, the artists can fill the "tablecloth" or "placemats" with their notions of the scariest jack-o-lantern or the most wicked witch.

Halloween Cakes in a Cup

Add a few drops of orange food coloring to frosting and ice top of each cup. Using chocolate chips, make a face on each iced cone. Or set out a bowl of small candies, such as chocolate chips, candy corn, and jelly beans, and have children make jack-o-lantern faces on the cakes.

1 (18.5-ounce) package white cake
    mix with pudding
2 boxes ice cream cups (with flat
    bottom surface)
1 (7.2-ounce) package fluffy white
    frosting mix

Red and yellow liquid food
    coloring
Small candies for decoration

Mix cake according to package directions. Fill ice cream cups with about ⅓ cup batter. Place cups on baking sheet. Bake at 350° for 30 minutes or until golden brown. Place on wire racks to cool.

Prepare frosting according to package directions; color with a few drops each of red and yellow food coloring.

Frost to resemble ice cream cone. Make a face on frosting using small candies. Cakes can be covered with plastic wrap and stored at room temperature up to 2 days. Yield: about 18 servings.

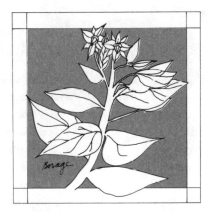

Popcorn Balls

3 quarts freshly popped popcorn,
    salted
1 cup molasses

1 cup light corn syrup
4 teaspoons vinegar
3 tablespoons butter or margarine

Spread popcorn evenly in a lightly greased 15- x 10- x 1-inch jellyroll pan; set aside.
Combine molasses, corn syrup, and vinegar in a medium saucepan; cook over low heat, stirring occasionally, until mixture reaches soft crack stage (270°). Remove from heat; stir in butter.

Pour syrup over popcorn; stir until all popcorn is coated. Let mixture cool slightly; shape into 2½-inch balls. Wrap individually in orange and black cellophane or store in airtight containers. Yield: 2 dozen.

Eudora's Niche

Cream of Artichoke and Oyster Soup
Crabmeat Supreme
Celebration Mushrooms
Medallion Squash
Celebration Torte
Toasted Pecans

Serves 6

This is the menu I created to honor my dear friend Eudora Welty when she was awarded the Medal of Freedom. The dinner was held in Jackson, Mississippi, on June 29, 1980. The recipes are special mementos of that day, and I hope you will enjoy them with your cherished friends.

Cream of Artichoke and Oyster Soup

5 artichokes
1 tablespoon salt
1 teaspoon Old Bay Seasoning
1 tablespoon vegetable oil
¼ cup chopped fresh parsley
1 (12-ounce) container Select
    oysters, undrained
1 medium onion, finely chopped
2 stalks celery, finely chopped
¼ cup plus 2 tablespoons butter or
    margarine
¼ cup all-purpose flour

4 (10¾-ounce) cans chicken broth
¼ cup lemon juice
1 bay leaf
¾ teaspoon salt
¼ teaspoon white pepper
¼ teaspoon ground mace
⅛ teaspoon dried whole thyme
½ teaspoon hot sauce
2 egg yolks, lightly beaten
1 cup whipping cream
Lemon slices
Chopped fresh parsley

Place artichokes in 2 inches of water in a large Dutch oven. Add 1 tablespoon salt, Old Bay Seasoning, oil, and parsley; bring to a boil. Reduce heat; cover and simmer 30 minutes. Drain and cool slightly.

Pull the leaf sections away on each artichoke, starting at the outside and working toward the center. Scrape the base of each leaf section with a knife; reserve pulp and set aside. Discard leaves. Scrape out the fuzzy thistle center (choke) with a spoon, leaving the heart. Trim rough edges from bottom of each heart. Chop hearts and set aside.

Drain oysters, reserving ⅓ cup oyster liquor. Set aside.

Sauté onion and celery in butter until tender; add flour and stir until smooth. Cook 1 minute, stirring constantly. Add chicken broth, lemon juice, bay leaf, ¾ teaspoon salt, pepper, mace, thyme, hot sauce, reserved oyster liquor, and reserved artichoke pulp. Stir well. Cover and simmer 20 minutes. (Recipe can be prepared to this point several hours in advance. Keep oysters refrigerated. Reheat soup before proceeding.) Add egg yolks, whipping cream, and oysters. Stir well, and continue cooking over low heat 5 minutes. Remove bay leaf. Garnish soup with lemon slices and chopped parsley; serve immediately. Yield: about 2 quarts.

Crabmeat Supreme

An elegant seafood creation for a summer luncheon or dinner.

1 cup mayonnaise	¼ teaspoon hot sauce
2 tablespoons chili sauce	⅛ teaspoon salt
2 tablespoons wine vinegar	1 pound fresh crabmeat, drained
2 tablespoons chopped green onion	and flaked
2 tablespoons chopped fresh	¼ cup whipping cream, whipped
parsley	6 medium tomatoes
1 tablespoon olive oil	¼ cup chopped salad olives
½ teaspoon Worcestershire sauce	

Combine mayonnaise, chili sauce, wine vinegar, green onion, parsley, olive oil, Worcestershire sauce, hot sauce, and salt in a medium mixing bowl; stir well. Gently fold in crabmeat and whipping cream. Chill 1 hour.

Wash tomatoes. Cut tops from tomatoes; scoop out pulp, leaving shells intact. Reserve pulp for use in other recipes. Spoon crabmeat mixture into tomato shells. Sprinkle top with chopped salad olives. Yield: 6 servings.

Celebration Mushrooms

A superb creation to complement the crabmeat entrée. This recipe would also be delicious with lamb, a prime rib roast, or turkey.

1½ pounds large mushrooms	1 cup whipping cream
¼ cup butter or margarine	1 teaspoon salt
1 cup minced fresh parsley	⅛ teaspoon white pepper
¾ cup chopped celery hearts	¼ teaspoon hot sauce
1 tablespoon minced fresh basil	Toast points
1 tablespoon chopped green onion	Fresh parsley (optional)

Clean mushrooms with damp paper towels. Remove mushroom stems, and reserve for other uses. Place mushrooms in a shallow baking pan; dot with butter. Combine parsley, celery, basil, and green onion; sprinkle over mushrooms.

Combine whipping cream, salt, white pepper, and hot sauce; pour over mushrooms. Bake at 325° for 30 minutes. Serve over toast points, and garnish with parsley, if desired. Yield: 6 servings.

Medallion Squash

Delicately flavored and delicious. In creating this recipe I chose one of Eudora's favorite vegetables. The recipe's simplicity reminded me of one of her most endearing traits—her complete lack of pretense. She is one of the most natural people I know.

6 small yellow squash	**1 teaspoon salt**
2 teaspoons dried green onion	**2 tablespoons butter or margarine**

Place squash in a steaming rack; sprinkle with green onion and salt. Steam 25 minutes or until tender; cool slightly. Cut a 1½-inch slit in the middle of each squash; place 1 teaspoon butter in each slit. Serve immediately. Yield: 6 servings.

Eudora Welty's Celebration Torte

My crowning effort to complete the dinner. It must be prepared a day ahead for proper aging.

6 egg whites	**2 (10-ounce) packages frozen**
1 teaspoon baking powder	**raspberries**
⅛ teaspoon salt	**1 cup whipping cream**
2 teaspoons vinegar	**¼ cup powdered sugar, sifted**
1 tablespoon vanilla extract,	**2 teaspoons grenadine**
divided	**¼ cup fresh blueberries**
2 cups superfine sugar	

Combine egg whites (at room temperature), baking powder, salt, vinegar, and 2 teaspoons vanilla in a large mixing bowl; beat until foamy. Gradually add sugar, 1 tablespoon at a time, beating until stiff peaks form. (Do not underbeat this mixture.)

Spoon meringue into 2 equal portions on unglazed brown paper. (Do not use recycled paper.) Using back of spoon, shape meringue into circles about 8 inches in diameter.

Bake at 250° for 1 hour. Cool away from drafts.

Thaw and drain raspberries, reserving 2 teaspoons liquid. Beat whipping cream until foamy; gradually add powdered sugar, beating until soft peaks form. Add reserved raspberry liquid, grenadine, and remaining 1 teaspoon vanilla; beat just until combined. Fold in raspberries.

Spread raspberry cream between layers and on top and sides of torte. Garnish with blueberries. Cover and refrigerate overnight. Yield: one 8-inch torte.

Toasted Pecans

4 cups pecan halves	**1 tablespoon salt**
¼ cup butter	

Place pecans on a baking sheet; avoid stacking. Bake at 325° for 10 minutes. Add butter and stir until pecans are coated. Sprinkle salt over pecans. Reduce heat to 250°, and bake for 20 to 30 additional minutes or until golden brown. Cool in pan. Yield: 4 cups.

Thanksgiving with a Difference

Consommé Madrilene
Elegant Quail
or
Honeyed Duck
Saffron Rice Amandine
Harvest Vegetable Platter
Cranberry Salad with Vinegar Dressing
Refrigerator Rolls
Apricot Brandy Pound Cake
Ambrosia

Serves 12

A tribute to American abundance with an untraditional twist. Choose quail cooked to moist perfection or ducks burnished with honey and spices. The only parts of this menu that should be cooked close to serving time are the game, rice, and vegetables. Make Consommé Madrilene, Cranberry Salad, and mix the dough for Refrigerator Rolls 1 day ahead. Prepare Ambrosia the morning of the dinner.

Wine Suggestion: A fruity red wine, such as a Beaujolais or a California Zinfandel, would complement the game. If you prefer a white wine, choose one that's not too dry, such as an Alsatian Riesling.

Consommé Madrilene

8 cups chicken broth	1 teaspoon salt
1 chicken-flavored bouillon cube	1 teaspoon Worcestershire sauce
3 cups tomato juice	½ teaspoon hot sauce
4 medium tomatoes, peeled, seeded, and chopped	Fresh parsley sprigs (optional)
	Green onion (optional)
2 egg whites	Hard cooked egg (optional)
1 teaspoon dried green onion	

Combine first 9 ingredients in a Dutch oven; stir well. Bring mixture to a boil. Remove from heat; strain liquid into container, and discard pulp. Serve soup hot or cold. Garnish with parsley, green onion, or hard cooked egg, if desired. Yield: 12 servings.

Charlotte Caper's Elegant Quail

The blend of seasonings and slow steaming make these quail superb.

1 teaspoon salt
¼ teaspoon freshly ground pepper
12 quail
1 cup butter or margarine

½ cup Chablis or other dry white
  wine
½ cup water
2 tablespoons lemon juice
2 teaspoons soy sauce

Sprinkle salt and pepper over the surface of each quail. Melt butter in a large oven-proof skillet over medium heat. Add quail; brown slowly for 15 minutes, turning as necessary.

Combine wine, water, lemon juice, and soy sauce; pour over quail. Cover, and bake at 325° for 1 hour and 15 minutes or until tender. Yield: 12 servings.

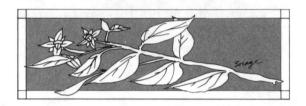

Linda Lacefield's Honeyed Duck

4 mallard ducks
2 tablespoons plus 2½ teaspoons
  salt, divided
1 tablespoon plus 1 teaspoon
  ground ginger
1 tablespoon plus 1 teaspoon basil
2 teaspoons pepper
3 cups honey
1 cup butter

¾ cup orange juice
1 tablespoon plus 2 teaspoons
  lemon juice
4 teaspoons orange peel
½ teaspoon dry mustard
4 to 6 oranges, sliced ½ inch thick
2 teaspoons cornstarch
3 tablespoons cold water

Boil ducks in 2 gallons salted water for 30 minutes. Dry ducks thoroughly inside and out. Combine 2 tablespoons plus 2 teaspoons salt with ginger, basil, and pepper. Rub half of this mixture inside of ducks.

Combine honey, butter, orange juice, lemon juice, orange peel, mustard, and remaining ½ teaspoon salt in small saucepan. Heat until butter melts. Rub 2 to 3 tablespoons of the mixture inside each duck. Stuff each duck with as many orange slices as possible. Pour 4 to 5 tablespoons honey mixture into each duck. Truss ducks. Rub remaining seasoning mixture on outside of ducks.

Place each duck on a large square of heavy-duty aluminum foil. Divide remaining honey mixture evenly, pour over ducks, and wrap securely. Place in large roasting pan. Bake at 325° for 1 hour and 45 minutes. Unwrap, baste, and bake 25 minutes longer until brown.

To make gravy, dissolve cornstarch in cold water. Stir cornstarch mixture into pan drippings; cook until thickened. Yield: 10 to 12 servings.

Saffron Rice Amandine

3 (5-ounce) packages
    saffron-seasoned yellow rice
    mix
4 cups boiling water
1 teaspoon salt
⅔ cup butter
2 tablespoons chopped green
    pepper

2 tablespoons chopped green onion
    tops
4½ cups chicken broth
1 (2-ounce) package slivered
    almonds

Combine rice, boiling water, and salt in a large bowl; stir well. Set aside 30 minutes; drain. Sauté rice in butter in a heavy skillet over low heat 5 minutes, stirring frequently. Add green pepper and green onion tops; cook 2 minutes over low heat, stirring frequently. Spoon mixture into a well-greased 2-quart baking dish. Pour chicken broth over rice mixture. Cover and bake at 350° for 45 minutes. Sprinkle almonds over rice mixture. Bake, uncovered, for 15 minutes or until all liquid is absorbed. Yield: 12 servings.

Harvest Vegetable Platter

1 pound brussels sprouts
1 to 2 tablespoons butter or
    margarine
¼ teaspoon salt
Dash of pepper

Squash-Turnip Sauté
Beet Purée (page 136)
Watercress or parsley sprigs

Steam brussels sprouts; toss with 1 to 2 tablespoons butter, salt, and pepper to taste. To assemble platter, mound Beet Puree in center of large serving platter. Arrange brussels sprouts in a ring around beets. Arrange Squash-Turnip Sauté in ring around brussels sprouts. Garnish with watercress or parsley sprigs. Yield: 10 to 12 servings.

Squash-Turnip Sauté

1 butternut squash
2 turnips
¼ cup butter
½ teaspoon sugar
1 tablespoon grated orange rind

¼ teaspoon ground cinnamon
1 tablespoon dry sherry
Salt and pepper
2 tablespoons chopped parsley

Bake squash at 325° for 15 minutes; let stand to cool. Cut squash in half crosswise; reserve seeded (bulb) half for other use. Peel seedless half; slice ⅛ inch thick. Cut slices into thin sticks.

Peel and slice turnips ⅛ inch thick; cut slices into thin sticks.

Melt butter in large skillet over medium heat. Add squash; sprinkle with sugar. Toss to coat with butter. Stir in orange rind and cinnamon; sauté 5 minutes. Add turnips and sherry; sauté until vegetables are tender, about 10 minutes. Sprinkle with salt and pepper to taste and parsley. Yield: 10 to 12 servings.

Beet Puree

1 pound fresh beets, cooked,
    peeled, and cut into chunks
2 tablespoons butter, melted
Salt and pepper

1 tablespoon port wine
¼ to ½ teaspoon sugar
⅛ teaspoon ground ginger

Process beets, melted butter, and salt and pepper to taste in food processor or blender until pureed; press through food mill for smoother texture, if desired. Stir in wine, ¼ to ½ teaspoon sugar, and ginger. Yield: 2 cups.

Cranberry Salad with Vinegar Dressing

1 (20-ounce) can pineapple chunks,
    undrained
3 envelopes unflavored gelatin
2 cups boiling water
1½ cups sugar
¼ teaspoon salt
2 oranges, peeled and sectioned

1 (12-ounce) package fresh
    cranberries
1 cup chopped pecans
½ cup lemon juice
Leaf lettuce
Wine Vinegar Dressing

Drain pineapple, reserving juice; set pineapple aside. Soften gelatin in reserved pineapple juice in a large bowl. Add water, sugar, and salt; stir until sugar is dissolved.

Position knife blade in food processor bowl; add orange sections and cranberries. Process 3 to 5 seconds or until fruits are finely chopped; add to gelatin mixture. Stir in pecans and lemon juice. Pour mixture into an 8-cup mold. Chill until firm. Turn out onto lettuce-lined serving plate. Serve with Wine Vinegar Dressing. Yield: 10 to 12 servings.

Wine Vinegar Dressing

½ cup mayonnaise
½ cup whipping cream
2 teaspoons wine vinegar

1 teaspoon lemon juice
½ teaspoon sugar

Combine all ingredients in a small mixing bowl; chill thoroughly. Yield: 1¼ cups.

Refrigerator Rolls

A delicious roll. Prepare the dough the day before; refrigerate.

1 package dry yeast
¼ cup warm water (105° to 115°)
1 cup shortening
½ cup sugar
3 eggs, lightly beaten

1 cup warm milk (105° to 115°)
1 teaspoon salt
5 cups all-purpose flour
⅓ cup butter, melted

Dissolve yeast in warm water; set aside.

Cream shortening; gradually add sugar, and beat until light and fluffy. Stir in eggs, milk, and yeast mixture; beat until smooth. Stir in salt and flour to make a sticky dough.

Place dough in a well-greased bowl, turning to grease top. Cover and refrigerate 24 hours. Remove dough from refrigerator 2 hours before serving.

Lightly grease muffin pans. Punch dough down, and shape into 1-inch balls. Place 3 balls in each muffin cup. Cover and let rise in a warm place (85°), free from drafts, 1 hour or until doubled in bulk.

Bake at 400° for 12 minutes or until light brown. Brush with butter and serve hot. Yield: 3 dozen rolls.

Apricot Brandy Pound Cake

1 cup butter, softened
3 cups sugar
6 eggs
1 (8-ounce) carton commercial sour
   cream
½ cup apricot brandy

1 teaspoon rum extract
1 teaspoon vanilla extract
1 teaspoon orange extract
3 cups all-purpose flour
¼ teaspoon baking soda
½ teaspoon salt

Cream butter; gradually add sugar, beating well. Add eggs, one at a time, beating well after each addition. Add sour cream, apricot brandy, and flavorings; stir well.

Combine flour, baking soda, and salt in a medium mixing bowl; stir well. Add flour mixture to batter; stir until smooth.

Pour batter into a greased, floured, and waxed paper-lined 10-inch tube pan. Bake at 325° for 1 hour and 20 minutes or until cake tests done. Cool in pan 10 minutes; remove from pan, and cool completely. Yield: one 10-inch cake.

Ambrosia

Known as food for the gods, ambrosia is often served at Thanksgiving and during the Christmas season in the South. Long ago, the best Louisiana and Florida oranges came in at that time.

8 large navel oranges
¾ cup superfine sugar
2 cups grated coconut

1 (8-ounce) can crushed pineapple,
   drained
Maraschino cherries, drained
   (optional)

Peel and section oranges. Layer one-third of oranges, sugar, coconut, and pineapple in a 2½-quart glass bowl. Repeat procedure twice with remaining oranges, sugar, pineapple and coconut. Cover and chill at least 3 hours. Garnish with maraschino cherries, if desired. Yield: 12 servings.

 Superfine Sugar: Grind granulated sugar in your food processor for superfine sugar. It dissolves instantly in liquid.

Tree-Trimming Supper

Wassail Bowl Punch
Party Mold
Shrimp Creole
Green Bean and Mushroom Salad
Cloud Nine Chocolate Pie
Assorted Christmas Cookies (Chapter VIII)

Serves 8

Greet tree-trimmers or carolers with Wassail Bowl Punch and appetizers. Invite guests to make some of the ornaments. You provide the supplies and give them room for activity. Do ask people to "sign" their ornaments with names or initials so that memories will be renewed when you trim future trees. Then relax afterwards with a festive supper of Shrimp Creole and Cloud Nine Chocolate Pie. Make the Party Mold, Cloud Nine Chocolate Pie, and the salad dressing up to 1 day in advance. Prepare the shrimp and sauce for Shrimp Creole just before guests are due to arrive; add shrimp to sauce and reheat just before serving.

Beverage Suggestion: If you wish to spike the Wassail Bowl Punch with rum or apple brandy, add the liquor after you've removed the punch from the stove. A California Gamay Beaujolais, a Portuguese rosé, or even beer would carry the lighthearted mood through supper.

Bitty Creekmore's Wassail Bowl Punch

Delicious and easy to make.

1 quart hot tea	2 cups orange juice
1 cup sugar	¾ cup lemon juice
1 (32-ounce) bottle cranberry juice cocktail	2 (3-inch) sticks cinnamon
1 (32-ounce) bottle apple juice	24 whole cloves, divided
	Orange slices

Combine hot tea and sugar in a large Dutch oven; stir in juices. Add cinnamon and 12 whole cloves; boil over medium heat 2 minutes. Remove from heat and cool.

Stud orange slices with remaining cloves. Pour Wassail into punch bowl; float orange slices on top. Yield: about 1 gallon.

Jane Brock's Party Mold

1 (8-ounce) plus 1 (3-ounce)
    package cream cheese, softened
½ cup butter or margarine,
    softened
½ cup commercial sour cream
⅓ cup sugar
1 teaspoon unflavored gelatin
¼ cup cold water
1 cup chopped almonds, toasted
½ cup golden raisins, chopped

⅓ cup chopped red maraschino
    cherries
⅓ cup chopped green maraschino
    cherries
Grated rind of 2 lemons
Additional red maraschino cherries
    (optional)
Additional green maraschino
    cherries (optional)
Sliced apples

Combine cream cheese and butter in a medium mixing bowl; beat until light and fluffy. Add sour cream and sugar, mixing well.

Combine gelatin and cold water in a small saucepan; cook over low heat, stirring constantly, until gelatin dissolves. Add to cream cheese mixture, mixing well.

Fold in almonds, raisins, chopped cherries, and lemon rind. Lightly grease a 4-cup mold with mayonnaise; spoon mixture into mold. Cover and refrigerate overnight.

Remove from refrigerator; let stand 20 minutes. Unmold onto a serving platter; garnish as desired with red and green cherries. Serve with apple slices. Yield: 8 servings.

Shrimp Creole

½ cup butter or margarine, melted
3 pounds medium shrimp, peeled
    and deveined
¼ cup all-purpose flour
1 cup finely chopped onion
1 medium-size green pepper, finely
    chopped
3 stalks celery, finely chopped
2 tablespoons finely chopped fresh
    parsley
2 cloves garlic, minced
1 beef-flavored bouillon cube

1 cup boiling water
1 (16-ounce) can whole tomatoes,
    undrained and chopped
2 tablespoons catsup
1 tablespoon Worcestershire sauce
2 teaspoons sugar
½ teaspoon salt
¼ teaspoon crushed red pepper
¼ teaspoon ground mace
¼ teaspoon dried whole thyme
1 bay leaf
Hot cooked rice

Heat butter in a large Dutch oven; add shrimp and cook, stirring constantly, 6 minutes. Remove shrimp and set aside. Add flour, stirring until smooth. Cook over medium heat, stirring constantly until lightly browned.

Sauté onion, green pepper, celery, parsley, and garlic in Dutch oven until tender. Dissolve bouillon in boiling water. Add bouillon, tomatoes, catsup, Worcestershire sauce, sugar, salt, red pepper, mace, thyme, and bay leaf; stir until well combined. Simmer, uncovered, 15 minutes; add sautéed shrimp and cook until thoroughly heated. Remove and discard bay leaf; serve over hot cooked rice. Yield: 8 servings.

Green Bean and Mushroom Salad

A crisp salad tossed with a tangy dressing.

½ pound fresh green beans,
    trimmed, cut in half crosswise
1 red onion, thinly sliced
½ pound mushrooms, sliced
1 large tomato, cut into thin
    wedges

1 hard-cooked egg white, thinly
    sliced
Salt and pepper
1 head romaine lettuce, torn into
    pieces
Olive Dressing

Cook green beans in boiling water just until they turn bright green; rinse immediately under cold water and drain well. Place green beans, onion, mushrooms, tomato, and egg white in large salad bowl; toss with salt and pepper to taste. Add lettuce and Olive Dressing; toss well. Yield: 8 servings.

Olive Dressing

1 hard-cooked egg yolk
2 tablespoons red wine vinegar
1 tablespoon lemon juice
1 tablespoon (1 ounce)
    pimiento-stuffed green olives
1 tablespoon juice from olives

3 large sprigs parsley
1 clove garlic
½ teaspoon dried oregano
½ cup vegetable oil
⅓ cup olive oil

Process egg yolk, vinegar, lemon juice, olives and juice, parsley, garlic, and oregano in food processor or blender until blended. Add oil; process until smooth. Yield: about 1 cup.

Cloud Nine Chocolate Pie

A super-rich dessert for chocolate-lovers. Serve small wedges.

20 Bordeaux cookies, crushed
1 tablespoon all-purpose flour
2½ tablespoons butter, melted
1 (4-ounce) package sweet baking
    chocolate
2 cups whipping cream, divided

1 (3-ounce) package cream cheese,
    softened
¼ cup sugar
¼ cup Tia Maria or Kahlua
¼ cup sifted powdered sugar

Combine cookie crumbs, flour, and melted butter in a small bowl; mix well. Press mixture into bottom and sides of a lightly greased 9-inch pieplate. Bake at 350° for 8 minutes. Cool.

Combine chocolate and 3 tablespoons cream in a heavy saucepan; cook over low heat until chocolate melts. Beat cream cheese in small mixing bowl; add sugar, 2 tablespoons cream, and chocolate mixture. Gradually add Tia Maria; set aside.

Whip remaining cream until stiff using high speed of electric mixer; add powdered sugar. Fold chocolate mixture into whipped cream, blending until smooth. Spoon into crust. Chill until firm. Store any leftover pie in freezer. Yield: one 9-inch pie.

Cheney
Christmas Dinner

Oysters with Cocktail Sauce
Crisp Celery Hearts and Ripe Olives
Turkey in a Bag
Giblet Gravy
Cornbread Dressing
Cranberry Sauce
Green Beans with Lemon-Chive Dressing
Broiled Tomato Halves
Sweet Potato Pecan Balls
Tipsy Cake
Toasted Pecans (page 132)

Serves 12

This Cheney Christmas menu holds all the family's favorites. It's a lavish dinner but quite easy to serve, since the cake should be completed three days ahead and everything but the oysters will hold until you're ready to eat. Bake the cornbread for the stuffing and make the cocktail sauce several days in advance and refrigerate. For freshest flavor, don't begin opening the oysters until the first guests arrive.

Wine Suggestion: The Cheneys prefer a California Pinot Blanc or Sauvignon Blanc with turkey. These dry white wines go well with the oysters too, but you might wish to start with champagne and serve a rosé or light-bodied red wine with the turkey.

Oysters with Cocktail Sauce

Arrange oysters on the half shell on a bed of finely crushed ice, or serve shucked oysters in cocktail glasses with a dollop of cocktail sauce and a slice of lemon.

1 cup catsup
½ cup chili sauce
1½ tablespoons lemon juice
1 tablespoon Worcestershire sauce
1 to 2 teaspoons prepared
   horseradish

½ teaspoon hot sauce
¼ teaspoon celery salt
6 dozen fresh oysters on the half
   shell
Lemon wedges

Combine first 7 ingredients in a small bowl; stir well. Chill thoroughly. Serve with oysters. Garnish with lemon wedges. Yield: 12 servings.

Turkey in a Bag

1 (13- to 15-pound) turkey
2 tablespoons salt
1½ teaspoons pepper
1 large onion, quartered
2 stalks celery with leaves, coarsely
   chopped

¼ teaspoon paprika
2 tablespoons boiling water
½ cup vegetable oil
Browning Bag
Giblet Gravy

Remove giblets and neck from turkey; reserve for gravy. Rinse turkey thoroughly with cold water; pat dry. Combine salt and pepper; sprinkle over surface and in cavity of turkey. Place onion and celery inside cavity of turkey; close with skewers.

Dissolve paprika in boiling water; stir well. Combine paprika mixture and oil, mixing well. Brush entire bird with oil mixture, reserving extra mixture. Insert meat thermometer in breast or meaty part of thigh, making sure it does not touch bone.

Place turkey in a browning bag. Tie bag securely; cut several slits in top of bag. Place turkey, breast side up, in a shallow roasting pan. Bake at 325° for 2½ hours until legs are easy to move or meat thermometer registers 185°.

Transfer turkey from browning bag to a serving platter. Let stand 30 to 45 minutes before carving. Serve with Giblet Gravy. Yield: 16 to 24 servings.

Giblet Gravy

Giblets and neck from turkey
1 teaspoon salt

1 teaspoon dried green onion
2 hard-cooked eggs, chopped

Place giblets, neck, salt, green onion, and water to cover in a medium saucepan. Bring to a boil. Reduce heat; cover, and simmer 1 to 2 hours or until giblets are fork tender. Drain, reserving broth. Remove meat from neck; coarsely chop neck meat and giblets.

Combine reserved broth, neck and giblet meat, and egg in a medium saucepan. Cook over medium heat 15 minutes, stirring occasionally. Yield: 2 cups.

Cornbread Dressing

1 cup finely chopped onion
1 medium-size green pepper, finely
   chopped
2 stalks celery with leaves, finely
   chopped
6 cups cornbread crumbs

2 cups soft breadcrumbs
1 teaspoon salt
¼ teaspoon pepper
4 eggs, lightly beaten
1½ cups turkey broth

Combine onion, green pepper, celery, and water to cover in a medium saucepan. Bring to a boil; reduce heat and simmer 10 minutes. Drain well.

Combine cooked vegetables, cornbread crumbs, breadcrumbs, salt, and pepper; mix well. Add eggs; stir well. Gradually add broth, stirring until well blended. Spoon into a lightly greased 12- x 7½- x 1½-inch baking pan. Bake, uncovered, at 400° for 45 minutes or until golden brown. Yield: 12 servings.

Green Beans with Lemon-Chive Dressing

½ cup fresh lemon juice
½ cup melted butter
2 tablespoons chopped chives

6 cups cooked green beans, fresh
  or canned

Mix lemon juice, butter, and chives together. Pour over cooked green beans and heat. Serve immediately. Yield: 12 servings.

Broiled Tomato Halves

1 cup fine dry breadcrumbs
¼ cup butter or margarine, melted

1 tablespoon chopped fresh parsley
6 medium tomatoes, halved

Combine breadcrumbs, butter, and parsley in a small mixing bowl; mix well.

Spoon breadcrumb mixture evenly over cut surface of each tomato half. Place prepared tomatoes on a rack in a shallow roasting pan. Broil about 8 inches from heat for 5 minutes or until topping is lightly browned. Yield: 12 servings.

Sweet Potato Pecan Balls

These may be made a day ahead, kept refrigerated, and baked just before serving. Good served hot, room temperature, or cold.

1 (16-ounce) can mashed sweet
  potatoes
½ cup sugar
2 tablespoons butter or margarine
½ teaspoon salt
¼ teaspoon cinnamon

1 teaspoon vanilla extract
3 cups finely chopped pecans or
  walnuts
12 teaspoons boysenberry or other
  berry jelly (orange or fig
  chutney may be substituted)

Combine all ingredients except pecans and jelly in large bowl and blend well with potato masher. Using a measuring tablespoon, shape mixture into 2-inch balls. Roll balls in finely chopped nuts. Place on large cookie sheet at least 2 inches apart. Indent top of ball with spoon and fill with ½ teaspoon jelly or chutney. Bake at 350° for 15 to 20 minutes or until nuts are toasted light brown. Yield: 24 balls. Allow two per serving.

Table Decorations: A small arrangement of cut poinsettia or evergreen boughs and pine cones, with red or white tapers, says "Merry Christmas" gracefully. To add drama to the Tipsy Cake, bring it to the table on a tray wreathed with holly sprigs or lemon leaves and frosted red and green grapes. To frost grapes, dip small bunches first in lightly beaten egg white and then in superfine sugar; allow grapes to dry on wire racks.

Tipsy Cake

6 eggs, separated
⅓ cup ice water
1½ cups sugar
½ teaspoon almond extract
½ teaspoon lemon extract
1½ cups sifted all-purpose flour
½ teaspoon baking powder
¼ teaspoon salt

¾ teaspoon cream of tartar
1 to 1½ cups sherry
1 cup crab apple jelly
3 tablespoons sliced almonds, toasted
Custard
2 cups whipping cream
¼ cup sugar

Place egg yolks in a large mixing bowl; beat at high speed of electric mixer until thick and lemon colored. Gradually add ice water, beating constantly until frothy. Gradually beat in 1½ cups sugar and flavorings.

Sift together flour, baking powder, and salt. Sprinkle flour mixture over yolk mixture ¼ cup at a time; gently fold in.

Beat egg whites (at room temperature) and cream of tartar until soft peaks form. Gently fold into batter.

Pour batter into 2 waxed-paper lined 9-inch cakepans, spreading evenly with a spatula. Bake at 350° for 30 minutes or until cake springs back when lightly touched. Cool cake 20 minutes, and remove from pan. Remove waxed paper and cool completely.

Pour ½ to ¾ cup sherry over each cake layer; let stand at least 3 hours.

Place a cake layer on cakeplate. Spread ½ cup jelly over layer; top with 1 tablespoon almonds. Spread custard over almonds. Cover with remaining layer, and repeat procedure with remaining jelly and 1 tablespoon almonds. Cover and refrigerate overnight.

Beat whipping cream until foamy; gradually add ¼ cup sugar, beating until soft peaks form. Spread over sides and top of cake; sprinkle with remaining almonds. Keep refrigerated. Yield: one 9-inch cake.

Custard

¾ cup sugar
2 tablespoons all-purpose flour
3 eggs

2 cups milk, heated
1 teaspoon vanilla extract

Combine sugar, flour, and eggs in a heavy saucepan; stir well. Gradually add hot milk, stirring constantly. Cook over medium heat, stirring constantly, 20 minutes or until thickened and mixture coats a metal spoon; cool slightly. Stir in vanilla. Chill thoroughly. Yield: 2 cups.

Page 145: *Gather your friends for A Tree Trimming Supper (page 138). Serve Wassail Bowl Punch and Party Mold as appetizers.*

Page 146: *This colorful Mexican Fiesta (page 173) features clockwise from right: Margaritas, Lime Grilled Chicken, Corn Kabobs, Guacamole, Salsa, and Chimi-Changas.*

The
Great Outdoors

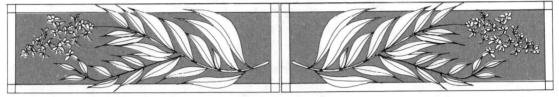

There are three ways to savor food outdoors. You can laze around a backyard barbecue. Or you can pack up and take off for a picnic at a park or beach. And sometimes you can take advantage of a mild evening in spring or late fall to move a dinner cooked indoors onto the patio.

The menus in this chapter play on the delight of each warm-weather opportunity. You can have the Pack Up-and-Go Picnic ready for a fast getaway anytime. For a concert under the stars or a romantic sunset, there's a Country French Picnic ready to go. For a change of pace from the same old burgers, there are barbecues built around beef ribs, a whole fish, and leg of lamb. When you're not sure which way the day will turn out, you can play it safe with the Easygoing Patio Supper or a memorable Spanish-style dinner that moves outdoors with ease.

The international flavor of some of the menus reflects the fact that dining outdoors is considered a special treat all over the world. For an all-American summer round-up, see the Big Fourth of July Barbecue on page 123. Whatever the culinary accent, the spirit is the same: lots of delicious food served any way you wish—from paper plates to china and linens.

Pack Up-and-Go Picnic

Cold Squash Soup
Energy-Packed Meat Loaf
Crusty Rolls
Gazpacho Salad
Crazy Chocolate Cake

Serves 6 to 8

These are cold, refreshing foods that can be kept in the refrigerator or freezer until you're ready to take off. The salad dressing can be refrigerated up to 1 week in a covered jar. The salad vegetables can be prepared a day ahead, but don't peel the avocados until you're ready to use them.

Cold Squash Soup

3 medium onions, finely chopped
3 tablespoons butter or margarine
8 small yellow squash, sliced
1½ cups chicken broth
1 teaspoon salt
⅛ teaspoon sugar

⅛ teaspoon ground nutmeg
2 tablespoons lemon juice
¼ teaspoon hot sauce
1 pint whipping cream
Chopped fresh parsley or chives

Sauté onion in butter in a large Dutch oven until onion is tender. Stir in squash and chicken broth; cover and simmer 15 minutes or until squash is tender. Add salt, sugar, nutmeg, lemon juice, and hot sauce. Spoon a fourth of squash mixture into container of electric blender, and process until smooth. Repeat with remaining squash mixture. (Recipe can be frozen at this point; stir in cream after thawing.)

Pour squash mixture into a large bowl; stir in whipping cream. Cover and chill thoroughly. Garnish with parsley or chives before serving. Yield: 7 cups.

Picnic Tips: Carry chilled soups in insulated jugs; serve them in plastic or paper cups, if you wish. Pack other cold food in styrofoam hampers with blocks of portable "ice" and wadded newspaper for additional insulation. Be especially careful to keep any food made with mayonnaise or seafood well chilled. Don't forget to pack serving utensils, including a slicing knife and a corkscrew, if appropriate.

Energy-Packed Meat Loaf

A succulent meat loaf that's delicious sliced cold for sandwiches. It can be refrigerated up to 2 days or frozen up to 1 month.

1½ pounds ground chuck
1 cup wheat germ
1¼ teaspoons salt
⅛ teaspoon pepper
¼ cup chopped onion
1 (4-ounce) can mushrooms,
   drained

1 cup catsup, divided
2 eggs, lightly beaten
1 tablespoon prepared horseradish
1 carrot, grated
3 slices bacon

Combine ground chuck, wheat germ, salt, pepper, onion, mushrooms, ⅔ cup catsup, eggs, horseradish, and carrot in a large bowl; mix well.

Shape meat mixture into a loaf; place on aluminum foil on a broiler rack. Brush with remaining ⅓ cup catsup and place bacon strips lengthwise over top. Cover with foil and bake at 300° for 45 to 50 minutes. Loaf may be served hot or cold. Yield: 6 to 8 servings.

Joe Middleton's Gazpacho Salad

This is a marvelous combination of layers of diced fresh vegetables and breadcrumbs with a tasty herbed garlic dressing.

3 cups diced tomatoes
2 tablespoons plus 2 teaspoons red
   wine vinegar, divided
1½ teaspoons salt, divided
3 medium cucumbers
¼ teaspoon sugar
1 large red onion, diced
2 medium-size green peppers
2 medium-size red peppers
3 stalks celery, diced

3 shallots, finely minced
⅓ cup minced fresh parsley
2 cups soft breadcrumbs
3 firm ripe avocados, halved,
   seeded, peeled, and diced
Herb and Garlic Dressing (page
   150)
1 (2-ounce) can anchovies, drained
3 tablespoons capers
½ cup ripe olives

Combine tomatoes, 1 teaspoon wine vinegar, and ½ teaspoon salt in a medium bowl; let stand 5 minutes. Place in a colander to drain and set aside.

Peel cucumbers, halve lengthwise, scoop out seeds, and dice. Combine diced cucumber with 1 tablespoon wine vinegar, ½ teaspoon salt, and ¼ teaspoon sugar; let stand 5 minutes. Place in colander to drain and set aside.

Cover diced onion with boiling water; drain. Rinse in cold water; drain again. Combine onion, peppers, and celery with ½ teaspoon salt and 1 tablespoon wine vinegar; set aside.

Combine shallots and parsley; set aside.

Spread ½ cup breadcrumbs in bottom of a 2-quart glass bowl; layer one-third each pepper and onion mixture, avocados, tomatoes, cucumbers, and one-fourth of the Herb and Garlic Dressing; repeat layers, ending with ¼ cup breadcrumbs and dressing. Sprinkle shallot and parsley mixture over salad. Cover and refrigerate 4 to 6 hours or overnight. Garnish with anchovies, capers, and olives. Yield: 10 servings.

Herb and Garlic Dressing

3 large cloves garlic, minced
1 teaspoon salt
⅛ teaspoon black pepper
1 tablespoon dried whole oregano
Zest of ½ lemon

3 tablespoons fresh lemon juice
3 tablespoons wine vinegar
½ cup olive oil
2 teaspoons Dijon mustard
¼ teaspoon hot sauce

Combine all ingredients in container of an electric blender; process until smooth. Chill. Yield: about ¾ cup.

Winifred Barron's Crazy Chocolate Cake

3 cups all-purpose flour
2 teaspoons baking soda
1 teaspoon salt
2 cups sugar
¼ cup plus 2 tablespoons cocoa
2 cups water

¾ cup vegetable oil
2 tablespoons cider vinegar
1 tablespoon vanilla extract
Chocolate Glaze
Chopped pecans

Sift together flour, soda, salt, sugar, and cocoa in a large mixing bowl. Pour water, oil, vinegar, and vanilla over flour mixture; beat on medium speed of electric mixer until thoroughly blended. Pour batter into a greased and floured 13- x 9- x 2-inch baking pan.

Bake at 350° for 35 minutes or until a wooden pick inserted in center comes out clean. Cool in pan. Drizzle Chocolate Glaze over cake, and garnish with chopped pecans. Yield: one 13- x 9-inch cake.

Chocolate Glaze

1½ cups sugar
¼ cup plus 2 tablespoons butter or
    margarine

¼ cup plus 2 tablespoons milk
1½ (1-ounce) squares unsweetened
    chocolate

Combine all ingredients in a medium-size heavy saucepan; cook over medium heat, stirring frequently, until chocolate melts. Bring to a boil; cover, and cook over high heat 2 minutes. Uncover and cook an additional 2 minutes. Remove from heat, and let glaze stand 8 to 10 minutes before drizzling over cake in pan. Yield: enough for one 13- x 9-inch cake.

Autumn Tailgate Picnic

Crunchy Crescent Tuna Buns
or
Chicken-Pimiento Casserole
Vegetable Salad
Deviled Eggs
Money-Saver Banana Cake
or
Chocolate Rum Cake

Serves 8

---

*I*f you're traveling some distance, wrap the tuna buns individually in aluminum foil — they'll hold up well. And carry the chicken casserole in the foil-wrapped baking pan. Wrap the deviled-egg halves in pairs for convenient carrying. The cakes will improve in flavor if baked 1 day ahead. Cover tightly with foil and store in a cool place. Two warming choices to fill the thermos are Hot Spiced Cranberry Punch (page 250) and Hot Buttered Rum (page 251). Remember plastic serving dishes and eating utensils for the chicken and salad.

Crunchy Crescent Tuna Buns

Finely chopped ham can be substituted for the tuna—omit the dillweed and add 1 tablespoon pickle relish.

1 (7-ounce) can solid white tuna in
    water, drained
3 tablespoons mayonnaise
¼ teaspoon hot sauce
¼ teaspoon dry mustard
¼ teaspoon dried whole dillweed

2 tablespoons finely chopped celery
2 water chestnuts, finely chopped
1 (8-ounce) can refrigerator
    crescent dinner rolls
2 tablespoons margarine, melted
½ cup crushed potato chips

Combine tuna and next 6 ingredients; mix well, and set aside.
Unroll crescent roll dough; separate into 4 rectangles. Firmly press perforations to seal. Cut each rectangle in half crosswise. Press dough to a 4-inch square. Spoon 1 tablespoon tuna mixture in center of square. Pull 4 corners up to the middle. Pinch seams to seal. Brush with melted margarine. Sprinkle with crushed potato chips. Bake at 375° for 15 to 20 minutes. Yield: 8 servings.

Miriam Mayo's Chicken-Pimiento Casserole

4 whole chicken breasts, split, boned, and skinned
1½ teaspoons salt
3 tablespoons vegetable oil
2 small onions, peeled and quartered
2 (4-ounce) jars sliced pimiento, undrained

2 cups hot water
1 tablespoon chicken-flavored bouillon granules
3 tablespoons cider vinegar
1 tablespoon soy sauce
1 tablespoon sugar
1 tablespoon cornstarch

Sprinkle chicken breasts with salt. Brown chicken in hot oil in a large skillet. Reduce heat, cover, and simmer chicken 15 minutes or until tender. Remove chicken to a 13- x 9- x 2-inch baking dish, reserving pan drippings in skillet. Sauté onion in pan drippings until tender.

Drain pimiento, reserving liquid. Place pimiento slices over chicken. Set aside.

Combine water, bouillon granules, reserved pimiento liquid, vinegar, soy sauce, and sugar; gradually stir mixture into cornstarch. Add cornstarch mixture to skillet. Cook over medium heat, stirring constantly, until thickened and bubbly. Pour mixture over chicken. Cover with heavy-duty foil. Bake at 375° for 15 minutes. Uncover and bake an additional 10 minutes. Yield: 8 servings.

Vegetable Salad

1 (17-ounce) can whole kernel corn, drained
1 (16-ounce) can French-style green beans, drained
1 (8.5-ounce) can green peas, drained
1 (2-ounce) jar chopped pimiento, drained
4 stalks celery, chopped

1 medium-size green pepper, chopped
1 small onion, chopped
1 cup vinegar
⅔ cup vegetable oil
2 tablespoons water
1½ cups sugar
Leaf lettuce

Combine corn, green beans, peas, pimiento, celery, green pepper, and onion in a large bowl, tossing lightly. Cover and refrigerate 1 hour.

Combine vinegar, oil, water, and sugar; mix well. Pour over vegetable mixture. Cover and refrigerate at least 24 hours. Drain and serve in a lettuce-lined bowl. Yield: 8 servings.

Deviled Eggs

12 hard-cooked eggs
1 tablespoon vinegar
1 (4½-ounce) can deviled ham
⅓ cup mayonnaise

2 teaspoons prepared mustard
1 tablespoon sweet pickle relish
Salt and pepper to taste
Paprika

Slice eggs in half lengthwise, and carefully remove yolks. Mash yolks; sprinkle with vinegar. Add remaining ingredients except paprika; stir well. Stuff egg whites with yolk mixture. Garnish eggs with paprika. Yield: 12 to 15 servings.

Money-Saver Banana Cake

Overripe bananas can be turned into an easy and delicious cake.

½ cup butter or margarine,
  softened
1 cup sugar
2 eggs
1 cup (2 large or 3 small) very ripe
  bananas, mashed
½ cup commercial sour cream or
  plain yogurt

1 teaspoon lemon extract
2¼ cups all-purpose flour
1 teaspoon baking powder
1 teaspoon baking soda
½ teaspoon salt
¾ cup chopped nuts (optional)

Cream butter; gradually add sugar, beating at medium speed of an electric mixer until light and fluffy. Add eggs, one at a time, beating well after each addition. Add bananas, sour cream or yogurt, and lemon extract; mix well.

Sift dry ingredients; stir into batter. Add nuts, if desired. Pour batter into a greased and floured 9-inch tube pan. Bake at 350° for 45 to 50 minutes, or until a wooden pick inserted in center comes out clean. Cool in pan 10 minutes. Remove from pan; cool completely. Yield: one 9-inch cake.

Gerry Beaird's Chocolate Rum Cake

1 (18.5-ounce) package yellow cake
  mix
1 (4.5-ounce) package instant
  chocolate pudding mix
1 tablespoon vanilla extract
1 (8-ounce) carton commercial sour
  cream

4 eggs
¼ cup dark rum or 1 tablespoon
  rum flavoring
½ cup vegetable oil
1 cup chocolate chips, divided
1 cup chopped pecans, divided
Sifted powdered sugar (optional)

Combine first 7 ingredients in large mixing bowl; beat 3 minutes on medium speed of electric mixer. Add ½ cup chocolate chips and ½ cup chopped nuts; beat 2 minutes longer. Fold in remaining ½ cup chocolate chips and ½ cup chopped nuts. The batter will be very stiff. Pour batter into a well-greased and floured 10-inch tube or Bundt pan. Bake at 350° for 1 hour, or until a wooden pick inserted in center comes out clean. Cool 30 minutes on wire rack before removing from pan. Allow cake to cool completely on a wire rack. Sprinkle top with powdered sugar, if desired. Yield: one 10-inch tube or Bundt cake.

Country French Picnic

Kir
Carrot Vichyssoise
Broccoli Quiche
Ratatouille
Assorted sausages, cold cuts, and cheeses
French Bread
Fresh Fruit
Pineapple Preserves Nut Cake

Serves 6 to 8

The names may sound a bit fancy, but vichyssoise, quiche, and ratatouille are typical French "convenience" foods—the kind of items a Parisian might purchase in a delicatessen on a day too hot for cooking. These quiches taste fine at room temperature and travel well in the piepans. Bring sausages to grill at the picnic site, if you wish, or serve cold cuts and cheese. Carry bottles of white wine and crème de cassis to mix Kir, or just serve chilled wine.

Kir

On more formal occasions substitute champagne for the wine to serve an elegant aperitif.

1 tablespoon crème de cassis   **¼ cup dry white wine**

Pour crème de cassis in the bottom of a wine glass. Pour in wine. Yield: 1 drink.

Carrot Vichyssoise

The classic cold potato and leek soup brightened with fresh carrots.

2 cups peeled, diced potatoes
1¼ cups sliced carrots
1 leek, sliced, white part only
3 cups chicken stock
⅛ teaspoon white pepper

1 teaspoon salt
3 dashes hot sauce
1 cup whipping cream
1 carrot, peeled and shredded
(optional)

Combine first 4 ingredients in saucepan and bring to a boil over medium high heat; reduce heat and simmer 25 minutes or until vegetables are tender.

Puree half the vegetables and liquid at a time in blender for 30 seconds on high speed. Be careful not to have too much in blender to avoid being burned. (Recipe can be frozen at this point; proceed after thawing.) Place liquid mixture in large mixing bowl; stir in pepper, salt, hot sauce, and cream. Chill in refrigerator until icy cold. Serve in chilled bowl, and garnish with shredded raw carrots. Yield: 6 servings.

Broccoli Quiche

A flavorful tart for a summer luncheon or supper. Make the pastry ahead of time.

3 eggs	1 (10-ounce) package frozen
1 cup half-and-half	broccoli spears, thawed and
¼ teaspoon salt	coarsely chopped
¼ teaspoon ground nutmeg	2 tablespoons grated Parmesan
⅛ teaspoon white pepper	cheese
3 dashes hot sauce	Pastry for one 10-inch pie
½ cup (2 ounces) shredded Swiss	
or Gruyère cheese	

Beat eggs in a large mixing bowl until foamy. Add half-and-half, salt, nutmeg, pepper, and hot sauce; beat well. Stir in Swiss cheese and broccoli. Pour into prepared pastry shell; sprinkle with Parmesan cheese. Bake at 375° for 30 minutes or until set. Yield: one 10-inch quiche.

Pastry

1¼ cups all-purpose flour	2 tablespoons shortening
⅛ teaspoon salt	¼ cup ice water
¼ cup plus 2 tablespoons butter or	1 tablespoon Dijon mustard
margarine	

Combine flour and salt in a medium mixing bowl; cut in butter and shortening with a pastry blender until mixture resembles coarse meal. Sprinkle ice water, 1 tablespoon at a time, evenly over surface; stir with a fork until all ingredients are moistened. Shape into a ball. Chill 30 minutes or overnight.

Roll dough to ⅛-inch thickness on a lightly floured surface. Line a 10-inch quiche dish with pastry; trim excess pastry around edges. Prick bottom and sides of pastry with a fork. Bake at 425° for 10 minutes. Remove from oven; brush bottom of pastry with mustard. Bake 2 additional minutes. Let cool. Yield: one 10-inch quiche shell.

Ratatouille

Equally good hot or cold. Serve on crackers for a party hors d'oeuvre.

2 pounds eggplant, peeled
2 pounds zucchini
¼ cup plus 1 tablespoon butter
3 green peppers, thinly sliced
2 medium onions, sliced
2 cloves garlic, minced
2½ pounds tomatoes, peeled, seeded and sliced

1 teaspoon dried basil
½ teaspoon celery seed
⅛ teaspoon thyme
2 teaspoons Worcestershire sauce
¼ teaspoon hot sauce
1 bay leaf
Salt to taste
1 large whole eggplant (optional)

Cut the eggplant and unpeeled zucchini into ½-inch slices. Sauté eggplant and zucchini in butter, several slices at a time; allow 2 or 3 minutes on each side. Remove and drain. Using same skillet, cook green peppers, onion, and garlic about 10 minutes over medium heat. Add tomatoes, herbs, Worcestershire sauce, hot sauce, and bay leaf; heat thoroughly. Salt to taste.

Place a layer of eggplant, zucchini, and half of tomato sauce in a 2-quart casserole. Repeat, ending with tomato sauce. Bake covered at 350° for 1 hour. Slice 1 inch off side of a large eggplant; scoop out pulp and reserve for other uses. Fill eggplant with ratatouille; mound remaining mixture around base of eggplant, if desired. Yield: 8 to 10 servings as a vegetable stew or salad; 45 to 50 as an hors d'oeuvre served on crackers or toasted rounds.

Note: Ratatouille can be served hot or cold.

Grace Auwarter's Pineapple Preserves Nut Cake

Scrumptious and easy to prepare.

1 cup margarine, at room temperature
2 cups sugar
4 eggs
3 cups all-purpose flour (reserve 1 tablespoon for nuts)
¼ teaspoon salt

1 tablespoon ground cinnamon
1 teaspoon cloves
1 cup buttermilk
1 teaspoon soda
1 tablespoon vanilla extract
1 cup pineapple preserves
1 cup chopped nuts

Cream margarine and sugar in large mixing bowl until light and fluffy. Add eggs, one at a time, beating well after each addition.

Sift together flour, salt, cinnamon, and cloves. Combine buttermilk and soda. Add flour mixture alternately with buttermilk, beginning and ending with flour, and mix well after each addition. Add vanilla, pineapple preserves, and nuts to which reserved tablespoon of flour has been added. Pour batter into greased and floured 10-inch tube pan; bake at 325° for 1 hour and 30 minutes. Do not open door for first hour. Yield: one 10-inch cake.

Birthday Cookout

Shrimp Dip
Green Pepper Crudité Cups
Roasted Beef Ribs
Grilled Herbed Potatoes
Tossed Salad Greens with Avocado Dressing
Short-Order Cheese Bread
Birthday Cake Supreme

Serves 6 to 8

This is a lavish but breezy celebration. The beef can be marinated overnight. The dip and salad dressing will keep refrigerated up to 2 days. Prepare the potato packets and bake the cake layers the night before. Frost the cake, cut up the crudités, and prepare the salad greens the day of the party.

Shrimp Dip

1 pound cooked, peeled, deveined, and chopped shrimp
1 (8-ounce) package cream cheese, softened
1 small onion, finely chopped
⅓ cup mayonnaise

3 tablespoons seafood cocktail sauce
Salt and pepper to taste
2 to 3 tablespoons finely chopped green pepper (optional)

Combine all ingredients in blender or food processor until thoroughly mixed. Serve with Green Pepper Crudité Cups or crackers. Yield: about 2 cups.

Green Pepper Crudité Cups

Red and green peppers
Carrot sticks
Celery sticks
Cucumber spears
Zucchini or yellow squash sticks

Blanched fresh snow peas
Blanched cauliflowerets or broccoli flowerets
Endive or curly endive leaves
Sprigs of parsley or dill

Cut around top of each pepper to remove core. Rinse out seeds under cold water and remove veins; place peppers upside-down on paper toweling to drain. Fill each pepper with an assortment of crudités, using endive leaves or herb sprigs to create "foliage." Arrange peppers around bowl of Shrimp Dip.

Roasted Beef Ribs

Easy to prepare and savory in taste.

6 beef ribs (5 to 6 pounds)
1 cup vegetable oil
½ cup Worcestershire sauce
Juice of 2 lemons

1 teaspoon garlic salt
1 teaspoon salt
1 teaspoon black pepper
2 medium onions, sliced

Trim fat from beef ribs. Place in a 13- x 9- x 2-inch baking dish.

Combine remaining ingredients. Pour sauce over beef ribs; cover and marinate overnight in refrigerator.

Drain marinade, and discard. Bake ribs at 350° for 30 minutes or until tender. Remove ribs from oven and place on barbecue grill over hot coals. Grill ribs 10 minutes on each side, or until crisp and brown. Serve hot. Yield: 4 to 6 servings.

Grilled Herbed Potatoes

¼ cup finely chopped celery
¾ cup butter or margarine
¼ teaspoon garlic powder
½ teaspoon salt
⅛ teaspoon pepper

1 teaspoon dried whole oregano
6 medium baking potatoes,
   unpeeled
1 large onion, thinly sliced

Sauté celery in butter in a small saucepan until tender. Stir in garlic powder, salt, pepper, and oregano.

Wash potatoes; slice each into ½-inch slices, cutting to, but not through bottom peel. Place a slice of onion between each slice of potato. Arrange potatoes on squares of heavy-duty aluminum foil; drizzle about 2 tablespoons of butter mixture over each potato. Fold foil edges over, and wrap each potato securely; cook on grill 1 hour or until done. Yield: 6 servings.

Avocado Dressing

Delightful on a tossed green salad or lettuce and endive. It's also a great sandwich spread with beef, ham, lamb, sliced chicken, or cold cuts.

½ cup avocado puree (about ½
   large avocado)
1 cup mayonnaise
2 cloves garlic, finely chopped, or
   ¼ teaspoon garlic powder
¼ cup whipping cream

¼ cup commercial sour cream
4 dashes hot sauce
2 teaspoons lemon juice
1 teaspoon Worcestershire sauce
1 teaspoon anchovy paste
¼ teaspoon salt

Blend together all ingredients in a small mixing bowl and serve as a dip, salad dressing, or spread. Keep refrigerated in a glass jar. Yield: approximately 2 cups.

Short-Order Cheese Bread

Easy enough to serve straight from the oven.

3¾ cups biscuit mix
1¼ cups (5 ounces) shredded sharp
    Cheddar cheese
1¼ cups milk

1 egg
½ teaspoon dry mustard
1½ tablespoons sesame seeds

Combine biscuit mix, cheese, milk, egg, and dry mustard in a large mixing bowl; beat on low speed of electric mixer until all ingredients are moistened. Increase speed to medium and beat an additional 1 minute.

Spoon batter into a greased 9- x 5- x 3-inch loafpan; sprinkle with sesame seeds. Bake at 350° for 1 hour and 10 minutes or until a wooden pick inserted in the center comes out clean. Immediately remove bread from pan and cool on a wire rack. Yield: 1 loaf.

Bill Cheney's Birthday Cake Supreme

Created especially to please the fancy of a college freshman. This light chocolate cake is reminiscent of one your grandmother used to make.

1 (18.5-ounce) package sour cream
    chocolate cake mix
3 eggs
1⅓ cups buttermilk
⅓ cup honey

1½ teaspoons brandy extract
Brandy Whipped Cream
¼ cup sweet baking chocolate,
    grated
3 candied cherries, halved

Combine cake mix, eggs, and buttermilk in large mixing bowl; blend for 1 minute with electric mixer on low speed, scraping bowl constantly. Beat on medium speed for 2 minutes, scraping bowl often.

Spoon batter into two greased, floured and waxed paper-lined 9-inch cake pans. Bake at 350° for 30 to 35 minutes or until cake tests done. Cool in pan 10 minutes. Remove layers from pan; cool on wire rack.

Warm honey in small saucepan over low heat; it should be liquid and not stiff. Stir in brandy flavoring and spoon over warm cake layers. Allow layers to cool completely.

Spread Brandy Whipped Cream between layers and on top and sides of cake. Chill for at least one hour.

Sprinkle top and sides lightly with grated sweet baking chocolate and dot with candied cherries. Refrigerate any leftover cake. Yield: one 2-layer cake.

Brandy Whipped Cream

2 cups whipping cream
½ cup sifted powdered sugar

1 tablespoon brandy or 1 teaspoon
    brandy extract

Beat cream in chilled bowl until standing in firm peaks. Continue to beat while gradually adding sugar and brandy. Mix well. Yield: enough for one 2-layer cake.

Baked Fish on the Grill

French-Fried Cauliflower
Grilled Stuffed Red Snapper
Dilled Carrots
Grill-Baked Potatoes
or
Corn on the Cob
Cucumber Salad
Blackberry Cobbler
or
Peach Pie

Serves 6

The French-Fried Cauliflower should be served hot from the pan, although it can be kept warm in a low oven. Plan to have everything else ready to go beforehand. Make the Bavarian Tartar Sauce, the Dilled Carrots, and the dressing for the cucumbers the night before. The stuffing and the basting sauce for the fish can be made and refrigerated several hours ahead. Bake either fruit dessert early in the day and reheat at serving time, or assemble before dinner and bake while the main course is served. The baked potatoes or corn can be wrapped in heavy-duty foil and placed over the coals while the fish is cooking. Allow about 45 minutes for the corn to cook and 1 hour for the potatoes to bake.

Margaret Garrett's French-Fried Cauliflower

1 small cauliflower, broken into
    flowerets
1 egg, lightly beaten
1 cup all-purpose flour
1 teaspoon baking powder
½ teaspoon salt

⅛ teaspoon pepper
Enough milk to make batter of
    medium consistency
Breadcrumbs
Vegetable oil
Bavarian Tartar Sauce (page 161)

Wash flowerets, drain, and dry thoroughly on paper towels. Make a batter of egg, flour, baking powder, salt, pepper, and enough milk to make batter of medium consistency. Dip flowerets in batter, roll in breadcrumbs, and fry in oil until golden. Drain on paper towels. Serve as hot hors d'oeuvres with Bavarian Tartar Sauce. Yield: 12 to 15 hors d'oeuvres.

Bavarian Tartar Sauce

1 hard-cooked egg
⅔ cup mayonnaise
½ small onion, minced
2 Gherkin pickles, minced
2 tablespoons minced parsley

2 anchovy fillets, rinsed, patted
   dry, and minced
¼ teaspoon chervil
⅛ teaspoon white pepper, coarsely
   ground

Force yolk and white of hard cooked egg through a sieve. Combine all ingredients; mix well. Cover and chill 2 hours. Yield: 1 cup.

Grilled Stuffed Red Snapper

Bass or trout can be substituted.

6 slices bread
1 cup beef or fish stock
¼ cup minced celery
¼ cup finely chopped green onion
2 tablespoons butter
2 tablespoons chopped parsley
1 (6½-ounce) can white crabmeat
2 tablespoons chopped fresh
   tomato or tomato catsup

⅛ teaspoon thyme
¼ teaspoon hot sauce
1 egg, lightly beaten
1 teaspoon salt, divided
¼ teaspoon white pepper
1 (4- to 6- pound) dressed red
   snapper
Basting Sauce

Soak bread in cold beef or fish stock; squeeze dry, and reserve liquid. Set aside.

Sauté celery and onion in butter over low heat. Add reserved bread, parsley, crabmeat, tomato, thyme, hot sauce, beaten egg, reserved liquid from bread, and ½ teaspoon salt. Stir to mix well.

Sprinkle fish inside and out with remaining salt and pepper. Stuff cavity with bread mixture; skewer opening closed. Place fish in a wire grilling basket; grill over hot coals 15 minutes on each side or until fish flakes easily when tested with a fork. Baste frequently with Basting Sauce. Yield: 6 servings.

Basting Sauce

3 tablespoons melted butter
1 teaspoon salt
3 tablespoons lemon juice

3 tablespoons Worcestershire sauce
¼ teaspoon hot sauce
¾ cup vegetable oil

Blend butter, salt, lemon juice, Worcestershire sauce, and hot sauce in small bowl. Add oil a little at a time and blend well. Yield: about 1 cup.

Buying Whole Fish: Don't discard the head and tail when buying whole fish. Cooked with the fish or by themselves, they make good fish stock for chowders, sauces, or aspics.

Lisa Walker Turner's Dilled Carrots

2 cups thinly sliced carrots
½ teaspoon salt
¾ teaspoon sugar, divided
1 beef-flavored bouillon cube
¼ cup finely chopped green onion

¼ cup commercial Green Goddess
  salad dressing
¼ cup commercial Italian salad
  dressing
1 tablespoon dillweed

Place carrots, water to cover, salt, ¼ teaspoon sugar, and bouillon cube in saucepan; simmer over medium heat. Cook, uncovered, about 15 to 20 minutes or until just tender. Drain and cool. Place in glass or stainless steel bowl and add green onion, salad dressings, dillweed, and ½ teaspoon sugar. Chill for 3 or 4 hours before serving. Make a day ahead if desired. Yield: 4 to 6 servings.

Cucumber Salad

A delightful salad to accompany a seafood or chicken entrée.

4 medium cucumbers
Salt
1 cup heavy cream, whipped
1 teaspoon chopped chives

1 teaspoon tarragon
⅛ teaspoon white pepper
1 to 2 tablespoons sherry wine
  vinegar to taste

Peel cucumbers; cut in half lengthwise and remove seeds. Cut into ½-inch slices. Sprinkle with salt and refrigerate.

Combine whipped cream, chopped chives, tarragon, salt and white pepper to taste. Add 1 tablespoon sherry wine vinegar and taste; add remaining tablespoon gradually, tasting as you add. Chill dressing. When ready to serve, drain cucumber and add to dressing. Yield: 6 servings.

Blackberry Cobbler

Pastry
4 cups fresh blackberries,
  washed and drained
2 cups sugar
½ teaspoon nutmeg

1 tablespoon plus 1 teaspoon
  vinegar
½ cup hot water
¼ cup butter or margarine,
  divided

Roll out half of pastry, and cut into 1-inch wide strips. Place strips on cookie sheet, and bake at 450° about 8 minutes or until lightly browned.

Combine blackberries, sugar, nutmeg, vinegar, and water; spoon half into a 3-quart baking dish, and dot with 2 tablespoons butter. Place baked pastry strips on top. Cover with remaining berry mixture and dot with 2 tablespoons butter.

Roll out remaining pastry and cut into 1-inch wide strips; arrange lattice-fashion on top of cobbler. Bake at 425° for 15 to 20 minutes or until lightly browned; reduce heat to 300° and bake 1 hour. Yield: 8 servings.

Pastry

2 cups all-purpose flour
½ teaspoon salt

¾ cup shortening
5 to 6 tablespoons cold water

Combine flour and salt; cut in shortening with a pastry blender until mixture resembles coarse meal. Sprinkle water, 1 tablespoon at a time, over surface; stir with a fork until all ingredients are moistened. Shape dough into a ball. Chill.

Peach Pie

1 (9-inch) unbaked pastry shell
4 large ripe peaches or nectarines
¼ cup sugar
½ cup whipping cream or
    undiluted evaporated milk

1 egg, lightly beaten
½ teaspoon almond extract
½ teaspoon vanilla extract
Crumb Topping
Cinnamon sugar

Bake pastry shell at 425° for 8 minutes. Cool on wire rack while preparing filling and topping.

Peel peaches and cut into thick slices; set aside. Combine milk, egg, and extracts. Place fruit in partially cooked pastry shell; cover with filling. Sprinkle topping over filling; then lightly sprinkle with cinnamon sugar. Bake at 350° for 45 minutes. Serve warm. Yield: one 9-inch pie.

Crumb Topping

2 tablespoons butter, softened
¼ cup sugar
¼ cup plus 2 tablespoons
    all-purpose flour

⅛ teaspoon salt
⅛ teaspoon cinnamon
½ teaspoon almond extract

Combine butter and sugar with a pastry blender until thoroughly blended; add flour, salt, cinnamon, and flavoring and continue mixing. Mixture should be crumbly.

Grill Tips: The most important element of a barbecue is a hot fire. So be sure to allow enough time for the charcoal to heat before you put the food on. Charcoal briquets require 40 minutes; lump charcoal only needs about 25 minutes because it burns more quickly. For extra smoky flavor, many cooks like to add chips or chunks of mesquite, hickory, alder, pecan, walnut, oak, or cherry wood to a bed of regular charcoal. For maximum smoke these should be soaked in water for an hour before they're added to the fire. But be frugal in your use of wood chips, or you'll risk overpowering the taste of the food. Never use pine or other softwood; the resin will ruin flavors. An instant-register thermometer (the kind you insert briefly — not the kind you leave in the meat) will save you from having to guess whether the food is done; beef and lamb should be about 145°F for medium-rare; chicken is cooked through at 190°F. Fish is done if it flakes when pierced with a fork; be careful not to overcook, because it dries out quickly.

Roast Lamb Outdoors, Mediterranean Style

Artichoke Dip
Grilled Butterflied Leg of Lamb
Eggplant au Gratin
Green Beans Vinaigrette
Mixer Method Egg Bread
Almond Tarts

Serves 8

This is a cookout to please the most sophisticated diners, but every recipe is do-ahead. For most relaxed pacing, marinate the lamb 2 days ahead. Make the dip, tarts, and bread 1 day ahead. Make the green beans and assemble the eggplant either the night before or the morning of the dinner.

Wine Suggestion: Grilled lamb goes beautifully with a robust red wine. Choose any red burgundy or a Mediterranean red, such as Dinga from Yugoslavia or a Dão from Portugal.

Margaret Emerson's Artichoke Dip

Tangy and easy to prepare, this dip must be made 1 day ahead.

2 (8½-ounce) cans artichoke hearts
1 (0.8-ounce) package dry Italian
    salad dressing mix
1½ cups mayonnaise

1 (4½-ounce) can shrimp, finely
    chopped
Pita bread triangles

Drain artichoke hearts; rinse with cold water, and drain again. Cut into small pieces; do not mash. Combine Italian salad dressing mix, artichoke pieces, mayonnaise, and finely chopped shrimp in small mixing bowl. Mix well and refrigerate overnight. Serve with pita bread triangles. Yield: approximately 3 cups dip.

 Cupcakes for a Picnic: When preparing cupcakes for a picnic basket or lunch boxes, split them in half and spread the icing inside.

Grilled Butterflied Leg of Lamb

1 (3½- to 4-pound) boneless leg of
    lamb roast
⅔ cup olive oil
3 tablespoons lemon juice
1 teaspoon salt
½ teaspoon freshly ground black
    pepper

1 teaspoon chopped parsley
1 teaspoon oregano
3 bay leaves, crumbled
1 cup thinly sliced onions
3 garlic cloves, thinly sliced

Trim fat and membrane from lamb. Blend together remaining ingredients. Marinate lamb in mixture 12 to 24 hours or up to 2 days in refrigerator. Drain lamb, reserving marinade.

Place lamb on grill over medium coals. Insert meat thermometer, if desired. Cover grill, and open vent. Grill until desired degree of doneness: about 2 hours or 140° (rare); about 2½ hours or 160° (medium); about 3 hours or 170° (well done).

Transfer lamb to a warm serving platter. Let stand 10 minutes before slicing. Yield: 8 to 10 servings.

Eggplant au Gratin

2 large eggplants
1 teaspoon salt
3 tablespoons olive or vegetable oil
Italian herb seasoning

2 cups tomato sauce
1 cup grated Parmesan or Swiss
    cheese
Vegetable oil

Trim off ends of eggplants; do not peel. Cut into 1½-inch-thick slices. Sprinkle both sides of each slice with salt. Let stand 30 minutes; rinse and drain well.

Place on an oiled jellyroll pan and brush tops with oil. Sprinkle each slice lightly with herb seasoning. Cover tightly with aluminum foil and bake at 400° until slices are tender. (This may be prepared several hours in advance.) Spread each slice with tomato sauce, and sprinkle with grated cheese; arrange slices overlapping in an oiled 13- x 9- x 2-inch baking dish or two 2½-quart casseroles. Drizzle oil on top. Bake at 400° for 15 minutes. Dish should be bubbling hot and cheese should be browned lightly. Yield: 6 to 8 servings.

Green Beans Vinaigrette

2 pounds fresh green beans,
    snapped
3 tablespoons vegetable oil
1 tablespoon vinegar

2 teaspoons sugar
1 tablespoon prepared mustard
1 tablespoon chopped fresh parsley
Salt and pepper to taste

Cook beans, covered, in a small amount of boiling salted water for 20 minutes. Drain. Combine oil, vinegar, sugar, mustard, parsley, salt, and pepper; mix well, and pour over beans. Cover and refrigerate several hours or overnight. Transfer to a serving dish; serve chilled. Yield: 8 servings.

Mixer Method Egg Bread

Attractive braided loaves from an easily mixed dough.

4 to 4¾ cups all-purpose flour,
  divided
2 packages dry yeast
½ cup milk
½ cup water
2 tablespoons shortening

2 tablespoons sugar
2 teaspoons salt
3 eggs
1 egg, lightly beaten
Poppy seeds

Combine 1¾ cups of flour and yeast in a large mixing bowl; blend well.

Combine milk, water, shortening, sugar, and salt in a medium-size saucepan. Cook over medium heat, stirring constantly, until mixture registers 120° to 130° on candy thermometer. Pour into flour-yeast mixture, mixing well. Add eggs and beat 30 seconds at low speed of electric mixer, scraping bowl constantly. Beat an additional 3 minutes at high speed.

Gradually stir in enough remaining flour to form a soft dough. Knead 5 to 10 minutes. Shape dough into a ball and place in a greased bowl, turning to grease top. Cover and let rise in a warm place (85°), free from drafts, 1 hour or until doubled in bulk. Punch dough down; cover and let rest 10 minutes.

Divide dough into 2 equal portions. Divide each portion into 3 equal pieces. Shape each piece into a 7½-inch rope. Braid 3 ropes together, pinching ends to seal. Place braided loaf in a greased 8½- x 4½- x 3-inch loafpan. Repeat procedure with remaining dough.

Repeat rising procedure. Brush loaves with beaten egg; sprinkle with poppy seeds. Bake at 400° for 30 minutes or until loaves sound hollow when tapped. Remove bread from pans; cool on wire racks. Yield: 2 loaves.

Priscilla Everett's Almond Tarts

The delicate flavor of almonds in a tantalizing cake. You can make one 8-inch square cake or 16 individual cake tarts.

1 cup butter, softened
¾ cup sugar
1 egg, separated
½ cup almond paste
1 teaspoon almond extract

2 cups all-purpose flour
½ teaspoon baking powder
¼ cup finely chopped almonds
½ cup apricot preserves

Cream butter in large mixing bowl; gradually add sugar, beating well. Add egg yolk and continue beating. Pinch off bits of almond paste and add to batter while beating. (The batter will not be smooth.) Add almond extract.

Sift flour and baking powder. Gradually add to creamed mixture. Mix well.

Spoon 1 heaping tablespoon batter into greased muffin pans. Smooth top of batter with spatula. Beat egg white until frothy. Brush tops of tarts with egg white and sprinkle with chopped almonds. Bake at 350° for 20 to 25 minutes. Cool completely before removing from pan. Fill indentation with apricot preserves. Yield: 16 tarts.

Easygoing Patio Supper

Scallops with Water Chestnuts
Spinach Shrimp Delight
Tomatoes Stuffed with Saffron Rice
Ribbon Salad
French Bread
Blueberries and Nectarines in Cointreau Custard

Serves 8

These are simple recipes, with almost no time pressure involved. Marinate the scallops at least 2 hours; assemble them and broil just before guests are due to arrive. Have the shrimp casserole and the stuffed tomatoes assembled in the refrigerator; put them in the oven while the scallops are served. The salad and salad dressing can be prepared early in the day, awaiting only tossing. The fruit for the dessert can be combined early in the day and the whipped cream added before serving.

Scallops with Water Chestnuts

1 pound scallops, fresh or frozen
1 (5-ounce) can water chestnuts, drained and cut into thirds

Spicy Marinade
15 slices bacon, cut in half

Thaw frozen scallops. Rinse with cold water to remove any shell particles. Cut large scallops in half. Place scallops and water chestnuts in medium-sized bowl; pour marinade over and allow to stand at least 2 hours or refrigerate overnight. Stir occasionally. Drain.

Place a scallop and a piece of water chestnut on each piece of bacon. Wrap bacon around scallop and secure with toothpick. Place on broiler pan and broil 4 inches from heat about 8 minutes. Turn carefully; broil 4 to 5 minutes longer or until bacon is crisp. Yield: about 30 hors d'oeuvres.

Spicy Marinade

⅓ cup salad oil
⅓ cup soy sauce
3 tablespoons catsup

1 tablespoon vinegar
¼ teaspoon black pepper
2 cloves garlic, crushed

Combine all ingredients; mix well. Yield: about 1 cup.

Spinach Shrimp Delight

Shrimp and spinach in an easy-to-prepare casserole.

2 (10-ounce) packages frozen
    chopped spinach
½ cup butter or margarine, melted
⅛ teaspoon garlic powder or 1
    clove garlic, minced
½ teaspoon salt, divided
1 tablespoon Worcestershire sauce
2 teaspoons anchovy paste

½ teaspoon hot sauce
2 tablespoons all-purpose flour
2 tablespoons butter or margarine
1¼ cups milk, warmed
¼ cup grated Parmesan cheese
2 cups cracker crumbs
1¼ pounds cooked shrimp, peeled
    and deveined

Cook spinach according to package directions, omitting salt; drain well, pressing out moisture with a spoon.

Combine spinach, ½ cup melted butter, garlic powder, ¼ teaspoon salt, Worcestershire sauce, anchovy paste, and hot sauce; set aside.

Melt butter in a heavy saucepan over low heat; add flour, stirring until smooth. Cook 1 minute, stirring constantly. Gradually add warm milk; cook over medium heat, stirring constantly, until thickened. Stir in ¼ teaspoon salt, Parmesan cheese, and spinach mixture.

Sprinkle bottom of greased 8-inch casserole with 1 cup cracker crumbs. Place ⅓ of spinach in casserole; top with ½ of shrimp. Repeat layers. Top with 1 cup cracker crumbs. Bake at 350° for 20 to 25 minutes. Yield: 6 servings.

Tomatoes Stuffed with Saffron Rice

A colorful combination that also goes well with ham or turkey.

1 medium onion, finely chopped
3 tablespoons butter or margarine,
    divided
1 (5-ounce) package yellow rice,
    cooked

8 large tomatoes
¼ teaspoon salt
1 teaspoon dried basil
½ teaspoon ground marjoram
Parmesan cheese

Sauté onion in 2 tablespoons butter in large skillet over medium heat; add cooked rice, and blend well.

Cut off tops of tomatoes and scoop out pulp. Add pulp, salt, basil, and marjoram to rice mixture. Stuff mixture into tomato shells; sprinkle with Parmesan cheese and dot each tomato with butter. Bake at 350° for 20 minutes. Yield: 8 servings.

Ribbon Salad

6 radishes, thinly sliced
2 green onions with tops, thinly
    sliced
1 head iceberg lettuce, cored and
    cut in half
1 small cucumber, peeled

2 carrots, peeled
1 hard-cooked egg, chopped
5 tablespoons chopped parsley
Ribbon Salad Dressing
Ripe olives (optional)

Place radishes and green onions in large salad bowl. Cut lettuce into ¼-inch slices; add to salad bowl, separating leaves. Using a vegetable peeler, cut cucumber lengthwise into ribbons, discarding seeded part. With vegetable peeler, cut carrots lengthwise into ribbons, discarding cores. Add cucumber and carrots to salad; sprinkle with egg and parsley. Toss with dressing. Garnish with ripe olives, if desired. Yield: 8 servings.

Ribbon Salad Dressing

1 teaspoon dried basil leaves
½ teaspoon dried dillweed
½ teaspoon sugar
3 tablespoons fresh lime or lemon
    juice

1 tablespoon white wine
3 tablespoons vegetable oil
3 tablespoons olive oil

Combine basil, dillweed, sugar, lime juice, and wine in small bowl; let stand 10 minutes. Whisk in oils. Chill. Spoon over Ribbon Salad. Yield: about ¾ cup.

Blueberries and Nectarines in Cointreau Custard

A perfect dessert to finish a summer meal.

1 pint fresh blueberries
3 nectarines, peeled, pitted and
    sliced
1 cup sugar, divided
6 egg yolks
2 tablespoons instant-blending
    flour

1¾ cups milk
⅓ cup Cointreau
1 cup whipping cream, whipped
3 tablespoons sifted powdered
    sugar

Place blueberries and nectarines in a large bowl; sprinkle ⅓ cup sugar over fruit, and set aside.

Beat egg yolks until thick and lemon colored. Add sugar and flour; mix well. Heat milk to 180° over medium heat. Gradually stir about one-fourth of hot milk into yolk mixture; add to remaining hot milk, stirring constantly. Cook over medium heat until mixture coats a metal spoon; cool.

Stir Cointreau into custard; pour mixture over fruit, and refrigerate. Combine whipped cream and powdered sugar; fold into fruit mixture before serving. Yield: 8 servings.

Sea Island Beach Party

Sea Island Shrimp
Salmon Potato Salad
Vegetable Pasta Salad
Sliced Tomatoes with Dill
Cheesecake with Blueberry Topping

Serves 12

A generous but carefree buffet. The shrimp should be prepared at least 1 day ahead. The salads will hold overnight. Sliced tomatoes sprinkled with chopped fresh chives offer a nice complement of flavors and texture, but they aren't essential. The cheesecake should be made the day of the party; if you would rather bake farther ahead, make Lemon Cream Loaf (page 253) to serve with the blueberry topping. This menu packs up easily, since only the Salmon Potato Salad and the shrimp must be kept chilled.

Sea Island Shrimp

5 pounds boiled shrimp, peeled
  and deveined
4 small white onions, thinly sliced
2 lemons, thinly sliced
1½ teaspoons salt
2 teaspoons celery seed

¾ cup tarragon vinegar
1½ cups vegetable oil
¼ cup prepared mustard
1 to 2 drops hot sauce
1 (3-ounce) jar capers

Alternate layers of shrimp, onions, and lemons in a large casserole. Combine remaining ingredients. Pour over shrimp mixture. Cover and refrigerate at least 24 hours. Drain shrimp before serving. Yield: 15 to 20 servings.

 A Note on Shrimp: When cooking shrimp, cabbage, or other foods that cause unpleasant odors, put a dozen cloves in a small pan of boiling water and let simmer. The aroma of the cloves will counteract the unpleasant odor with a delightful fragrance.

Salmon Potato Salad

2 (15½-ounce) cans salmon, flaked
6 small new potatoes, peeled,
    cooked, and diced
6 hard-cooked eggs, chopped
6 radishes, minced
1 medium cucumber, peeled and
    diced
1 cup chopped onion
¼ cup plus 2 tablespoons lemon
    juice

1½ cups mayonnaise
2 teaspoons salt
¼ teaspoon garlic salt
1 teaspoon Worcestershire sauce
8 drops hot sauce
Lettuce leaves
Paprika
Tomato wedges (optional)

Combine salmon, potatoes, eggs, radishes, cucumber, and onion; mix well. Sprinkle lemon juice over salmon mixture; toss lightly.

Combine mayonnaise, salt, garlic salt, Worcestershire sauce, and hot sauce; mix well. Combine salmon mixture and mayonnaise mixture; toss until thoroughly blended. Cover and chill 1 hour and 30 minutes.

Spoon salmon mixture onto a lettuce-lined platter. Sprinkle with paprika. Garnish platter with tomato wedges, if desired. Yield: 12 servings.

Vegetable Pasta Salad

A colorful combination of crisp vegetables and tender pasta.

10 to 12 ounces ziti or macaroni,
    cooked and drained
2 carrots, cut lengthwise into
    quarters and sliced
2 stalks celery, thinly sliced
¼ cup sliced pitted ripe olives
3 tablespoons grated Parmesan
    cheese
4 to 6 ounces pepperoni, coarsely
    chopped

¼ cup white wine
1 small head cauliflower, cored and
    broken into small flowerets
1 bunch broccoli
1 yellow squash, cut lengthwise
    into quarters and sliced
Salt
Garlic Dressing (page 172)

Combine ziti, carrots, celery, olives, and Parmesan cheese in large salad bowl.

Cook pepperoni in medium skillet over medium heat until lightly browned. Pour wine into skillet, stirring to scrape up bits of meat; cook 1 minute. Pour over ziti mixture and toss well.

Cook cauliflower in boiling water 2 minutes; rinse immediately under cold water and drain well. Break off broccoli flowerets and slice stems; cook in boiling water 2 minutes. Rinse immediately under cold water and drain well. Add cauliflower, broccoli, and yellow squash to salad bowl; sprinkle with salt to taste. (Salad can be made to this point and refrigerated overnight.) Toss with dressing. Yield: 12 servings.

Garlic Dressing

1 clove garlic	2 tablespoons red wine vinegar
1 tomato, cored, cut into pieces	Salt
6 small sprigs parsley	½ cup vegetable oil
1½ teaspoons Dijon mustard	⅓ cup olive oil

Process garlic, tomato, parsley, mustard, vinegar, and salt to taste in food processor or blender until blended. With machine running, slowly pour in oils. Process until well combined. Dressing can be refrigerated up to 1 week. Yield: about 1 cup.

Winifred's Cheesecake with Blueberry Topping

A very nice cheesecake with a slight taste of orange. For a quick dessert, serve Blueberry Topping over sliced pound or sponge cake with a dollop of whipped cream.

2 cups graham cracker crumbs	5 eggs
2 tablespoons sugar	1 cup half-and-half
½ cup butter or margarine	1 tablespoon Grand Marnier
5 (8-ounce) packages cream cheese, softened	½ cup less one tablespoon fresh orange juice
1¾ cups sugar	Blueberry Topping
2 tablespoons freshly grated orange rind	

Combine first 3 ingredients, mixing well. Firmly press mixture into bottom of a greased 9-inch springform pan, and chill thoroughly.

Beat cream cheese, 1¾ cups sugar, and orange rind in a large bowl on medium speed of electric mixer until mixture is light and fluffy. Add eggs, one at a time, beating well after each addition. Add half-and-half gradually; then slowly add Grand Marnier and orange juice. Spoon batter into prepared pan. Set aside.

Pour hot water into a shallow baking pan about 1½ to 2 inches deep. Place baking pan in 300° oven. When water begins to simmer, place cheesecake pan in simmering water. Bake for 2 hours to 2 hours and 15 minutes or until a wooden pick inserted in center come out clean. Cake will be golden brown on top and slightly leaving sides of pan. When cake is completely cold, release side of springform pan. Do not refrigerate. To serve, slice cake and spoon topping over each slice. Yield: 12 to 14 servings.

Blueberry Topping

2 pints fresh blueberries, divided	1½ tablespoons cornstarch
1 cup sugar	1 tablespoon lemon juice

Puree 1 pint blueberries. Combine puree, sugar, and cornstarch in medium saucepan. Cook over medium heat until mixture is thickened, stirring constantly. Remove from heat. Stir in remaining blueberries and lemon juice. Cool to room temperature; refrigerate until ready to serve. Yield: 4 cups.

Mexican Fiesta

Margaritas
Guacamole
Chimi-Changas
Lime Grilled Chicken
Corn Kabobs
Sliced Pineapple and Mango or Papaya
Coconut Surprise Cake

Serves 8

To be sure that everything tastes best, without the flurry of last minute preparations, follow this sequence: make the cake and the salsa, and refrigerate up to 2 days ahead; refrigerate the chicken in the lime juice mixture up to 8 hours ahead or overnight; and make the Chimi-Changas up to 2 hours in advance, and keep warm.

Margaritas

Lime juice
Salt
4 cups crushed ice
1½ cups tequila
⅔ cup lime juice

2 tablespoons Triple Sec
½ cup powdered sugar
1 egg white
Lime slices

Dip rims of cocktail glasses in lime juice, and then in a shallow dish of salt; shake to remove excess salt.

Combine remaining ingredients except lime slices in container of an electric blender; process until frothy. Pour into prepared glasses; garnish with lime slices. Yield: about 6 servings.

Guacamole

4 large avocados, peeled and
   mashed
1 medium onion, finely chopped
3 green chile peppers, seeded,
   rinsed, and minced
2 medium tomatoes, peeled and
   coarsely chopped

1 tablespoon plus 1½ teaspoons
   lemon juice
Juice of 1 lime
1 teaspoon salt
Hot sauce to taste
Tortilla chips

Combine all ingredients except tortilla chips; mix well. Cover and chill thoroughly. Serve with tortilla chips, or spoon over Chimi-Changas. Yield: about 6 cups.

Gwen Malvaney's Chimi-Changas

This unusual name translates to "monkeying around"; in other words, the cook can be creative. So feel free to vary the filling ingredients. But be sure the filling is stove hot, so that the cheese will melt.

¼ pound ground round
1 large onion, finely chopped
1 large green pepper, finely chopped
1 clove garlic, minced
1 tablespoon vegetable oil
2 tablespoons chili powder
½ teaspoon red pepper
½ cup refried beans

1 cup (4 ounces) shredded Monterey Jack cheese
Flour tortillas
Vegetable oil
Shredded lettuce
Guacamole (optional)
Sour cream (optional)
Salsa (optional)

Combine ground round, onion, green pepper, garlic, and vegetable oil in a large skillet; cook until beef is browned, stirring to crumble meat. Drain off pan drippings. Stir in chili powder, red pepper, and refried beans. Add cheese, and stir until cheese melts.

Spoon ¼ cup meat mixture off center of each tortilla. Fold the edge nearest meat filling up and over filling, just until mixture is covered. Fold in sides of each tortilla to center; roll up. Secure with wooden picks. Repeat with remaining mixture and tortillas.

Fry in deep hot oil (370°) 2 to 3 minutes or until golden brown, turning once. Drain well on paper towels.

Remove wooden picks. Arrange Chimi-Changas on shredded lettuce; top with Guacamole, sour cream, and Salsa, if desired. Yield: 12 servings.

Salsa

2 tablespoons chopped onion
1 clove garlic, finely chopped
3 tablespoons olive oil
1 (14½-ounce) can whole tomatoes, undrained and chopped
½ cup water

1 (4-ounce) can chopped green chiles, undrained
2 teaspoons vinegar
½ teaspoon dried whole oregano
½ teaspoon salt

Sauté onion and garlic in olive oil in a medium saucepan until tender. Stir in remaining ingredients; simmer, uncovered, 20 minutes, stirring occasionally. Serve warm with Chimi-Changas. Yield: about 1½ cups.

Storing Spices: Red spices (chili powder, paprika, and red pepper) will maintain flavor and retain color longer if stored in a cool place and away from any direct source of heat.

Lime Grilled Chicken

Six pounds of assorted chicken pieces can be used.

½ cup lime juice
½ cup vegetable oil
1 tablespoon grated onion
2 teaspoons tarragon leaves
1 teaspoon seasoned salt

¼ teaspoon freshly ground black
   pepper
2 (3- to 3½-pound) broiler-fryers,
   cut up

Combine first 6 ingredients in a small mixing bowl; mix well. Place chicken, skin side down, on grill. Grill over medium coals 50 minutes or until chicken is tender. Turn chicken, and brush with sauce every 10 minutes. Serve immediately. Yield: 6 to 8 servings.

Corn Kabobs

4 ears corn, cut into 3-inch pieces
4 medium-size red onions,
   quartered
4 medium zucchini, cut into 2-inch
   chunks

¼ cup margarine or butter, melted
2 tablespoons chopped fresh
   coriander or parsley
½ teaspoon chili powder
½ teaspoon ground cumin

Thread vegetables, alternately, onto eight long skewers. Combine remaining ingredients; brush part of mixture over vegetables. Place skewers on grill about 6 inches above heat. Grill 20 minutes, turning and brushing several times with butter mixture. Yield: 8 servings.

Coconut Surprise Cake

1 (18.5 ounce) package white cake
   mix
3 egg whites
1¼ cups water
⅓ cup vegetable oil
1 (14-ounce) can sweetened
   condensed milk

1 (12-ounce) carton frozen whipped
   topping, thawed
1 (12-ounce) package frozen
   coconut, completely thawed
   and dried on paper towel

Blend cake mix, egg whites, water, and oil in large bowl at low speed of electric mixer until moistened. Beat 2 minutes at highest speed or by hand 800 strokes. Pour batter into a well-greased and floured 13- x 9- x 2-inch pan. Bake at 350° for 25 to 35 minutes. Remove from oven and immediately pierce holes with toothpick over entire cake top; dribble condensed milk over the cake in the pan. (You will think no more milk will go in, but it will.)

Allow to cool on wire rack. When cake is completely cold, spread with whipped topping and sprinkle coconut over top. Refrigerate until served. Yield: 20 servings.

Spanish Dining al Fresco

Sangría
Curry Cream
Paella
Asparagus Pimiento
Zucchini Salad
Chocolate Mousse

Serves 8

The wonderful flavors of this dinner reflect the mingled European and Moorish traditions of Spain. The food is not at all fragile—it moves outside easily and can stand awhile. The molded Curry Cream, Chocolate Mousse, and salad should all be done ahead; the Paella and Asparagus Pimiento can be served at room temperature— they needn't be piping hot.

Sangría

2 quarts Burgundy or other dry red
   wine
1 quart orange juice
1 quart club soda, chilled
⅔ cup lemon juice
½ cup lime juice

3 dashes Angostura bitters
1 cup sugar
Lemon slices
Lime slices
Orange slices

Combine first 6 ingredients in a large punch bowl; add sugar. Stir gently. Garnish with fruit slices; serve over ice. Yield: about 1 gallon.

Curry Cream

The flavors of this appetizer go well with Sangría or sherry.

1 envelope unflavored gelatin
¼ cup cold water
2½ cups chicken broth, heated
6 hard-cooked egg yolks

1 teaspoon curry powder
Chutney, your choice (mango, fig,
   apple, peach, or nectarine)

Sprinkle gelatin over ¼ cup cold water in a medium saucepan. Place over low heat, stirring until gelatin dissolves; add hot chicken broth. Pour broth mixture, egg yolks, and curry powder into blender. Blend 30 seconds. Taste and add more curry, if desired. Pour mixture into well-oiled 5-cup ring mold and chill until firm. Unmold on serving dish; fill center with chutney. Yield: 8 servings.

Betty Kruger's Paella

8 chicken breast halves, skinned
  and boned
½ cup olive oil
1 slice bacon
1 cup chopped onion
3 cloves garlic, minced
1 (28-ounce) can whole tomatoes,
  undrained and chopped
2 pounds fresh shrimp, peeled and
  deveined
⅛ teaspoon garlic salt

2 cups uncooked regular rice
½ teaspoon ground saffron
2 cups chicken broth
1 (6½-ounce) can minced clams,
  undrained
1 (10-ounce) package frozen
  English peas
1 (2-ounce) jar chopped pimiento,
  undrained
½ cup dry white wine
Lemon wedges

Brown chicken in hot oil in a large skillet; remove chicken, and set aside, reserving oil. Cook bacon in a large Dutch oven over medium heat; remove bacon. Sauté onion and garlic in bacon drippings until tender. Add tomatoes and reserved chicken; cook over low heat 30 minutes.

Sauté shrimp with garlic salt in reserved oil in skillet 3 minutes; remove mixture and set aside. Sauté rice with saffron in skillet. Stir rice and pan drippings into chicken mixture. Add chicken broth. Cover and simmer 20 to 25 minutes. Add shrimp, clams, peas, pimiento, and wine; cover, and cook 5 minutes. Remove to a large serving dish. Garnish with lemon wedges. Yield: 8 servings.

Asparagus Pimiento

2 pounds fresh asparagus spears,
  cleaned

1 (2-ounce) jar pimiento strips
Vinaigrette Dressing

Place asparagus spears in boiling water to cover. Cover and return to a boil. Uncover; reduce heat and simmer 12 minutes or until a knife point will easily pierce the spears. Drain well, and place asparagus spears on a serving dish. Arrange pimiento strips over spears, and serve with Vinaigrette Dressing. Serve warm or chilled. Yield: 8 servings.

Vinaigrette Dressing

2 teaspoons sugar
1 teaspoon prepared mustard
1 tablespoon chopped fresh parsley

1 tablespoon vinegar
3 tablespoons vegetable oil

Combine all ingredients, and stir until smooth. Yield: about ¼ cup.

Betty Kruger's Zucchini Salad

2 medium zucchini	6 large mushrooms, sliced
4 radishes	Lettuce leaves
1 stalk celery, finely chopped	Horseradish Dressing
3 green onions, finely chopped	¼ cup grated Parmesan cheese

Slice zucchini in half lengthwise; remove seeds. Grate zucchini and radishes. Combine zucchini, radishes, celery, onions, and mushrooms; toss well. Spoon into a lettuce-lined bowl. Cover and refrigerate several hours. Before serving, pour dressing over salad and sprinkle with Parmesan cheese. Yield: 8 servings.

Horseradish Dressing

1 (8-ounce) carton commercial sour cream	¼ teaspoon ground cumin
1 teaspoon Dijon mustard	⅛ teaspoon garlic powder
1 teaspoon prepared horseradish	⅛ teaspoon salt
	Pinch of pepper

Combine all ingredients in a small mixing bowl; stir well. Cover and refrigerate several hours. Yield: about 1 cup.

Chocolate Mousse

4 (1-ounce) squares semi-sweet chocolate	4 egg yolks
⅓ cup water	2 tablespoons brandy
¾ cup sugar	3 cups whipping cream
	1 egg white

Melt chocolate over hot water in top of double boiler.

Place water and sugar in a small saucepan; cook over medium heat, stirring frequently, until sugar is dissolved.

Pour melted chocolate into container of electric blender or food processor. Process chocolate, slowly adding hot syrup in a thin stream. Continue processing while adding egg yolks, one at a time. Add brandy; process until mixture is smooth. Set aside to cool.

Combine whipping cream and egg white in a large bowl; beat until stiff peaks form. Fold chocolate mixture into whipped cream. Spoon into 8 (6-ounce) individual serving dishes; chill at least 2 hours. Yield: 8 servings.

Page 179: *A loaf of crusty bread, a bottle of wine, Broccoli Quiche, Ratatouille, and Pineapple Preserves Nut Cake add up to a Country French Picnic (page 154).*

Page 180: *An opulent array of hors d'oeurves sets the tone of the New Year's Eve Party (page 182). Meatballs with Sweet and Sour Sauce, Artichoke Appetizers, Champagne Punch, and an array of cheese and fruit are served from the dining room buffet.*

Cooking For A Crowd

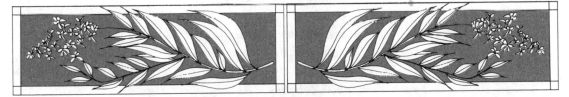

There is no feeling quite like the pride you can take in catering a family reception or the excitement of welcoming as many as 50 guests. Yet the work is proportionately less than would be required to prepare as much food for separate small dinners. The menus in this chapter provide patterns of food quantities and recipe selections for five types of large gatherings. Look carefully at each meal pattern, and you'll see how other recipes can also fit the occasion.

The New Year's Eve Party, for example, includes two seafood hors d'oeuvres—crisp Zesty Shrimp Morsels that can be made weeks in advance and creamy Crabmeat Supreme, which should be made close to serving time. Other elements of the cocktail party pattern are a finger sandwich, a dip, one meat, one meatless hot dish, and three bite-size sweets. Think of the menu as the sum of these elements, and you can vary it as you wish.

Take the Wedding Rehearsal Dinner for Forty-eight as the pattern for a large sit-down dinner. It has been designed around three elements: appetizers that can be frozen ahead and reheated whenever you're ready to pop open the champagne, desserts that can be made and frozen weeks in advance, and entrée ingredients—chicken, rice, and carrots—that are fairly sturdy and not too expensive. Study the other menus in the book, and you'll realize that you can use them repeatedly as big-party guidelines without ever serving the same fare twice.

New Year's Eve Party for Forty

Champagne Punch
Artichoke Appetizers
Almond Chicken Sandwiches
Cheese and Fruit Platter
Elegant Crab Dip
Fresh Vegetable Relishes with Eggplant Dip
Meatballs with Sweet and Sour Sauce
Zesty Shrimp Morsels
Assorted Breads
Miniature Pecan Tarts
Rocks

Serves 40

Schedule cooking sessions over a month to make the cookies, tarts, Shrimp Morsels, Eggplant Dip, and meatballs. Cut up the vegetable relishes, prepare the punch and the filling for the canapés, and make the Artichoke Appetizers up to a day ahead. Prepare Elegant Crab Dip a few hours in advance. Leave the fruit and cheese platter for last, so that the fruit will look fresh. Plan to reheat half of the hot foods at the beginning of the party and the rest later on, so that it all will remain tempting.

Mrs. B. M. Walker's Champagne Punch

The punch base of lemonade, Sauterne, and cranberry juice may be made early in the day or even the day before and kept chilled. Add the chilled soda and champagne just before serving.

3 (6-ounce) cans frozen pink
    lemonade, thawed
4½ cups water
2 (750 ml) bottles Sauterne, chilled
1 quart plus 2 cups cranberry juice

2 (32-ounce) bottles club soda,
    chilled
4 (750 ml) bottles champagne,
    chilled

Blend pink lemonade, water, Sauterne, and cranberry juice in large glass or stainless steel container. Chill. When ready to serve, pour into punch bowl, and add soda and champagne. Yield: approximately 4 gallons.

Elly Launius's Artichoke Appetizers

2 (6-ounce) jars marinated
   artichoke hearts
1 small onion, finely chopped
1 clove garlic, minced
4 eggs, beaten
¼ cup fine dry breadcrumbs
½ teaspoon salt

⅛ teaspoon pepper
⅛ teaspoon ground oregano
⅛ teaspoon hot sauce
2 cups (8 ounces) shredded sharp
   Cheddar cheese
2 tablespoons minced fresh parsley

Drain liquid from artichoke hearts; reserve half the liquid. Chop artichoke hearts. Sauté onion and garlic in reserved artichoke liquid 5 minutes.

Combine eggs, breadcrumbs, salt, pepper, oregano, and hot sauce in a large bowl. Add cheese, parsley, sautéed vegetables, and chopped artichokes; mix well. Press mixture into a greased 10- x 6- x 2-inch baking dish. Bake at 325° for 40 minutes or until lightly browned. Cut into 1-inch squares to serve. Serve hot or cold. Yield: about 2½ dozen squares.

Almond Chicken Sandwiches

1½ cups cooked chicken, finely
   chopped
1 teaspoon lemon juice
½ cup chopped almonds
⅛ teaspoon nutmeg

1½ cups (6 ounces) shredded Swiss
   cheese
Mayonnaise
18 slices bread, crusts removed

Blend all ingredients except bread in large bowl. Add enough mayonnaise to spread well. (Filling can be refrigerated up to 2 days.) Divide filling among 9 sandwiches; cut sandwiches into fourths. Yield: 36 finger sandwiches.

Ice Molds for Punch Bowls: You can either freeze some of the punch recipe in a decorative mold or use plain water. If you're using water, boil it and then chill it; the ice will be clearer than if made with water straight from the tap. Ring and heart shaped molds are especially appropriate for Christmas and wedding parties, but any pan or other container can be used. Half-fill the mold with liquid and freeze solid. Then arrange strawberries, pineapple rings, citrus slices, melon balls, grapes, and any other fruit or greenery you wish on the ice in a decorative pattern. Add about one-half inch of punch or water and freeze long enough to anchor the fruit. Fill the mold with liquid and freeze solid. To unmold, dip briefly in warm water.

To make decorative ice cubes, half fill ice trays with chillled boiled water and freeze. Place a berry, citrus wedge, or mint leaf on each cube. Then fill trays and freeze.

Elegant Crab Dip

You can easily increase this recipe by multiplying all ingredients by 1½ or by doubling the ingredients.

1 pound crabmeat, flaked
½ cup butter
¼ cup plus 2 tablespoons
    all-purpose flour
2 cups half-and-half
1 (4-ounce) jar chopped pimiento,
    drained
¼ cup plus 2 tablespoons finely
    chopped celery

1 tablespoon dried green onion
1 teaspoon finely chopped onion
¾ teaspoon salt
⅛ teaspoon white pepper
¼ teaspoon ground mace
½ teaspoon hot sauce
¼ cup Sauterne
Melba toast or assorted crackers

Chill crabmeat in ice water. Drain well, and set aside.

Melt butter in a heavy saucepan over low heat; add flour, stirring until smooth. Cook 1 minute, stirring constantly. Gradually add half-and-half; cook over medium heat, stirring constantly, until thickened and bubbly. Stir in pimiento, celery, onion, salt, pepper, mace, and hot sauce. Cook mixture 5 minutes, stirring often. Add Sauterne and crabmeat; stir well and heat through. Remove mixture to a chafing dish or keep warm in top of a double boiler over simmering water. Serve crab dip hot with melba rounds or assorted crackers. Yield: about 4½ cups.

Eggplant Dip

This mixture can be served as a salad over shredded lettuce.

1 large onion, chopped
2 medium-size green peppers,
    chopped
2 cloves garlic, minced
½ cup olive oil
3 medium eggplant, peeled and
    chopped
1 (10-ounce) can tomatoes and
    green chiles

2 teaspoons salt
½ cup catsup
3 tablespoons Chablis or other dry
    white wine
1 tablespoon sugar
1 tablespoon Worcestershire sauce
1 (3-ounce) bottle capers, drained
Vegetable relishes

Sauté onion, green pepper, and garlic in olive oil in a small Dutch oven until tender. Add eggplant; stir well. Cook over low heat 20 minutes, stirring occasionally.

Add tomatoes and green chiles, salt, catsup, Chablis, sugar, and Worcestershire; stir well. Cook, uncovered, over low heat 30 minutes, stirring occasionally. Remove from heat; cool. Stir in capers. Serve as dip with assorted vegetable relishes. Yield: about 8 cups.

Meatballs with Sweet and Sour Sauce

Use freshly ground meat for best results. Serve meatballs hot with Sweet and Sour Sauce for dipping. The recipe doubles easily, and any leftovers will freeze well.

1 pound ground beef	¼ teaspoon chives
1 egg, lightly beaten	⅛ teaspoon tarragon leaves
2 slices bread, crusts removed	2 tablespoons finely chopped onion
¼ cup plus 2 tablespoons milk	½ cup all-purpose flour
1½ teaspoons salt	¼ cup butter
¼ teaspoon freshly ground pepper	Sweet and Sour Sauce

Combine ground beef and beaten egg in a large mixing bowl. Chop bread coarsely in the container of an electric blender. Soak bread in milk and squeeze dry. Combine next 5 ingredients and beef mixture; add soaked bread, and mix well. Shape mixture into small balls; roll lightly in flour. Refrigerate for 20 to 30 minutes.

Sauté meatballs in butter in large heavy skillet over medium heat until well browned, about 10 minutes. Yield: approximately 40 appetizer meatballs.

Sweet and Sour Sauce

1 cup water	2 tablespoons catsup
½ cup dark brown sugar	3 teaspoons cornstarch
⅓ cup lemon juice	¼ cup cold water

Combine first 4 ingredients in a small saucepan. Cook over medium heat until mixture boils. Combine cornstarch and cold water; stir to dissolve. Slowly add cornstarch mixture to sauce, stirring constantly. Bring to a boil over medium heat and boil 1 minute. Yield: about 2 cups sauce.

Vegetable Dippers: Line a large basket with cabbage leaves; fill it with "bundles" of carrot and celery sticks and cucumber and zucchini spears held in green and red pepper rings. Or arrange the vegetables in a cabbage-lined, hollowed-out small pumpkin or turban squash. For color and variety, add blanched broccoli flowerets and cauliflowerets, fresh pea pods, sliced jicama and kohlrabi, Belgian endive leaves, and radish rosettes to the assortment of dippers. Remember to blanch broccoli, cauliflower, and pea pods for 1 minute in boiling water; then chill quickly in ice water.

Zesty Shrimp Morsels

Make these a day or two ahead and refrigerate. Or freeze them prior to baking.

1 pound boiled shrimp, deveined
    and finely chopped
⅛ to ¼ teaspoon salt
1 teaspoon dry mustard
¼ teaspoon mace
3 tablespoons grated green pepper

3 tablespoons mayonnaise
1 teaspoon Worcestershire sauce
1 dash hot sauce
Cream Cheese Pastry
1 egg yolk, beaten
2 tablespoons water

Blend shrimp, salt, mustard, mace, green pepper, mayonnaise, Worcestershire sauce, and hot sauce in a large mixing bowl.

Place a scant teaspoon of shrimp filling in center of each prepared pastry round; fold in half, and pinch edges to seal or press with fork tines. Prick tops with fork. (Recipe can be made to this point and frozen; don't thaw before baking.) Brush with beaten egg yolk diluted with 2 tablespoons water. Bake on lightly greased cookie sheet at 375° for 15 to 20 minutes or until golden brown. Serve hot. Yield: about 45 appetizers.

Cream Cheese Pastry

½ cup butter or margarine, cold
1 (8-ounce) package cream cheese,
    softened

1½ cups all-purpose flour
¼ cup cream or undiluted canned
    milk

Cut butter and cream cheese into flour until mixture resembles coarse meal. Add cream, stirring to form a soft dough; shape dough into a ball, and chill. Roll out on well-floured surface to ⅛-inch thickness. Cut into 3-inch rounds. Yield: about 45 pastry rounds.

Miniature Pecan Tarts

Bake this dessert when you have time and freeze for later use.

1 egg, lightly beaten
3 tablespoons butter, melted
¾ cup firmly packed dark brown
    sugar
⅛ teaspoon salt

1 teaspoon vanilla extract
1 cup chopped pecans
Tart shells
Sifted powdered sugar (optional)

Combine first 5 ingredients in a small mixing bowl; beat well. Spoon 1 teaspoon pecans into each tart shell. Cover with 2 teaspoons filling. Bake at 325° for 30 minutes. Cool on wire rack. Sprinkle with powdered sugar before serving, if desired. Yield: enough filling for 2 dozen miniature tart shells.

Tart Shells

1 (3-ounce) package cream cheese, softened

½ cup butter, softened
1 cup all-purpose flour

Combine cream cheese and butter; cream until smooth. Add flour, mixing well. Refrigerate dough at least 2 hours.

Shape the dough into 24 (1-inch) balls; put each ball into a paper-lined 1¾-inch muffin pan, and shape into a shell. Yield: 2 dozen tart shells.

Rocks

Here's a cookie that's especially good for a finger-food buffet.

1 cup butter, softened
2 cups firmly packed dark brown
  sugar
3 eggs
1 teaspoon soda
½ cup cold water
3 cups all-purpose flour

1 teaspoon ground allspice
2 teaspoons ground cinnamon
1 teaspoon ground nutmeg
1 teaspoon vanilla extract
1½ pounds (3½ cups) shelled
  pecans, coarsely chopped
3 pounds raisins

Cream butter in large bowl of electric mixer; gradually add sugar, beating well. Add eggs, one at a time, beating well after each addition. Dissolve soda in water; set aside.

Combine flour, allspice, cinnamon, and nutmeg; add to creamed mixture alternately with soda mixture, beginning and ending with flour mixture. Stir in vanilla, pecans, and raisins.

Drop batter by heaping teaspoonfuls onto greased baking sheet. Bake at 350° for 15 to 20 minutes. Remove to wire rack at once and allow to cool completely; place in airtight containers. The cookies will keep fresh for a month or longer. If they should lose their crispness, bake at 350° for 1 or 2 minutes. Yield: about 9 dozen.

Cheese and Fruit Platter: This is an easy opportunity to brighten the buffet table or another corner of your party area. Choose cheeses of contrasting shapes — perhaps a small round of Brie or Camembert, a wedge of Swiss or Emmenthal, and a block of Cheddar or Muenster. Or serve just one large cheese — a wide wheel of French Brie or Cheddar can look even more dramatic than several varieties. Then assemble four or five kinds of fruit around the cheese. Remember that pineapple spears, black and red grapes, pomegranate and orange sections, kiwi slices, and whole strawberries not only look more colorful but also won't discolor as fast as apples and pears. Nutmeats are also delicious with cheese and can enhance the presentation.

Holiday Buffet Dinner for Twenty

Frozen Punch
or
Swizzle Punch
Hot Turnip Green Dip
Shrimp-Stuffed Mushrooms
Baked Ham with Cumberland Sauce
Acorn Squash Rings
Braised Brussels Sprouts
Party Carrot Loaf
Apple Chutney
Quick and Easy Biscuits
Stained Glass Fruitcake

Serves 20

As festive as this menu is, it's also very easy to serve. Bake the fruitcake months ahead. Freeze the biscuits, stuffed mushrooms, and punch, if you wish. Make the dip, ham, and Acorn Squash Rings 1 to 3 days ahead. That leaves only the carrot loaf and brussels sprouts to finish the day of the dinner.

Mildred Reynolds's Frozen Punch

This is a great do-ahead punch. Freeze it in large juice cans, if you wish—there will be no need for ice at serving time. The almond extract is the secret ingredient; add ½ to 1 teaspoon according to taste.

1 (3-ounce) package lime-flavored
   gelatin
2½ cups sugar
1 cup boiling water
7 cups cold water
1 (12-ounce) bottle lemon juice

1 (46-ounce) can unsweetened
   pineapple juice
2 or 3 drops green food coloring
1 teaspoon almond extract
1 quart ginger ale, chilled

Dissolve gelatin and sugar in boiling water in a large saucepan; add cold water, lemon juice, pineapple juice, food coloring, and almond extract. Freeze punch; remove from freezer several hours before serving so that it will be slushy and not frozen hard. Pour in punch bowl (no ice is needed); add ginger ale just before serving. Yield: about 1 gallon.

Note: If an alcoholic beverage is desired, add light rum to taste. Any colored gelatin may be used to suit the occasion.

Swizzle Punch

1 (750 ml) bottle 151 proof dark rum
1 (6-ounce) can frozen lime juice, thawed
1 (12-ounce) can frozen concentrated orange juice, thawed
1 (40-ounce) can unsweetened pineapple juice

3 tablespoons (1½ ounces) Angostura bitters
½ cup (4 ounces) passion fruit mix or ¼ cup grenadine
¼ cup plus 2 tablespoons (3 ounces) orange Curaçao
Water to make a gallon

Combine all ingredients in gallon container and fill to top with water. Mix and pour into punch bowl over a block of ice or ice ring. Yield: 40 servings.

Note: A new plastic trash can makes a handy container for mixing and storing large quantities of punch.

Cynthia Morse Taylor's Hot Turnip Green Dip

Prepare this ahead of time and keep refrigerated; then serve hot from a chafing dish.

½ cup finely chopped onion
½ cup finely chopped celery
2 tablespoons butter or margarine
1 (3-ounce) can sliced mushrooms, drained
1 (10-ounce) package frozen chopped turnip greens
¼ teaspoon grated lemon rind

1 (10¾-ounce) can cream of mushroom soup, undiluted
1 (6-ounce) package garlic cheese spread
1 teaspoon Worcestershire sauce
5 drops hot sauce
Corn chips
Assorted crackers

Sauté onion and celery in butter until tender; stir in mushrooms. Set aside.

Cook turnip greens according to package directions; drain well. Combine drained turnip greens and lemon rind in the container of an electric blender or food processor; process until smooth.

Combine sautéed vegetables, pureed turnip greens, soup, cheese, Worcestershire sauce, and hot sauce in the top of a double boiler; stir frequently until mixture is well blended and heated. Serve hot with corn chips or assorted crackers. Yield: about 6 cups.

Note: Frozen chopped spinach can be substituted for turnip greens.

Shrimp-Stuffed Mushrooms

Make these ahead and freeze before broiling.

2 pounds large fresh mushrooms
2 tablespoons vegetable oil
¾ teaspoon salt
¼ cup chopped green onion
1 tablespoon finely chopped celery
2 tablespoons butter or margarine
1 tablespoon Worcestershire sauce
¼ teaspoon garlic powder
⅛ teaspoon white pepper
⅛ teaspoon ground mace
⅛ teaspoon hot sauce

1 egg, lightly beaten
½ pound cooked fresh shrimp, peeled, deveined, and finely chopped
⅓ cup soft breadcrumbs
2 teaspoons grated Parmesan cheese
1 tablespoon butter or margarine, melted
¼ teaspoon paprika

Remove stems from mushrooms; finely chop stems and set aside. Wipe mushrooms caps with a damp paper towel. Place mushroom caps, cap side down, on lightly greased baking sheets. Drizzle oil over caps and sprinkle with salt. Bake at 425° for 10 minutes. Drain on paper towels.

Sauté onion and celery in 2 tablespoons butter in a large skillet until tender. Add chopped mushroom stems, Worcestershire sauce, garlic powder, white pepper, mace, hot sauce, and egg; stir well. Cook over medium heat until mixture is thoroughly heated and liquid has evaporated. Remove from heat, and stir in shrimp.

Return mushroom caps, cap side down, to baking sheets. Fill each with shrimp mixture. Combine breadcrumbs, Parmesan cheese, melted butter, and paprika; stir until well blended. Sprinkle mixture evenly over stuffed mushrooms. (Recipe can be prepared to this point, and refrigerated up to 2 days or frozen up to 1 month.) Broil 3 to 4 minutes or until lightly browned. Yield: about 50 servings.

Baked Ham with Cumberland Sauce

Once the ham is fully cooked, it can be refrigerated up to a week.

1 (16- to 17-pound) smoked, uncooked ham
1 (8-ounce) jar Dijon mustard
1 (11-ounce) jar red currant jelly

1 cup apple juice or apple brandy
2 teaspoons whole cloves
Cumberland Sauce

Place ham, fat side up, in heavy foil; wrap tightly. Place in a shallow roasting pan; bake at 325° for 2½ hours.

Remove ham from oven; insert meat thermometer, making sure it does not touch fat or bone. Score fat in a diamond design, and stud with cloves.

Combine mustard, jelly, and apple juice; stir well, and pour over ham. Bake, covered, at 325° for 2½ to 3 hours or until meat thermometer registers 160°. Remove cover the last hour and baste ham every 15 minutes. Cover lightly with aluminum foil if ham gets too brown. Serve hot or cold with Cumberland Sauce. Yield: 20 to 24 servings.

Cumberland Sauce

1 green onion, finely chopped
1 tablespoon butter or margarine
1 (11-ounce) jar red currant jelly
⅓ cup orange juice
1 tablespoon orange rind

¼ cup lemon juice
1 tablespoon lemon rind
1 teaspoon Dijon mustard
1 cup port wine

Sauté onion in butter in a medium saucepan over low heat until tender. Add jelly, orange juice, orange rind, lemon juice, lemon rind, and mustard; cook over low heat until jelly dissolves, stirring occasionally. Add wine, and cook 5 minutes. Sauce can be refrigerated in a covered container up to 1 week; reheat over low heat, stirring often, before serving. Yield: 2 cups.

Betty Kruger's Acorn Squash Rings

Garnish with spiced red crabapples for festive color.

5 medium acorn squash
¼ teaspoon salt
⅔ cup orange juice
½ cup butter or margarine

1 cup firmly packed brown sugar
½ cup corn syrup
1 tablespoon grated lemon rind

Wash squash thoroughly in cold water. Cut squash into ½-inch slices to form rings, and remove seeds. Place squash rings in a lightly greased 2½-quart shallow baking dish; sprinkle with salt. Pour orange juice over squash rings. Cover with aluminum foil, and bake at 350° for 30 minutes.

Melt butter in a small saucepan; add brown sugar, corn syrup, and lemon rind, mixing well. Bring mixture to a boil; reduce heat, and simmer 5 minutes, stirring frequently. Immediately spoon mixture over squash rings. Return to oven, and bake, uncovered, 30 minutes or until squash is tender. Yield: 20 servings.

Braised Brussels Sprouts

Fresh brussels sprouts have a milder taste than frozen ones.

1 pound brussels sprouts
2 tablespoons butter or margarine

2½ cups chicken broth or veal stock

Remove any discolored leaves from brussels sprouts. Cut off stem ends, and make 2 diagonal slashes in base of each sprout. Wash sprouts thoroughly.

Sauté brussels sprouts in butter in a large skillet until tender. Add chicken broth or veal stock, and bring to a boil. Reduce heat, and simmer, uncovered, 20 minutes. Remove brussels sprouts to serving dish; continue to cook broth or stock until it is reduced to a syrup. Pour over brussels sprouts, and serve immediately. Yield: 4 servings.

Party Carrot Loaf

Double the carrot loaf recipe to serve 20, and bake in two pans.

1½ pounds carrots, scraped and
    sliced
2 cups water
1½ teaspoons salt, divided
1 cup half-and-half
1 cup soft breadcrumbs
3 tablespoons minced onion
2 tablespoons minced green pepper
1½ tablespoons prepared
    horseradish

1 tablespoon minced parsley
1 tablespoon chopped pimiento
¼ teaspoon hot sauce
2 eggs
2 tablespoons butter or margarine,
    melted
6 to 8 very small carrots, cooked
    (optional)
Parsley sprigs (optional)

Combine carrots, water, and ½ teaspoon salt in a large saucepan. Bring to a boil; reduce heat, cover, and simmer 40 minutes or until carrots are tender. Drain well, and mash carrots with a fork.

Combine mashed carrots, half-and-half, breadcrumbs, onion, green pepper, horseradish, parsley, pimiento, hot sauce, and remaining salt in a large mixing bowl; beat until well blended.

Beat eggs in a small mixing bowl until foamy. Add beaten eggs and butter to carrot mixture; beat until well blended.

Pour mixture into a greased and waxed paper-lined 7½- x 3- x 2-inch loafpan. Bake at 350° for 40 minutes or until a wooden pick inserted in center comes out clean. Cool in pan on a wire rack 20 minutes; invert on serving platter, and remove pan. Peel off waxed paper, and garnish with small cooked carrots and parsley sprigs, if desired. Serve immediately. Yield: one 7½- x 3- x 2-inch loaf.

Apple Chutney

You might make a batch of this chutney for Christmas giving and keep a jar to accompany the ham or turkey on your own table.

10 cups (about 14) firm ripe apples
3 cups golden raisins
Peel of 2 oranges, finely chopped
5½ cups sugar
1 teaspoon salt
½ teaspoon ground cloves
1 teaspoon cinnamon

½ cup cider vinegar
¼ cup lemon juice
1 hot pepper, finely chopped
2 tablespoons fresh gingerroot,
    finely chopped
½ cup red currant jelly
1 cup pecans, finely chopped

Peel and core apples; cut into large pieces. Combine apples and remaining ingredients except pecans in a large Dutch oven. Stir until sugar is dissolved. Cook over medium heat 45 to 50 minutes or until thick. Stir often to prevent sticking. Add pecans about 5 minutes before removing from heat. Pour mixture into sterilized jars, leaving ½-inch headspace. Cover at once with metal lids, and screw bands tight. Process in boiling-water bath 10 minutes. Yield: 11 half-pints.

Natchez Quick and Easy Biscuits

Partially bake and freeze these biscuits any time you wish; then finish baking just before serving.

2 cups self-rising flour
¼ teaspoon salt
½ cup shortening

1 cup buttermilk
2 tablespoons butter or margarine, melted

Combine flour and salt; stir well. Cut in shortening until mixture resembles coarse meal. Gradually add buttermilk, stirring until dry ingredients are moistened.

Turn dough out onto a floured surface. Knead lightly. Roll to ½-inch thickness; cut with a 1½-inch biscuit cutter. Place biscuits on a greased baking sheet; brush with butter. Bake at 450° for 8 minutes or until lightly browned. Yield: 2 dozen.

Lewis Crouch's Stained Glass Fruitcake

1 (8-ounce) package chopped dates
1 (8-ounce) package chopped candied citron
½ (12-ounce) package candied red cherries
½ (12-ounce) package candied green cherries
1 (4-ounce) package green chopped candied pineapple
1 (4-ounce) package red chopped candied pineapple
1 (4-ounce) package yellow chopped candied pineapple
1 (4-ounce) package candied orange peel
2 cups pecan halves
2 cups walnut halves

1½ cups golden raisins
3 cups all-purpose flour, divided
½ cup butter or margarine, softened
¾ cup sugar
4 large eggs
¼ teaspoon salt
¾ teaspoon ground cinnamon
¾ teaspoon ground cloves
¾ teaspoon mace
¾ teaspoon ground nutmeg
1 (14-ounce) can sweetened condensed milk
3 tablespoons dark rum
¼ cup plus 2 tablespoons brandy, divided

Combine first 11 ingredients in a large mixing bowl; add ½ cup flour, and stir gently until ingredients are coated. Set aside.

Cream butter in a very large mixing bowl; gradually add sugar, beating until light and fluffy. Add eggs, one at a time, beating well after each addition.

Combine remaining flour, salt, cinnamon, cloves, mace, and nutmeg; set aside. Add sweetened condensed milk, rum and 3 tablespoons brandy to creamed mixture, beating until well blended. Add flour mixture, one cup at a time, beating until batter is smooth. Stir in fruit and nut mixture.

Spoon batter into a greased 9-inch springform pan. Bake at 275° for 3½ hours or until a wooden pick inserted in the center comes out clean. Let fruitcake cool completely on a wire rack. Loosen and remove sides of springform pan. Sprinkle top of fruitcake with remaining brandy. Place fruitcake in an airtight container. Yield: one 9-inch cake.

Bridal Shower Brunch for Twenty-four

Party Punch
Individual Spinach Quiche
Chicken Mousse
Cucumber Cream Cheese Filling
Watermelon Basket with Fruits in Season
Sour Cream Rolls
Party Mints
Petits Fours
Toasted Pecans (page 132)

Serves 24

You should be able to complete everything except the rolls and the sandwiches by the night before, so that there won't be much cooking left for the morning of the brunch. Start by making the mints and baking the cake weeks in advance. Complete the petits fours, make the chicken mousse and the punch, and prepare the fruit the day before. The Individual Spinach Quiche can be made ahead and reheated, but the recipe is simple enough to make early in the day or just before serving.

Dot Taylor's Party Punch

1 (46-ounce) can unsweetened
    pineapple juice
1 cup lemon juice
2 cups sugar

2 quarts water
Ice ring (page 183)
1 quart ginger ale
½ gallon pineapple sherbet

Combine pineapple juice, lemon juice, sugar, and water. Chill several hours. Pour mixture over ice ring in a punch bowl; add ginger ale and sherbet. Yield: about 5 quarts.

Individual Spinach Quiche

1 (12-ounce) package frozen
    spinach soufflé, thawed
1 cup (4 ounces) shredded Swiss
    cheese

2 eggs, lightly beaten
3 tablespoons milk
½ teaspoon curry powder
Tart shells (page 187)

Combine first 5 ingredients, and stir well; pour into prepared pastry shells. Bake at 350° for 30 minutes. Yield: about 4 dozen.

Note: Double the tart shell recipe to make 48 quiches.

Hester Faser Chicken Mousse

4 chicken breast halves
1 medium onion, quartered
1 stalk celery, sliced
1 carrot, peeled and sliced
¼ cup chopped fresh parsley
1½ teaspoons salt, divided
6 peppercorns
3 envelopes unflavored gelatin
¼ cup lemon juice

¼ teaspoon white pepper
¼ teaspoon hot sauce
1 cup mayonnaise
1 cup minced celery
¼ cup minced green pepper
1 tablespoon minced pimiento
1 cup whipping cream, whipped
Caper Mayonnaise Sauce

Combine chicken, onion, celery, carrot, parsley, 1 teaspoon salt, and peppercorns in a medium Dutch oven; add water to cover. Bring to a boil; reduce heat and simmer, covered, 45 minutes or until chicken is tender. Remove chicken from broth; cool. Bone chicken, and chop; set aside. Strain broth, reserving 3½ cups; set aside.

Soften gelatin in 1½ cups reserved broth in a medium Dutch oven; cook, stirring constantly, over low heat 5 minutes or until gelatin dissolves. Remove from heat, and stir in lemon juice, white pepper, hot sauce, remaining 2 cups broth, and ½ teaspoon salt. Let cool 10 minutes. Add mayonnaise, and stir until smooth. Chill mixture until it reaches the consistency of unbeaten egg whites. Add reserved chicken, celery, green pepper, and pimiento; stir until well combined. Fold in whipping cream; pour mixture into a lightly oiled 9-cup mold. Chill.

Unmold mousse on a chilled serving plate; slice and serve with sauce. Yield: 24 servings.

Caper Mayonnaise Sauce

1 cup mayonnaise
2 tablespoons chopped fresh
    parsley
2 tablespoons capers

2 tablespoons finely chopped green
    onion
2 teaspoons chopped dill pickle

Combine all ingredients; stir well. Yield: about 1 cup.

Watermelon Basket: To make an attractive basket, choose a long watermelon. Measure its length and mark the center; make cuts on either side of the center to form a handle for the basket. Cut away the melon quarters around the handle; reserve for other use. Cut the edges of the basket in any pattern you wish: scalloped, zigzagged, or curved upward on both sides like a double-prowed boat. Scoop out the melon and cut the fruit into pieces; combine in a large bowl with honeydew or cantaloupe melon balls, seedless grapes, and assorted seasonal fruits and berries. You will have more fruit than you can fit into the basket; use it to refill the basket during the party.

Cucumber Cream Cheese Filling

Easy to make and colorful. Use as a filling for raw vegetables or tiny sandwiches.

2 (8-ounce) packages cream cheese, softened
1 cucumber, peeled, seeded, and grated
1 small onion, peeled and grated
¼ teaspoon salt

2 teaspoons dried dillweed
3 tablespoons mayonnaise
Cherry tomatoes (optional)
Celery sticks (optional)
Mushroom caps (optional)
Zucchini slices (optional)

Combine cream cheese, cucumber, onion, salt, and dill in small bowl of electric mixer; add mayonnaise, mixing until thoroughly blended and smooth. Mixture can be piped into cherry tomatoes, celery sticks, or mushroom caps. This spread also can be used as filling for finger sandwiches. Yield: about 2 cups spread.

Note: For prettiest presentation, pipe the cream cheese mixture into the vegetables. Use a pastry bag and decorative tip—perhaps a star tip for the cherry tomatoes, a scroll tip to fill celery sticks, and a small plain tip to write the initial of the guest of honor on diagonally cut slices of zucchini. The keys to smooth piping are to keep the bag tightly twisted around the filling as you work and to pipe with a light touch.

Sour Cream Rolls

2 cups self-rising flour
1 cup butter, melted

2 (8-ounce) cartons commercial sour cream

Combine all ingredients in a medium mixing bowl; mix well. Spoon batter into greased miniature muffin pans, filling three-fourths full. (Recipe can be made to this point and refrigerated, covered, overnight. Bring to room temperature before baking.) Bake at 450° for 15 minutes or until golden brown. Serve hot. Yield: 4 dozen.

Party Mints

¼ cup plus 1 tablespoon butter, softened
2 tablespoons evaporated milk

1 teaspoon peppermint extract
3 drops food coloring
3 cups sifted powdered sugar

Combine butter, milk, peppermint extract, and food coloring in a medium-size mixing bowl; beat well. Gradually add 2½ cups powdered sugar, beating well. Lightly grease hands with butter, and knead in remaining powdered sugar. Continue kneading until candy is smooth.

Mold candy into small patties and place on waxed paper-lined baking sheets or press mixture into lightly greased individual candy molds. Let dry, uncovered, at least 12 hours. Yield: about 1 pound.

Note: Mints may be arranged in an airtight container, with waxed paper between the layers, and frozen for later use.

Paula Ellis's Petits Fours

1 (18.25-ounce) package	2 eggs
commercial white cake mix	1 teaspoon vanilla extract
1⅓ cups milk	Butter Cream Icing, divided
¼ cup vegetable oil	Cooked Icing

Combine cake mix, milk, oil, and eggs; blend until moistened. Add vanilla; beat 2 minutes at medium speed of electric mixer. Pour batter into greased and floured 13- x 9- x 2-inch baking pan. Bake at 350° for 25 minutes or until a wooden pick inserted in center comes out clean.

Cool in pan 10 minutes; remove from pan and cool on wire rack. Wrap cake tightly in foil; freeze for several hours or until firm. (Cake can be frozen up to 1 month.)

Remove cake from foil and carefully trim crust from all surfaces, making sure top of cake is flat. Frost top of cake with Butter Cream Icing. Cut cake into 40 (1½-inch) squares. Place squares two inches apart on a wire rack; place rack in a large shallow pan. Quickly pour a thin layer of warm Cooked Icing over the cakes, completely covering top and sides. Repeat procedure, if necessary, for a thicker layer of icing.

Spoon up all the icing that drips through rack, and reheat to pouring consistency; add a small amount of water, if necessary, to maintain original consistency. Continue pouring and reheating until all cakes are frosted. Repeat procedure 2 additional times to coat all petits fours. Allow icing to dry. Place cakes on a cutting board; trim any excess frosting from the bottom of each cake with a sharp knife.

Decorate the petits fours as desired, using a decorating cone and remaining Butter Cream Icing. Yield: 40 (1½-inch square) petits fours.

Butter Cream Icing

1 (16-ounce) package powdered	Dash of salt
sugar, sifted	1 teaspoon vanilla extract
½ cup shortening	¼ teaspoon butter extract
¼ cup water	

Combine powdered sugar and shortening in a large mixing bowl; beat at low speed until smooth. Add water slowly, beating constantly. Add salt and vanilla, and mix well. Beat 5 minutes at medium speed of electric mixer.

Divide icing into separate portions for frosting cake, and for each color that will be used for decorating. Tint each with desired color. Icing will keep in airtight container in refrigerator for up to 1 week. Yield: about 2¼ cups icing.

Cooked Icing

¼ cup plus 3 tablespoons water	½ teaspoon almond extract
¼ cup plus 1 tablespoon light corn	6 cups sifted powdered sugar
syrup	Food coloring

Combine water, corn syrup, and almond extract in the top of a double boiler. Add sugar, mixing well. Place over boiling water, stirring until powdered sugar is melted and mixture is smooth and glossy. Add food coloring to obtain desired color. Yield: about 4 cups.

Wedding Rehearsal Dinner for Forty-eight

Champagne
Cheese Puffs
Chicken Veronique
Curried Carrots
Wild Rice Amandine
Avocado Salad Mold
Chocolate Cheesecakes
or
Miniature Cheesecakes

Serves 48

---

*D*on't let the numbers frighten you, for this is manageable quantity-cooking if you have enough large pots and pans. Prepare and freeze the Cheese Puffs and dessert up to 1 month ahead. Refrigerate the salad and pre-cook the chicken two or three days ahead. Cook the rice and the carrots, and finish the chicken the day of the dinner. Bake the Cheese Puffs when guests arrive. Reheat the chicken, tightly covered, and the rice in the oven; reheat the carrots on top of the stove—all while the Cheese Puffs are being served. Be sure to have someone available to help with the serving; the hardest part of this menu is keeping all of the food warm from cooking pots to dinner plates.

Charlotte Charles's Cheese Puffs

½ (14-ounce) loaf French bread, crusts removed
1 cup (4 ounces) shredded extra sharp Cheddar cheese
1 (3-ounce) package cream cheese, softened

½ cup butter
1 teaspoon Worcestershire sauce
½ teaspoon dry mustard
⅛ teaspoon Old Bay seasoning
1 clove garlic, minced
2 egg whites

Cut bread into 1-inch cubes. Set aside.

Combine Cheddar cheese, cream cheese, and butter in the top of a double boiler. Cook over boiling water until cheese melts, stirring frequently.

Add Worcestershire sauce, mustard, Old Bay seasoning, and garlic; stir well. Remove cheese mixture from heat.

Beat egg whites (at room temperature) until stiff peaks form. Gently fold into cheese mixture. Dip bread cubes into cheese mixture, coating well. Place cubes on a greased baking sheet, and freeze 1 hour. (Recipe can be made to this point up to 1 month ahead. When cubes are completely frozen, transfer to freezer bags for easier storage. Do not thaw. Bake on greased baking sheets as directed.) Bake at 350° for 10 minutes or until lightly browned. Serve hot. Yield: about 4 dozen.

Note: This recipe doubles easily.

Chicken Veronique

To serve 48, make 2 double recipes in 2 roasting pans.

2 teaspoons salt	2 stalks celery, chopped
½ teaspoon white pepper	2 tablespoons chives
1 teaspoon paprika, divided	1 teaspoon tarragon leaves
12 chicken breast halves, skinned	½ cup butter or margarine, divided
1 cup Chablis or other dry white wine, divided	1 cup whipping cream
	¼ cup all-purpose flour
¼ cup lemon juice	1 pound seedless green grapes

Combine salt, white pepper, and ½ teaspoon paprika; mix well. Place chicken in a lightly greased 13- x 9- x 2-inch baking dish. Sprinkle salt mixture evenly over chicken. Add ½ cup wine, lemon juice, celery, chives, and tarragon; dot with ¼ cup butter. Bake, covered, at 350° for 1 hour. Baste chicken with remaining ½ cup wine every 20 minutes. (Recipe can be made to this point and refrigerated up to 2 days ahead; reheat in oven before proceeding.) Remove chicken to a warm serving platter; reserve pan drippings.

Add whipping cream to pan drippings; cook over medium heat 2 minutes, stirring constantly. Melt remaining ¼ cup butter in a small saucepan over low heat. Add flour, stirring until a smooth paste is formed. Gradually add flour to pan liquid; cook over low heat, stirring constantly until thickened.

Pour sauce over chicken and cover with grapes. Sprinkle remaining ½ teaspoon paprika over chicken. Yield: 12 servings.

Curried Carrots

Multiply all ingredients by 4 to serve 48.

3 chicken-flavored bouillon cubes	2 tablespoons lemon juice
1½ cups boiling water	1 tablespoon curry powder
3 pounds medium carrots, peeled and sliced	1 teaspoon salt
	½ teaspoon pepper
3 tablespoons butter or margarine	½ teaspoon sugar
3 tablespoons chopped parsley	

Dissolve bouillon cubes in boiling water. Combine dissolved bouillon cubes, carrots, butter, parsley, lemon juice, curry powder, salt, pepper, and sugar in a medium Dutch oven. Add water to cover; bring to a boil. Reduce heat and simmer, uncovered, 10 minutes or until tender. Yield: 12 servings.

Wild Rice Amandine

Make 2 double recipes, baking them in two 3-quart casseroles, to serve 48.

2 (4-ounce) packages wild rice
2 teaspoons salt
4 cups boiling water
⅔ cup butter
2 tablespoons chopped chives

2 tablespoons finely chopped green pepper
3 cups chicken broth
½ cup sliced almonds

Combine rice, salt, and boiling water in a medium mixing bowl; set aside 30 minutes. Drain well.

Sauté rice in butter in a heavy skillet over low heat 5 minutes, stirring frequently. Add chives and green pepper; cook 3 minutes, stirring frequently.

Pour rice mixture into a well-greased 1½-quart casserole. Add chicken broth. Cover, and bake at 350° for 45 minutes. Sprinkle almonds over the rice and bake, uncovered, an additional 25 minutes or until liquid is absorbed. (If rice is to be reheated, bake only 15 minutes with almonds; cover with foil until serving time. Reheat, uncovered, in oven.) Yield: 12 servings.

Avocado Salad Mold

Make 2 double recipes in two 2-quart molds to serve 48. The salads can be refrigerated up to 3 days.

1 (3-ounce) package lime-flavored gelatin
1 envelope unflavored gelatin
1¼ cups boiling water
1 (3-ounce) package cream cheese, softened
½ cup mayonnaise
1 medium avocado, peeled and chopped

1 medium-size green pepper, finely chopped
1 cup finely chopped celery
2 tablespoons finely chopped onion
1 teaspoon lemon juice
½ teaspoon salt
¼ teaspoon hot sauce
Lettuce leaves
Cherry tomatoes (optional)

Dissolve gelatin in boiling water; let cool slightly.

Combine cream cheese and mayonnaise in a medium mixing bowl; beat well. Add avocado, green pepper, celery, onion, lemon juice, salt, and hot sauce; mix well. Add gelatin mixture to avocado mixture, stirring until well blended. Pour gelatin mixture into a lightly oiled 4-cup ring mold. Chill until firm. Unmold on a lettuce-lined serving platter. Garnish with cherry tomatoes, if desired. Yield: 12 servings.

Charlotte Charles's Chocolate Cheesecakes

Refrigerate these cakes up to 5 days ahead, or freeze them up to 1 month. If they are frozen, don't thaw completely before serving; they should be served cold.

16 chocolate wafer cookies, finely crushed	3 eggs
1 (12-ounce) package semi-sweet chocolate morsels	⅛ teaspoon salt
	1 teaspoon vanilla extract
3 (8-ounce) packages cream cheese, softened	1 (8-ounce) carton commercial sour cream
1 cup sugar	Whipped cream (optional)

Line 1¾-inch muffin pans with miniature paper liners. Sprinkle bottom of liners with chocolate cookie crumbs.

Place chocolate morsels in top of a double boiler; bring water to a boil. Reduce heat to low; cook until chocolate melts.

Beat cream cheese with electric mixer until light and fluffy; gradually add sugar, mixing well. Add eggs, one at a time, beating well after each addition. Stir in melted chocolate, and beat until blended. Stir in salt, vanilla, and sour cream. Pour 1 tablespoon mixture into each liner. Bake at 350° for 10 minutes. (Center may be soft but will firm up when chilled.) Let cool to room temperature on a wire rack; refrigerate overnight. Garnish with a dollop of whipped cream, if desired. Yield: 6½ dozen.

Winifred Barron's Miniature Cheesecakes

These cheesecakes freeze beautifully. Take them out of the freezer 30 minutes to 1 hour before serving and allow them to reach room temperature.

4 (8-ounce) packages cream cheese, softened	1 tablespoon lemon juice
	1 cup graham cracker crumbs
1 (14-ounce) can sweetened condensed milk	1 teaspoon ground cinnamon
	Chopped maraschino cherries

Beat cream cheese; gradually add milk and lemon juice, beating well. Chill thoroughly.

Combine graham cracker crumbs and cinnamon in a small mixing bowl; drop 1 teaspoon chilled cream cheese mixture onto the graham cracker crumbs. Shake bowl to completely coat cream cheese. Shape cream cheese mixture into a ball and place in a petit four paper cup. Repeat procedure with remaining cream cheese mixture. Garnish each cheesecake with chopped maraschino cherries. Chill thoroughly. Yield: about 5 dozen.

Teenage Party for Twenty

Easy Fruit Punch (page 251)
Confetti Dip
Cheese Crispies
Snazzy Dogs
Po'Boy Sandwiches
Crisp Garden Slaw
Chocolate Sheet Cake (page 126)
Chocolate Delight Ice Cream Squares

Serves 20

These recipes are easy enough for any teenager to lend a helping hand. Make the cake and Cheese Crispies up to a week ahead, the slaw and ice cream squares several days ahead. The dip should be made the day before. Prepare the Snazzy Dogs just before guests arrive, and let your guests make their own Po'Boy Sandwiches.

Mary Edwards's Confetti Dip

Make a day ahead for best flavor. This recipe doubles easily.

1 (8-ounce) package cream cheese, softened
2 tablespoons butter, softened
½ teaspoon celery salt
Dash of paprika
½ teaspoon Worcestershire sauce
½ teaspoon soy sauce

1 cup finely chopped radishes
¼ cup finely chopped green onions
2 tablespoons whipping cream (optional)
Potato Chips
Pretzels

Blend first six ingredients until smooth. Stir in radishes and onions. Chill in refrigerator for several hours to blend flavors. Serve as a spread, or add enough whipping cream for dipping consistency. Serve with chips and pretzels. Yield: 1½ cups.

Quick Teenage Snack: Press an indentation in the center of a refrigerated biscuit, fill with your favorite pizza sauce, and top with a pepperoni slice and shredded mozzarella cheese. Bake at 425° for 10 to 15 minutes. One medium jar spaghetti sauce is enough to make one hundred mini-pizzas.

Cheese Crispies

½ cup butter or margarine,
  softened
1 cup (4 ounces) shredded New
  York extra sharp Cheddar
  cheese
1 cup all-purpose flour
1 cup oven-toasted rice cereal
¼ teaspoon salt
⅛ teaspoon red pepper
Additional all-purpose flour

Combine butter and cheese; mix well. Add flour, cereal, salt, and red pepper; stir until all ingredients are well blended. Shape mixture into ½-inch balls; place 2 inches apart on ungreased baking sheets. Dip a fork in flour, and flatten balls slightly. Bake at 375° for 10 minutes or until lightly browned. Remove to wire racks, and cool completely. Store in an airtight container up to 1 week. Yield: about 3 dozen.

Snazzy Dogs

This is a favorite of my teenage grandchildren, Ruth and Reynolds. You can easily make 3 or 4 batches at a time.

½ cup crushed corn chips
⅓ cup finely chopped onion
¼ cup tomato sauce
1 teaspoon Worcestershire sauce
1 cup (4 ounces) shredded
  American cheese
1 (16-ounce) package frankfurters
10 hot dog buns

Combine corn chips, onion, tomato sauce, Worcestershire sauce, and cheese; mix well. Slice frankfurters lengthwise to make a pocket. Spoon stuffing mixture inside each pocket. Place frankfurters in a 13- x 9- x 2-inch baking pan. Bake uncovered at 350° for 20 minutes or until cheese mixture is melted. Serve in hot dog buns. Yield: 10 servings.

Po'Boy Sandwiches

Arrange the following ingredients on large trays, and let the teenagers assemble their favorite combinations.

20 to 24 hard rolls, horizontally
  split
Mayonnaise
Dijon mustard
Leaf lettuce
4 medium tomatoes, sliced
2 (8-ounce) packages sliced bologna
2 (8-ounce) packages sliced cotto
  salami
2 (8-ounce) packages sliced breast
  of turkey
2 (8-ounce) packages mild Cheddar
  cheese slices
2 (8-ounce) packages Provolone
  cheese slices
2 (8-ounce) packages Swiss cheese
  slices

Spread cut side of top of each roll with mayonnaise and bottom side with mustard. Line bottom of each roll with leaf lettuce and tomato slices. Top with desired meat and cheese, alternating slices. Cover each with top of hard roll. Yield: 20 to 24 servings.

Crisp Garden Slaw

To double the recipe, use a very large head of cabbage and a medium onion, and double all other ingredients.

2 small heads cabbage, about 8 cups, shredded
1 small white onion, finely chopped
1 medium-size green pepper, chopped
1 medium-size red pepper, chopped
2 small carrots, grated

¼ cup minced parsley
⅔ cup cider vinegar
½ cup sugar
1½ teaspoons salt
¼ teaspoon pepper
2 teaspoons celery seed
1 envelope unflavored gelatin
⅔ cup salad oil

Combine cabbage, onion, peppers, carrots, and parsley. Toss to mix. Combine vinegar, sugar, salt, pepper, and celery seed in a small saucepan; boil over medium heat. Add gelatin; stir until dissolved. Allow to cool. Gradually beat in salad oil. Pour dressing over vegetables and mix. Cover and chill. Gently toss at serving time. This slaw will keep for several days in refrigerator. Yield: 10 servings.

Note: The gelatin preserves the crispness; do not mold the salad.

Chocolate Delight Ice Cream Squares

A delectable confection and ideal for a large group. Make this dessert a day or two ahead of serving time.

1 (half-gallon) carton vanilla ice cream, softened
1 (15-ounce) package cream-filled chocolate sandwich cookies

1 (12-ounce) carton frozen whipped topping, thawed

Allow ice cream to soften in large mixing bowl. Break up cookies into very small pieces (not fine crumbs) in plastic bag with rolling pin. Stir into softened ice cream; fold in thawed whipped topping. Pour into 9- x 13- x 2-inch pan and freeze. Cut into 2-inch squares when ready to serve. Yield: 24 (2-inch) squares.

New Orleans Buffet for Sixteen

Ramos Gin Fizz
Jambalaya
Salad Vinaigrette
Bread Pudding with Cognac Sauce

Serves 16

Be careful not to overcook the seafood in this menu. Everything else can be prepared well in advance. The bread pudding and the salad dressing will hold overnight. Clean the salad greens and start the jambalaya early in the day, if you wish. Add the seafood to the jambalaya after guests have arrived.

Ramos Gin fizz can be increased for a crowd. To make four drinks at a time, quadruple the quantities and mix all ingredients except seltzer in blender. Pour into tall glasses, and add a dash of seltzer to each.

Ramos Gin Fizz

During the 1920s and 30s, Ramos was the renowned bartender at the old Hotel Roosevelt in New Orleans.

1 jigger (1½ ounces) gin
¼ teaspoon lemon juice
¼ teaspoon lime juice
¼ teaspoon orange flower water
¼ cup plus 2 tablespoons milk or
    half-and-half

1 egg white
1 tablespoon powdered sugar
Cracked ice
1 dash seltzer water

Combine all ingredients except seltzer water in a cocktail shaker; shake until foamy. Pour into a tall glass, and add a dash of seltzer water. Yield: 1 serving.

Serving a Buffet: Brightly colored cloths can turn folding tables, carts, and other furniture into makeshift buffets. When space is limited, consider serving each course in a separate room.

Jambalaya

This recipe originated at the famous Bon Ton Restaurant in New Orleans. To serve 16, double the ingredients.

½ cup shortening
3 cups chopped onion
3 medium-size green peppers, chopped
3 stalks celery, chopped
1 teaspoon minced garlic
2 tablespoons fresh parsley
2 teaspoons salt
¼ teaspoon red pepper

½ teaspoon dried whole thyme
2 (8-ounce) cans tomato sauce
2¼ cups water
4 (12-ounce) cans Select oysters, drained
1 pound small uncooked shrimp, peeled and deveined
4 cups cooked rice

Melt shortening in a large Dutch oven; add next 10 ingredients, mixing well. Bring mixture to a boil. Reduce heat; simmer, uncovered, 2 hours, stirring occasionally. (Recipe can be made to this point up to 8 hours in advance; reheat sauce over low heat before adding seafood.)

Add oysters to vegetable mixture; cook 10 minutes. Add shrimp; cook an additional 5 minutes. Add rice, mixing well; cook until rice is thoroughly heated. Yield: 10 servings.

Salad Vinaigrette

3 heads bibb lettuce, torn
2 head romaine lettuce, torn

1 head red leaf lettuce
Vinaigrette Dressing

Combine bibb, romaine, and red leaf lettuce in a large salad bowl; toss lightly. Serve with Vinaigrette Dressing. Yield: 16 servings.

Vinaigrette Dressing

½ cup vegetable oil
⅓ cup white wine vinegar
1 small onion, finely chopped
2 tablespoons finely chopped green pepper
2 tablespoons finely chopped pimiento, drained

1 tablespoon India Relish
1 tablespoon chopped fresh parsley
½ teaspoon salt
Dash of pepper
1 teaspoon sugar
½ teaspoon dry mustard

Combine all ingredients in a jar. Cover, and shake vigorously. Chill. Shake well before serving. Yield: 1½ cups.

Bread Pudding with Cognac Sauce

To serve 16, prepare 2 bread puddings and double the sauce ingredients. The sauce is delicious on fruit or pound cake.

1 cup golden raisins
1 (6-ounce) package dried apricots,
   coarsely chopped
¼ cup cherry-flavored brandy
5 eggs
3 egg yolks
1 cup sugar
1 cup whipping cream
1 quart milk, scalded

1 teaspoon vanilla extract
⅓ cup butter or margarine,
   softened
8 to 10 ¼-inch-thick slices French
   bread
3 tablespoons sifted powdered
   sugar
Cognac Sauce

Combine raisins and apricots in a small bowl; cover with boiling water for 5 minutes. Drain fruit and add brandy; stir until well blended. Spoon evenly into a well-greased 13- x 9- x 2-inch baking dish. Set aside.

Combine eggs, egg yolks, and sugar in a large bowl; mix well. Combine whipping cream and scalded milk; gradually add to egg mixture. Stir in vanilla.

Generously spread butter on both sides of bread; place on top of fruit and pour milk mixture over top.

Place baking dish in pan of hot water; bake at 325° for 1 hour. Sprinkle powdered sugar on top, and place under broiler until lightly browned. Serve at room temperature with Cognac Sauce. Sauce will hold at room temperature for several hours or may be refrigerated up to 3 days and served cold. Yield: 10 servings.

Cognac Sauce

3 egg yolks
1 cup sugar
1½ cups milk, scalded
1 tablespoon cornstarch

3 tablespoons water
1 tablespoon plus 2 teaspoons
   Cognac

Combine egg yolks and sugar in top of a double boiler; beat well. Gradually add scalded milk. Place mixture over simmering water, and cook until thoroughly heated.

Combine cornstarch and water in a small bowl, stirring well; add to milk mixture. Cook, stirring constantly, until mixture coats a metal spoon. Remove from heat; cool 10 minutes. Stir in cognac. Yield: 2 cups.

Double Boiler: If you don't have a double boiler, you can substitute a saucepan placed over a larger pan of boiling water. Remember that the top pan should not touch the water. In most recipes the water should be simmering, not boiling.

Covered-Dish Supper for Eighteen

Vegetable Relishes with Finger Lickin' Dressing
Pork Chops Southern Style
or
Zucchini-Beef Casserole
or
Zesty Broccoli-Shrimp Casserole
Potato Whole Wheat Health Bread
Yummy Brownies

Serves 18

D ivide up the preparation of these do-ahead, portable recipes when you're planning a covered-dish supper. But any of the recipes can be doubled or tripled if you'd rather serve fewer dishes. You might want to add another batch of cookies or a simple cake from the desserts in Chapter VIII. Percolator Hot Spiced Cranberry Punch (page 250) would be a good beverage choice.

Vegetable Relishes with Finger Lickin' Dressing

1 bunch broccoli
1 small head cauliflower
1 (14-ounce) can artichoke hearts, drained
1 cup mayonnaise
1 (8-ounce) carton commercial sour cream
2 tablespoons lime juice

3 tablespoons commercial blue cheese salad dressing
2 teaspoons anchovy paste
¼ teaspoon finely chopped chives
¼ teaspoon salt
¼ teaspoon paprika
¼ teaspoon hot sauce

Trim off large leaves of broccoli, and remove tough ends of lower stalks. Wash broccoli thoroughly, and break into flowerets. Remove outer green leaves of cauliflower, and break into flowerets; wash thoroughly. Blanch broccoli and cauliflower in boiling water for 1 minute. Plunge in cold water; drain well. Attractively arrange broccoli, cauliflower, and artichoke hearts on a serving platter; cover, and chill thoroughly.

Combine mayonnaise, sour cream, lime juice, blue cheese dressing, and anchovy paste in a small mixing bowl. Beat until well blended. Stir in remaining ingredients. Cover, and chill thoroughly. Pour dressing into serving bowl, and serve with chilled vegetables. Yield: 8 servings.

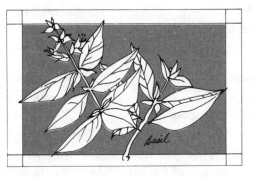

Pork Chops Southern Style

My version of a colorful and delicious dish served at the historic Lee's Inn at Highlands, North Carolina.

1½ tablespoons Worcestershire
    sauce
2¼ teaspoons salt, divided
¾ teaspoon lemon-pepper
    marinade, divided
6 (1-inch-thick) center-cut pork
    chops

3 tablespoons butter or margarine
3¾ cups boiling water
4 beef-flavored bouillon cubes
1½ cups uncooked regular rice
12 (½-inch-thick) slices onion
6 (½-inch-thick) slices tomato
6 medium-size green peppers

Sprinkle Worcestershire sauce, 2 teaspoons salt, and ½ teaspoon lemon-pepper marinade evenly on both sides of pork chops.

Melt butter in a large heavy skillet; brown pork chops on both sides. Transfer chops to large roasting pan, reserving pan drippings in skillet. Add water, bouillon cubes, and rice to skillet. Cover, and cook 8 minutes.

Place 1 slice onion, then 1 slice tomato, then 1 slice onion on each pork chop. Sprinkle remaining salt and lemon-pepper marinade evenly on pork chops.

Slice off tops of green peppers; remove seeds, and discard. Place green peppers around pork chops in roasting pan. Fill green peppers equally with partially cooked rice. Pour 2 tablespoons bouillon mixture into each green pepper. Pour remaining mixture in bottom of pan. Cover with foil. Bake at 350° for 1 hour. Serve hot. Yield: 6 servings.

When Cooking for a Crowd: Plan you menu so you can utilize several cooking appliances rather than just your oven. Don't forget to use the stove top, microwave, electric skillet, and toaster oven.

Zucchini-Beef Casserole

Prepare this tasty casserole in the morning, and refrigerate it; then pop it into the oven about 35 minutes before serving time.

1 pound ground chuck
1 (8-ounce) can tomato sauce
1 teaspoon salt
½ teaspoon sugar
1 teaspoon Worcestershire sauce
¼ teaspoon hot sauce
2 green onions, finely chopped
1 pound zucchini, thinly sliced

1 (3-ounce) package cream cheese, softened
1 (8-ounce) carton commercial sour cream
2 tablespoons seasoned dry breadcrumbs or grated Parmesan cheese
Paprika

Brown meat in a large skillet over medium heat, stirring to crumble. Add tomato sauce, salt, sugar, Worcestershire sauce, and hot sauce; cook over medium heat, stirring occasionally, 5 minutes. Remove from heat, and stir in green onion.

Spoon half of meat mixture into a greased 10- x 6- x 2-inch baking dish; top with half of the zucchini slices. Repeat layers.

Combine cream cheese and sour cream in a small mixing bowl, mixing well. Spread evenly over casserole. Sprinkle with breadcrumbs or Parmesan cheese, then paprika. Bake at 350° for 35 minutes. Serve hot. Yield: 6 servings.

Zesty Broccoli-Shrimp Casserole

A spicy, change-of-pace entrée.

1 (10-ounce) package frozen broccoli flowerets
½ cup uncooked regular rice
1 large onion, chopped
½ cup chopped celery
¼ cup butter or margarine
1 (4-ounce) can mushroom pieces and stems, drained
1 (10¾-ounce) can cream of mushroom soup, undiluted

1 cup uncooked medium shrimp, peeled, deveined and halved
1 teaspoon Worcestershire sauce
¼ teaspoon ground mace
4 ounces Monterey Jack cheese with jalapeño peppers, cut into cubes
Paprika

Cook broccoli and rice according to package directions. Set each aside.

Sauté onion and celery in butter in a large skillet until vegetables are tender. Stir in mushrooms, mushroom soup, shrimp, Worcestershire sauce, and mace. Cook over medium heat, stirring often, until shrimp are pink. Stir in reserved rice and cheese.

Place broccoli in bottom of a greased 10- x 6- x 2-inch baking dish. Spread shrimp mixture evenly over broccoli; sprinkle with paprika. Bake at 350° for 25 minutes or until bubbly. Serve hot. Yield: 6 servings.

Potato Whole Wheat Health Bread

A light and very nutritious bread.

2 medium potatoes, peeled and sliced	1 cup milk
2½ cups water	½ cup plus 1 tablespoon butter or margarine, melted and divided
1 package dry yeast	¼ cup honey
1 tablespoon sugar	3¾ cups bread flour
2 eggs	3¼ cups whole wheat flour
1 tablespoon salt	

Combine potatoes and water in a medium saucepan; bring to a boil. Reduce heat, cover, and simmer 20 minutes or until potatoes are tender. Drain, reserving ½ cup cooking liquid. Mash potatoes, reserving 1 cup; reserve remaining potatoes for other uses.

Cool cooking liquid to 105° to 115° in a small mixing bowl; dissolve yeast and sugar in warm liquid. Let stand 5 minutes or until bubbly.

Combine 1 cup reserved potatoes, eggs, salt, milk, ½ cup melted butter, and honey in a large mixing bowl; mix well. Stir in yeast mixture, mixing well.

Combine flour in a medium mixing bowl; add to potato mixture, one cup at a time, beating well after each addition.

Turn dough out onto a lightly floured surface; knead 10 minutes or until dough is smooth and elastic. Place dough in a large greased bowl, turning to grease top. Cover, and let rise in a warm place (85°), free from drafts, 1 hour or until doubled in bulk.

Punch dough down. Turn out onto a lightly floured surface; knead 3 minutes.

Divide dough in half. Shape each half into a loaf; place in greased 9- x 5- x 3-inch loafpans. Brush loaves with remaining melted butter. Cover, and repeat rising procedure 1 hour and 15 minutes or until doubled in bulk.

Bake at 375° for 35 minutes or until loaves sound hollow when tapped. Remove from pans immediately; cool completely on wire rack. Yield: 2 loaves.

Note: After first rising, dough may be divided into 4 portions, and placed in 4 greased 7½- x 3- x 2-inch loafpans. Repeat rising procedure; bake at 375° for 30 minutes.

Cooking Potatoes: New potatoes should be cooked in boiling water. Old potatoes should start in cold water and be brought to a boil.

Yummy Brownies

A very moist, cake-like brownie that takes about 10 minutes to make and that freezes well.

½ cup butter or margarine,
   softened
1 cup sugar
4 eggs
1 (16-ounce) can chocolate syrup
1 teaspoon vanilla extract

1 cup plus 1 tablespoon all-purpose
   flour, divided
½ teaspoon baking powder
¼ teaspoon salt
1 cup chopped pecans
½ cup semisweet chocolate morsels

Cream butter in a large mixing bowl; gradually add sugar, beating well. Add eggs, one at a time, beating well after each addition. Gradually add chocolate syrup and vanilla, beating until well blended.

Sift 1 cup flour, baking powder, and salt together into a small mixing bowl; gradually add to chocolate mixture, beating well after each addition. Dredge pecans and chocolate morsels in remaining flour in a small mixing bowl; fold into batter.

Spoon batter evenly into a greased and floured 15- x 10- x 1-inch jellyroll pan. Bake at 350° for 30 minutes or until a wooden pick inserted in center comes out clean. Cool 10 minutes in pan. Cut into 3-inch squares and serve. Yield: about 1½ dozen.

Page 213: *After the big game or after graduation, the Teenage Party for Twenty (page 202) is sure to satisfy ravenous appetites. From top: Fruit Punch, Snazzy Dogs, Chocolate Sheet Cake, Po'Boy Sandwiches, and potato chips.*

Page 214: *Come home from the theater or a movie to a late supper of Egg Rolls with Sweet and Sour Sauce or Hot Mustard Sauce, Pepper Steak, and Frozen Orange Cream. With some do-ahead preparation, this After Theater Chinese Supper (page 235) is completed in a snap.*

Ready
When You Are

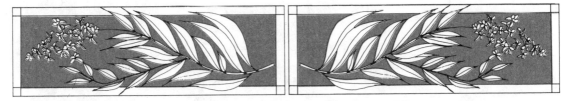

Fortunately, a meal doesn't have to be elaborate to warrant sharing. A Favorite Sunday Supper of Savory Stuffed Cabbage and homemade bread can provoke fondest memories. An Easy Company Dinner that takes only about an hour to prepare can turn a surprise visit into a warm celebration. Sometimes an impromptu Chili or Hearty Soup Supper can suit relaxed conversation even better than a more formal menu.

The meals in this chapter are either fast-cooking or do-ahead, so that the food can be ready to serve whenever you're ready to dine. Some of the menus offer answers for specific situations. What to serve after a movie or show? An entertaining After Theater Chinese Supper. How to make yesterday's ham or turkey look good enough to eat? A Day After the Big Dinner entrée that makes it taste fresh again. And what to plan to please houseguests when you want to spend your time with them? A delicious menu for A Relaxed Evening.

A few tips for general readiness: Any braised meat dish will taste even better after a night in the refrigerator. Baked breads freeze well and can be thawed and reheated when needed. Cooked vegetables can be reheated in a microwave oven.

Chili Supper

Nachos
Cabbage Slaw with Golden Dressing
Chili con Carne
Onion-Rye Bread
Mile High Ice Cream Pie
or
Fresh Apple Cake

Serves 8

This is a fun menu for impromptu entertaining after a football game or on any let's-get-together Saturday night. You can keep the chili in the freezer and the chocolate sauce in the refrigerator for just such occasions. A food processor will make quick work of the slaw and the garnishes for the chili.

Nachos

1 (12-ounce) bag plain tortilla chips
8 to 10 jalapeño peppers, sliced

4 cups (16 ounces) shredded extra sharp Cheddar cheese

Place tortilla chips on a baking sheet or ovenproof platter. Place a slice of jalapeño pepper and 1 tablespoon cheese on each chip. Broil 8 inches from heat just until cheese melts. Serve immediately. Yield: 8 to 10 appetizer servings.

Cabbage Slaw with Elly's Golden Dressing

2 pounds cabbage, finely shredded
2 carrots, grated
1 medium-size green pepper, chopped (optional)
¼ cup sugar

½ teaspoon salt
½ cup Dijon mustard
1 cup whipping cream
¼ cup rice wine vinegar

Combine cabbage, carrots, and green pepper, if desired, in large bowl. Combine remaining ingredients in medium bowl. Whisk until blended and slightly thickened; pour over salad and stir well. Yield: 8 servings.

Charles G. Smith's Chili con Carne

2 pounds lean beef for stewing, cut
    into 1-inch cubes
1½ pounds pork, cut into 1-inch
    cubes
1 tablespoon vegetable oil
2 medium-size green peppers, cut
    into strips
2 large onions, chopped
1 tablespoon minced garlic
1 tablespoon salt
1 teaspoon ground cumin
2 tablespoons chili powder
1 teaspoon dried whole thyme

3 cups water
2 (8-ounce) cans tomato sauce
1 (6-ounce) can pitted ripe olives,
    cut into halves
2 (4-ounce) cans mushroom pieces
    and stems
1 (1-ounce) square unsweetened
    chocolate, coarsely chopped
Cooked kidney beans
Hot cooked rice
Chopped onions (optional)
Shredded cheese (optional)

Brown meat in vegetable oil in a large Dutch oven over medium heat; drain, and return meat to Dutch oven. Add green pepper, onion, and garlic; cook over medium heat 10 minutes or until vegetables are tender. Stir in salt, cumin, chili powder, thyme, and water; bring to a boil. Reduce heat to low; cover and simmer 45 minutes.

Stir in tomato sauce, olives, mushrooms, and chocolate; cover and simmer an additional 30 minutes. Serve over kidney beans and rice. Top with chopped onions and shredded cheese, if desired. Yield: about 4 quarts.

La Verne Hester's Onion-Rye Bread

2 packages dry yeast
2 tablespoons plus 1 teaspoon
    sugar, divided
½ cup warm water (105° to 115°)
1 cup milk, scalded
2 tablespoons shortening

2 teaspoons salt
3 cups sifted all-purpose flour
5 teaspoons caraway seeds
3 tablespoons grated onion
About 1½ cups unsifted rye flour
Vegetable oil

Combine yeast, 1 teaspoon sugar, and warm water in a mixing bowl; stir well. Let stand 5 minutes or until bubbly.

Combine milk, shortening, salt, and remaining sugar; stir until shortening is melted. Add cooled milk mixture to yeast mixture; stir well.

Gradually add 3 cups all-purpose flour, stirring until smooth. Sprinkle caraway seeds on dough. Add grated onion and enough rye flour to make a firm dough.

Place dough in a lightly greased bowl, turning to grease top. Cover and place in a cold oven beside a bowl of very hot water. Allow to rise until doubled in bulk, about 1½ hours. Punch dough down. Turn out onto a floured surface; let rest 15 minutes. Shape dough into a loaf; place in greased 9- x 5- x 3-inch loafpan, and brush top with vegetable oil. Cover and repeat rising procedure 1 hour or until doubled in bulk. Bake at 350° for 45 to 50 minutes or until loaf sounds hollow when tapped. Remove bread from pan immediately; cool on wire rack. Yield: 1 loaf.

Mile High Ice Cream Pie

From the Pontchartrain Hotel comes this spectacular dessert. Elegant Chocolate Sauce is also marvelous over plain cake or ice cream. Serve either hot or cold.

1 baked (9-inch) pastry shell, cooled	4 large egg whites
1 pint vanilla ice cream, softened	¼ teaspoon cream of tartar
1 pint chocolate ice cream, softened	½ teaspoon vanilla extract
	½ cup sugar
	Elegant Chocolate Sauce

Spoon vanilla ice cream evenly into bottom of pastry shell; freeze until firm. Spoon chocolate ice cream evenly over vanilla layer, and return to freezer.

Combine egg whites (at room temperature), cream of tartar, and vanilla in a large mixing bowl; beat until foamy. Gradually add sugar, 1 tablespoon at a time, beating until stiff peaks form. Quickly spread meringue over frozen pie, sealing to edge. Place 6 inches from heat, and broil about 1 minute or until meringue is lightly browned. Return to freezer until serving time.

Cut into wedges, and place on individual serving plates. Drizzle each serving with Elegant Chocolate Sauce, and serve immediately. Yield: 8 servings.

Elegant Chocolate Sauce

1 (14-ounce) can sweetened condensed milk	3 tablespoons butter
1 (16-ounce) can chocolate syrup	⅛ teaspoon salt
	1 teaspoon vanilla extract

Blend condensed milk and chocolate syrup in top of a double boiler over rapidly boiling water and cook for 5 minutes, stirring occasionally. Add butter and salt; remove from heat and add vanilla. Yield: 1½ pints.

Fresh Apple Cake

This luscious cake stays moist and fresh for days.

2 cups sugar	1 teaspoon salt
1 cup vegetable oil	2 teaspoons apple pie spice
3 eggs	2 cups peeled and coarsely chopped apples
2 teaspoons vanilla extract	
3 cups all-purpose flour	1¼ cups pecans, chopped
1 teaspoon baking soda	

Combine sugar, oil, eggs, and vanilla in a large mixing bowl; beat about 1 minute at medium speed of electric mixer. Combine flour, soda, salt, and apple pie spice; gradually add to sugar mixture, beating at low speed of electric mixer until blended.

Stir apples and pecans into batter. Spoon batter into a greased and floured 10-inch tube pan. Bake at 325° for 1 hour and 30 minutes or until wooden pick inserted in center comes out clean. Cool in pan 15 minutes; remove from pan, and let cool completely. Yield: one 10-inch cake.

Beef Stew Supper

Favorite Beef and Vegetable Stew
Crunchy Layered Vegetable Salad
Cherry-Pear Dessert

Serves 8 to 10

*I*f you like to cook ahead when you do have time, for those days when you don't, you'll appreciate the salad, stew, and dessert in this menu. All will hold several days in the refrigerator.

Favorite Beef and Vegetable Stew

The recipe can be doubled and will taste even better if refrigerated overnight and reheated.

2½ pounds boneless beef chuck, cut into 1-inch cubes
2 tablespoons all-purpose flour
1 teaspoon salt
½ teaspoon lemon-pepper marinade
3 tablespoons butter or margarine
2 tablespoons vegetable oil
3 medium-size red onions, finely chopped

2 cloves garlic, minced
8 carrots, scraped and sliced
2 cups sliced fresh mushrooms
2 large potatoes, peeled and cubed
3 bay leaves
1 quart beef broth
2 cups burgundy or other dry red wine
2 tablespoons Worcestershire sauce

Combine beef, flour, salt, and lemon-pepper marinade in a paper bag; shake to coat beef. Melt butter and vegetable oil in an 8-quart stock pot over medium heat. Brown beef on all sides. Remove beef, and set aside, reserving pan drippings.

Sauté onion and garlic in pan drippings until vegetables are tender. Add beef and remaining ingredients, stirring well. Bring to a boil. Reduce heat; cover, and simmer 1 hour. Uncover, and simmer an additional 30 minutes, stirring occasionally. Discard bay leaves. Spoon into serving dishes, and serve immediately. Yield: about 1 gallon.

To Thicken Soups: Gradually add instant potato flakes to soups, gravies, or sauces. The flakes never lump when added directly as flour and cornstarch do. And they add texture.

Crunchy Layered Vegetable Salad

This salad must be made a day ahead.

1 large head iceberg lettuce,
washed and torn into bite-size
pieces
12 slices bacon, cooked, crumbled,
and divided
1 medium-size red onion, sliced
and separated into rings

1 (10-ounce) package frozen
English peas, thawed
1½ cups mayonnaise
1 tablespoon sugar
½ cup grated Parmesan cheese
½ cup grated Romano cheese

Layer lettuce, two-thirds of the bacon, onion, and peas in a 4-quart serving bowl. Place remaining bacon in a covered container, and set aside.

Combine mayonnaise and sugar in a small mixing bowl; mix well. Spread evenly over top of salad, sealing to edge of bowl. Combine Parmesan and Romano cheese; mix well, and sprinkle over salad. Cover tightly with plastic wrap, and chill 24 hours. Garnish with remaining crumbled bacon. Yield: 8 to 10 servings.

Margaret Ragland Thompson's Cherry-Pear Dessert

This recipe can also be served on lettuce leaves as a salad.

1 (29-ounce) can pear halves,
undrained
1 (6-ounce) package cherry-flavored
gelatin

1 (8-ounce) package cream cheese,
softened
2 envelopes whipped topping mix
½ cup chopped pecans

Drain pears, reserving 1⅓ cups syrup. Set pears aside. Heat syrup to boiling point; pour over gelatin in a medium-size mixing bowl. Stir until gelatin dissolves.

Puree pear halves in blender, and fold into gelatin mixture. Chill until mixture becomes the consistency of unbeaten egg whites.

Beat cream cheese until smooth, and fold into gelatin mixture. Prepare whipped topping mix according to package directions; fold into gelatin mixture along with chopped pecans.

Pour mixture into a lightly oiled 12- x 8- x 2-inch baking dish and chill until firm. Cut into 2-inch squares to serve. Yield: 24 squares.

Easy Company Dinner

Tossed Salad with Herb Croutons
Apricot Chicken
or
Piquant Pork Chop Casserole
Creole Carrots
Sally Lunn
Easy Baked Alaska Pie
or
Chocolate Bread Pudding

Serves 6

---

*T*he ingredients for this menu can be kept on hand for surprise guests, and the whole meal can be prepared in a little over an hour. Make the dessert and side dishes while either easy casserole is in the oven.

Tossed Salad with Herb Croutons

This salad is simple and subtle enough to serve with almost any entrée. Try making Herb Croutons if time permits—if not, the commercial croutons are fine with the salad.

1 medium head romaine lettuce, washed and torn into bite-size pieces
1 medium-size green pepper, thinly sliced
1 cucumber, peeled, scored, seeded, and sliced
4 ounces mushrooms, sliced

½ medium-size red onion, sliced
Freshly ground black pepper
Herb Dressing (page 222)
3 slices Italian bread, cubed
2 ounces sliced ham, cut into thin strips
2 tablespoons grated Parmesan cheese

Combine lettuce, green pepper, cucumber, mushrooms, and onion in salad bowl; sprinkle with ground pepper to taste.

Heat 2 tablespoons Herb Dressing in a medium skillet over medium heat. Add bread cubes; cook, tossing often, until lightly toasted. Remove croutons to salad bowl. Add ham to skillet; sauté until slightly crisped. Add ham to salad. Sprinkle Parmesan cheese over salad. Toss with remaining dressing. Yield: 6 servings.

Herb Dressing

3 tablespoons fresh lemon juice
2 teaspoons dried basil leaves
½ teaspoon celery seed
¼ teaspoon ground cardamom

¼ cup plus 2 tablespoons vegetable oil
2 tablespoons sesame oil

Mix lemon juice, basil, celery seed, and cardamom in small bowl; let stand 10 minutes. Whisk in oils. Yield: about ¾ cup.

Apricot Chicken

6 chicken breast halves, skinned
Salt and pepper
1 (21-ounce) can apricot pie filling
1 tablespoon lemon juice

½ teaspoon salt
½ teaspoon ground nutmeg
½ cup pecan or almond halves
Hot cooked rice

Arrange chicken in a 13- x 9- x 2-inch baking dish; sprinkle with salt and pepper.

Combine pie filling, lemon juice, ½ teaspoon salt, nutmeg, and pecan or almond halves; stir well. Spread mixture evenly over chicken. Cover, and bake at 375° for 1 hour or until chicken is tender. Arrange chicken over rice; spoon sauce over chicken. Serve immediately. Yield: 6 servings.

Ruth Whitney's Piquant Pork Chop Casserole

6 (1-inch-thick) pork chops (about 2½ pounds)
1 clove garlic, halved
¾ cup catsup
2 tablespoons firmly packed brown sugar

2 teaspoons prepared horseradish
2 teaspoons prepared mustard
½ teaspoon Worcestershire sauce

Rub chops with garlic; place in a greased 13- x 9- x 2-inch baking dish.

Combine catsup, brown sugar, horseradish, mustard, and Worcestershire sauce in a small mixing bowl; mix well. Spoon over pork chops. Bake, uncovered, at 350° for 1 hour. Serve hot. Yield: 6 servings.

Fresh Salads: Purchase salad greens the day of serving. Freshness is necessary to create a delicious salad. If purchased the day before serving, place the greens in a clean, wet dish towel and keep refrigerated.

Creole Carrots

Colorful carrots with a zesty flavor.

1½ pounds carrots, scraped and thinly sliced
2 cups water
1 beef-flavored bouillon cube
½ teaspoon salt
1 (3-ounce) package cream cheese, softened
1 (8-ounce) carton commercial sour cream

3 tablespoons finely chopped green pepper
2 tablespoons finely chopped green onion
½ teaspoon grated lemon rind
¼ teaspoon hot sauce
Fresh parsley sprigs

Combine carrots, water, bouillon cube, and salt in a medium saucepan; bring to a boil. Cover, and simmer 20 minutes or until carrots reach desired degree of doneness; drain.

Return carrots to saucepan; add cream cheese, sour cream, green pepper, green onion, lemon rind, and hot sauce, mixing well. Cook over medium heat until thoroughly heated. Garnish with parsley; serve immediately. Yield: 6 servings.

Sally Lunn

Fifteen minutes to prepare and 45 minutes to bake. This delightful bread will add spark to any meal.

1 tablespoon vegetable shortening
¼ cup butter, softened
2 tablespoons sugar
3 large eggs

1 cup milk
2 cups all-purpose flour
1 tablespoon baking powder
1 teaspoon salt

Cream shortening, butter, and sugar in a large mixing bowl until light and fluffy. Combine eggs and milk; add to creamed mixture.

Combine flour, baking powder, and salt; add to creamed mixture and beat until thoroughly blended. Pour into a well-greased 8½- x 4½- x 3-inch loaf pan, and bake at 325° for 45 minutes. Serve hot with plenty of butter. Yield: 1 loaf.

Note: This is good reheated but it is best when first taken from oven.

Maxine Randolph's Easy Baked Alaska Pie

1 quart vanilla ice cream, softened
1 baked (9-inch) graham cracker
    piecrust, cooled
16 large marshmallows
1 tablespoon pineapple juice

3 egg whites
¼ cup sugar
Chocolate Sauce (page 108)
Sliced fresh strawberries

Spoon softened vanilla ice cream into piecrust, spreading evenly; freeze until firm.

Place marshmallows and pineapple juice in the top of a double boiler; place over boiling water, and cook, stirring frequently, until marshmallows melt. Remove from heat, and set aside.

Beat egg whites (at room temperature) in a large mixing bowl until soft peaks form; gradually add sugar, 1 tablespoon at a time, beating until stiff peaks form. Gently fold marshmallows into beaten egg whites. Quickly spread meringue over frozen pie, sealing to edge. Place frozen pie 6 inches from heat, and broil 1 minute or until meringue is lightly browned.

Return to freezer until serving time. Cut pie into wedges; place on individual serving plates, drizzle with Chocolate Sauce, and top with strawberries. Yield: 6 servings.

Allan Glover Walker's Chocolate Bread Pudding

From Rosemount, the grand old mansion in Alabama, comes this special occasion dessert. It is one of the choice recipes compiled by generations of the Glover family.

2½ cups milk
4 (1-ounce) squares unsweetened
    chocolate
5 slices day-old bread, torn into
    small pieces
1 tablespoon butter or margarine
5 eggs, separated

1 cup sugar
1 teaspoon vanilla extract
1 cup whipping cream
¼ cup sifted powdered sugar
1 tablespoon crème de menthe,
    Grand Marnier, or brandy

Combine milk and chocolate in a heavy saucepan. Cook over low heat, stirring constantly, until chocolate melts. Remove from heat. Add breadcrumbs and butter; stir until butter melts. Cool.

Beat egg yolks; add to cooled milk mixture, stirring constantly. Add sugar and vanilla, mixing well.

Beat egg whites (at room temperature) until soft peaks form. Fold into chocolate mixture. Pour into a 2-quart baking dish. Place baking dish in a pan of water. Bake at 300° for 1 hour and 30 minutes or until a knife inserted in center comes out clean.

Beat whipping cream until foamy; gradually add powdered sugar, beating until soft peaks form. Stir in crème de menthe, Grand Marnier, or brandy.

Serve pudding warm with whipped cream mixture. Yield: 8 to 10 servings.

Note: Pudding may be refrigerated and reheated in a pan of warm water.

Day After the Big Dinner

Creole Turkey Casserole
or
Sesame Crêpes with Herbed Turkey
or
Butter Bean and Ham Casserole
Sliced Tomatoes with Cucumber Cream Dressing
Rum Yum Apples

Serves 8

---

*P*lan to enjoy the big-dinner ham or turkey all over again. The light salad and baked apples for dessert add a fresh note. You might want to dice and freeze additional leftover ham or turkey in pre-measured quantities, so that it will be ready to combine with the ingredients for another day's entrée.

Creole Turkey Casserole

This freezes well; reheat at 350° until bubbly.

2 medium onions, finely chopped
1 green pepper, finely chopped
⅓ cup bacon drippings
1 (8-ounce) can mushroom pieces
  and stems, undrained
1 (14½-ounce) can tomatoes,
  undrained and chopped
1 (8-ounce) can tomato sauce
1 (6-ounce) can tomato paste

¼ cup sherry
1 tablespoon garlic salt
Dash of pepper
Dash of hot sauce
Dash of Worcestershire sauce
4 cups hot cooked rice
3 cups cooked, cubed turkey
Green pepper rings
Fresh parsley sprigs

Sauté onion and chopped green pepper in bacon drippings in a large skillet until vegetables are tender. Add next 9 ingredients. Bring to a boil. Reduce heat, cover, and simmer 12 minutes.

Spoon rice evenly in bottom of a 13- x 9- x 2-inch baking dish; top with turkey. Spoon sauce over turkey. Bake, uncovered, at 350° for 15 minutes or until thoroughly heated. Garnish with green pepper rings and parsley. Serve hot. Yield: 8 servings.

Louise C. Hamilton's Sesame Crêpes With Herbed Turkey

Try the unusual flavor of sesame crêpes filled with herbed turkey.

1 medium onion, chopped
¼ cup butter or margarine
½ cup all-purpose flour
2 cups milk, divided
1 cup half-and-half
¼ cup Chablis or other dry white wine

2 teaspoons tarragon leaves, crumbled
1½ teaspoons salt
⅛ teaspoon black pepper
3 cups diced, cooked turkey
Sesame Crêpes

Sauté onion in butter in a large skillet over medium heat 6 minutes. Add flour, stirring well; cook 1 minute. Add 1½ cups milk, half-and-half, Chablis, tarragon, salt, and pepper. Cook over medium heat, stirring constantly, until thickened; remove from heat, and reserve 1 cup sauce mixture. Stir turkey into remaining sauce mixture.

Spoon about 3 tablespoons mixture onto each crêpe. Roll up, and place seam side down in a buttered 13- x 9- x 2-inch baking dish. Cover, and bake at 350° for 30 minutes.

Combine reserved sauce and remaining milk in a small saucepan; cook over medium heat, stirring constantly, until thoroughly heated. Spoon over hot crêpes, and serve immediately. Yield: 8 servings.

Sesame Crêpes

⅔ cup whole wheat flour
½ cup all-purpose flour
2 tablespoons sesame seeds
1 tablespoon onion powder
1 tablespoon dried parsley flakes

¼ teaspoon salt
⅛ teaspoon black pepper
3 large eggs, beaten
1¼ cups milk
¼ cup vegetable oil, divided

Combine flour, sesame seeds, onion powder, parsley flakes, salt, and pepper in a medium mixing bowl. Make a well in the center of mixture; add eggs, milk, and 2 tablespoons vegetable oil, beating until smooth. Cover and refrigerate 1 hour.

Coat the bottom of a 6-inch crêpe pan or heavy skillet with some of remaining oil, adding additional oil as needed; place pan over medium heat until oil is just hot, not smoking.

Pour 3 tablespoons batter into pan. Quickly tilt the pan in all directions so that batter covers bottom of pan. Cook crêpe 1 minute.

Lift edge of crêpe to test for doneness. Crêpe is ready for flipping when it can be shaken loose from pan. Flip crêpe, and cook 30 seconds. (This side is rarely more than spotty brown, and is the side on which the filling is placed.) Place on paper towels to cool. Stack crêpes between layers of waxed paper to prevent sticking. Repeat procedure until all batter is used, stirring batter occasionally. Yield: 16 crêpes.

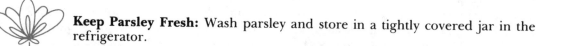 **Keep Parsley Fresh:** Wash parsley and store in a tightly covered jar in the refrigerator.

Butter Bean and Ham Casserole

1 (16-ounce) package frozen butter
  beans, thawed
2 cups cooked, cubed ham
1 cup water
¾ cup (3 ounces) shredded sharp
  Cheddar cheese
½ cup chopped onion

¼ cup plus 1 tablespoon catsup
2 tablespoons butter or margarine,
  melted
½ teaspoon seasoned salt
2 medium tomatoes, peeled and
  sliced
¼ cup seasoned, dry breadcrumbs

Combine first 8 ingredients in a large mixing bowl; stir gently to combine. Pour mixture into a greased 12- x 8- x 2-inch baking dish. Arrange tomato slices over mixture; sprinkle with breadcrumbs. Bake, uncovered, at 350° for 1 hour. Serve hot. Yield: 6 to 8 servings.
Note: Cooked, cubed chicken may be substituted for ham.

Sliced Tomatoes with Cucumber Cream Dressing

A light salad that goes well with casseroles.

2 tablespoons vinegar
2 tablespoons sugar
1 cup peeled and diced cucumber

1 cup whipping cream, whipped
Sliced tomatoes

Add vinegar and sugar to diced cucumber in small mixing bowl; fold in whipped cream. Serve with sliced tomatoes. Yield: 2 cups.

Rum Yum Apples

These can be made ahead and refrigerated—good served warm or cold.

¼ cup apricot preserves
3 tablespoons grated orange rind,
  divided
⅓ cup orange juice
½ cup sugar

½ cup water
2 tablespoons dark rum
8 medium-size baking apples,
  peeled and cored
Sweetened whipped cream

Combine preserves, 2 tablespoons grated orange rind, orange juice, sugar, and water in a small saucepan; cook over medium heat 5 minutes or until mixture thickens slightly. Add rum, stirring well. Set aside.
Cut a thin slice from stem end of each apple. Arrange apples, cut side down, in a buttered 13- x 9- x 2-inch baking dish. Spoon preserve mixture over apples. Cover loosely with aluminum foil, and bake at 350° for 45 minutes or until tender. Cool to room temperature; garnish each apple with a dollop of whipped cream, and sprinkle with remaining grated orange rind before serving. Yield: 8 servings.

Hearty Soup Supper

Canadian Cheese Soup
or
Creole Oyster Soup
or
German Potato Soup
Winter Vegetable Salad with Fennel Dressing
Honey Wheat Bread
Apple Pie

Serves 6

What could be more enticing than a rich soup served with homemade bread and a satisfying salad? A scrumptious apple pie for dessert! The potato soup takes the most time to make, the oyster soup the least. But this meal can be scheduled any way you wish. Even the salad will hold overnight in the refrigerator; toss with the dressing just before serving.

Martha Cheney's Canadian Cheese Soup

This delectable soup, a favorite of my son Garner, ranks high on my list of soups to serve company for a late supper or after a football game. It may be prepared early in the day and reheated.

2 large carrots, scraped and cut into 2-inch slices
2 stalks celery, cleaned and cut into 2-inch slices
1 small onion, quartered
2 cups water
2 chicken-flavored bouillon cubes
2 cups milk

¼ cup all-purpose flour
8 ounces Cheddar cheese, cut into cubes
2 teaspoons Worcestershire sauce
½ teaspoon salt
⅛ teaspoon pepper
2 slices bacon, cooked and crumbled

Combine carrots, celery, onion, water, and bouillon cubes in container of electric blender; process at medium speed until finely chopped. Pour into large saucepan, and cook over medium heat 25 minutes or until vegetables are tender. (If a smoother soup is desired, place this mixture in container of electric blender and process at high speed until smooth.)

Combine milk, flour, cheese, Worcestershire sauce, salt, and pepper in container of electric blender; process at high speed until smooth. Stir into hot vegetable mixture; cook over medium heat 25 minutes or until thickened, stirring often. Ladle into individual soup bowls, and sprinkle with crumbled bacon. Serve hot. Yield: 6 servings.

Creole Oyster Soup

5 green onions, finely chopped
½ cup sliced fresh mushrooms
1 stalk celery, finely chopped
½ teaspoon garlic powder
¼ cup butter or margarine
¼ cup all-purpose flour
1 chicken-flavored bouillon cube
1 cup boiling water

2 (12-ounce) containers Standard
   oysters, undrained
4 saltine crackers, coarsely
   crumbled
¼ teaspoon ground mace
2 cups milk, scalded
Salt to taste
⅛ teaspoon pepper

Sauté onion, mushrooms, celery, and garlic powder in butter in a small Dutch oven until vegetables are tender. Gradually add flour, stirring until smooth. Cook 1 minute, stirring constantly.

Dissolve bouillon cube in boiling water; gradually add to vegetable mixture. Cook over medium heat, stirring constantly, until thickened and bubbly. Stir in oysters, crumbled crackers, and mace. Continue cooking over medium heat, stirring constantly, until mixture is heated and oyster edges curl. Add milk; stir in salt to taste and pepper. Ladle into individual bowls; serve warm with crackers. Yield: 6 servings.

German Potato Soup

6 cups chicken broth
2 stalks celery with leaves, chopped
2 carrots, scraped and sliced
1 medium onion, quartered
1 clove garlic, sliced
3 whole peppercorns
1 bay leaf, crushed
2 sprigs fresh parsley

1¾ teaspoons salt, divided
½ teaspoon celery salt
5 medium potatoes, peeled and
   quartered
¼ cup butter or margarine
¼ teaspoon white pepper
Commercial sour cream (optional)

Combine chicken broth, celery, carrots, onion, garlic, peppercorns, bay leaf, parsley, ½ teaspoon salt, and celery salt in a large Dutch oven, bring to a boil. Reduce heat, and simmer 15 minutes or until carrots are tender, stirring occasionally. Cool slightly. Strain broth; discard whole spices. Set aside cooked vegetables and 2 cups broth, reserving remaining broth in Dutch oven.

Place reserved vegetables and 2 cups broth in the container of an electric blender; process until smooth. Return pureed vegetable mixture to remaining broth in Dutch oven, stirring well. Set aside.

Combine potatoes, ½ teaspoon salt, and water to cover in a large saucepan. Bring to a boil; reduce heat, and cook, uncovered, 20 minutes or until tender. Drain liquid, reserving potatoes in saucepan; add butter, white pepper, and remaining salt. Beat on medium speed of electric mixer until smooth and creamy. Gradually add potatoes to broth in large Dutch oven, stirring to blend well; cook over medium heat, stirring frequently, until thoroughly heated. Serve immediately; dollop with sour cream, if desired. Yield: about 2 quarts.

Winter Vegetable Salad with Fennel Dressing

2 slices bacon
½ (10-ounce) package frozen baby
    lima beans
¼ teaspoon dried thyme leaves
1 cup canned garbanzos, rinsed and
    drained
1 tablespoon sliced pimiento
Pepper to taste
8 to 10 ounces winter greens:
    purple savoy cabbage, spinach,
    celery cabbage, kale, and/or
    iceberg lettuce, cleaned and
    torn into pieces

1 small green pepper, seeded and
    chopped
½ small red onion, finely chopped
¼ teaspoon salt
1 cup canned diced beets, rinsed
    and drained
1 hard-cooked egg, chopped
Fennel Dressing

Cook bacon in a medium skillet until crisp; remove bacon, reserving drippings in skillet. Crumble bacon, and set aside. Rinse lima beans to separate and thaw slightly; drain well. Stir lima beans and thyme into bacon drippings; sauté lima beans until tender. Set aside.

Combine garbanzos and pimiento in a small mixing bowl; add pepper to taste.

Combine greens, green pepper, onion, and salt in a large mixing bowl. Arrange tossed greens on a large platter. Mound beets in center of platter. Arrange garbanzo mixture around beets; arrange lima beans around garbanzos. Sprinkle with reserved bacon and egg. Serve with Fennel Dressing. Yield: 6 servings.

Fennel Dressing

1 tablespoon fennel seeds
3 tablespoons lemon juice
3 tablespoons white wine
1 tablespoon dried whole oregano

2 cloves garlic, finely chopped
¼ cup vegetable oil
¼ cup olive oil
2 tablespoons plain yogurt

Place fennel seed in a small heavy skillet; cook over medium heat 5 minutes, stirring occasionally, until lightly browned. Combine browned fennel seed, lemon juice, wine, oregano, and garlic in a small mixing bowl. Whisk in oils and yogurt until smooth. Repeat whisking process before serving with salad. Yield: 1 cup.

Sarah Kilgore's Honey Wheat Bread

2 packages dry yeast
2 cups warm skim milk (105° to
    115°)
2 tablespoons vegetable oil
2¼ teaspoons salt
2 tablespoons honey
¼ cup wheat germ

2 tablespoons regular oats,
    uncooked
½ cup whole wheat flour
4¼ cups bread flour
2 tablespoons butter or margarine,
    melted

Dissolve yeast in warm milk; stir well and let stand 5 minutes. Combine milk mixture, vegetable oil, salt, honey, wheat germ, oats, and whole wheat flour in a large mixing bowl. Blend mixture at medium speed of electric mixer until smooth. Stir in enough bread flour to make a soft dough.

Turn dough out onto a floured surface; knead 8 minutes or until smooth and elastic. Place in a greased bowl, turning to grease top. Cover and let rise in a warm place (85°), 1 hour or until doubled in bulk.

Punch dough down; turn out onto a lightly floured surface, and divide in half. Shape into loaves and place in two lightly greased 8½- x 4½- x 3-inch loafpans. Repeat rising procedure 1 hour or until doubled in bulk. Bake at 350° for 30 minutes or until loaves sound hollow when tapped. Remove bread from pans; cool on wire rack. Brush with melted butter. Yield: 2 loaves.

Note: Dough may be divided into 4 portions, shaped into loaves, and placed in 4 lightly greased 6- x 3½- x 2-inch baking pans. Repeat rising procedure, letting rise 20 minutes or until doubled in bulk. Bake at 350° for 30 minutes or until loaves sound hollow when tapped.

Mary Frances Blake's Apple Pie

Shredded apples make this pie different from most others and utterly delectable.

Pastry for 1 double-crust 9-inch pie
2 eggs
2 cups sugar
½ cup butter or margarine, melted
4 cups shredded unpeeled apples

2 teaspoons ground cinnamon
1 teaspoon vanilla extract
¼ teaspoon salt

Roll half of pastry to ⅛-inch thickness on a lightly floured surface; fit into a 9-inch pieplate. Chill remaining pastry.

Place eggs in a large mixing bowl, beating well. Gradually add sugar and butter, beating well. Stir in apples, cinnamon, vanilla, and salt. Spoon apple mixture into pastry shell.

Roll remaining pastry to ⅛-inch thickness; cut into ¾-inch-wide strips, and arrange in a lattice design over filling. Trim edges; seal and flute. Bake at 350° for 1 hour and 15 minutes or until set. Serve warm. Yield: one 9-inch double-crust pie.

Tempting
Fish Supper

Fish Fillets Piquant
or
Baked Ocean Perch with Ripe Olive Sauce
Steamed New Potatoes
or
Cooked Rice
Hazelnut Carrot Coins
Pear Upside-Down Cake with Raspberry Sauce

Serves 4

---

ish should be cooked quickly—making it a good choice for a fast supper. But these recipes also add the appeal of unusual sauces. If you're too busy to bake, serve the Raspberry Sauce over berries or peaches and ice cream.

Fish Fillets Piquant

1 clove garlic, sliced
1 tablespoon plus 1½ teaspoons
    vegetable oil
1 tablespoon all-purpose flour
1 stalk celery, minced
2 green onions, minced
1 tablespoon minced green pepper
1 beef-flavored bouillon cube
1 cup boiling water
¼ cup plus 2 tablespoons catsup

1 tablespoon chopped fresh parsley
1 small bay leaf
Salt to taste
⅛ teaspoon white pepper
⅛ teaspoon ground mace
Pinch of ground thyme
⅛ teaspoon hot sauce
1 pound catfish, flounder, or trout
    fillets, sliced into 6 to 8 pieces
Fresh parsley sprigs

Sauté garlic in oil in a large skillet until browned; remove garlic and discard. Reserve oil in skillet.

Add flour to reserved oil, stirring until smooth. Cook, stirring constantly, over medium heat until browned. Add celery, onion, and green pepper; stir well. Continue to cook over medium heat, stirring occasionally, until vegetables are tender.

Dissolve bouillon cube in boiling water; stir into vegetable mixture. Add catsup, chopped parsley, and bay leaf; stir well. Stir in salt to taste, pepper, mace, thyme, and hot sauce. Bring mixture to a boil; reduce heat to low. Simmer, uncovered, 10 minutes. Add fish.

Continue to simmer, uncovered, 15 minutes or until fish flakes easily when tested with a fork. Remove bay leaf and discard.

Transfer fish and sauce to a warm serving platter. Garnish with parsley sprigs, and serve immediately. Yield: 4 servings.

Baked Ocean Perch with Ripe Olive Sauce

The baked fish is good plain, but the sauce enhances it.

4 perch fillets (about 1 pound)	¼ teaspoon lemon-pepper marinade
2 tablespoons vegetable oil	¼ teaspoon paprika
2 tablespoons lemon juice	4 lemon slices
¼ teaspoon salt	Ripe Olive Sauce

Brush surface of fish with vegetable oil; sprinkle with lemon juice, and place in a lightly greased 13- x 9- x 2-inch baking dish. Combine salt, lemon-pepper marinade, and paprika; sprinkle over fish fillets. Place 1 lemon slice on each fish fillet.

Bake, uncovered, at 400° for 15 minutes or until fish flakes easily when tested with a fork. Transfer to a warm platter, and serve immediately with Ripe Olive Sauce. Yield: 4 servings.

Ripe Olive Sauce

1 (2.2-ounce) can sliced ripe olives, undrained	¾ cup milk
1 tablespoon plus 1½ teaspoons butter or margarine	1 egg yolk, lightly beaten
	1 tablespoon lemon juice
1 tablespoon plus 1½ teaspoons all-purpose flour	½ teaspoon Angostura bitters
	¼ teaspoon salt

Drain olives, reserving 2 tablespoons olive liquid. Chop olives; set aside.

Melt butter in a heavy saucepan over low heat; add flour, stirring until smooth. Cook 1 minute, stirring constantly. Gradually add milk and reserved olive liquid; cook over medium heat, stirring constantly, until thickened and bubbly. Combine egg yolk, lemon juice, and Angostura bitters, stirring well. Slowly pour egg yolk mixture into sauce, stirring constantly. Cook over medium heat, stirring constantly, 1 minute. Remove from heat; stir in reserved olives and salt. Yield: about 1 cup.

Hazelnut Carrot Coins

2 pounds carrots, sliced	½ cup butter
3 ounces blanched hazelnuts, chopped	Pinch of ground cinnamon

Steam carrots until tender. Spread hazelnuts in large, heavy skillet; cook over medium heat, stirring occasionally, 15 to 20 minutes or until golden. Reduce heat to low; stir in butter until melted. Add carrots and cinnamon; toss to coat. Yield: 6 to 8 servings.

Pear Upside-Down Cake with Raspberry Sauce

Substitute canned pear halves in light syrup when fresh ones are not in season. Either way, this is an easy cake that can be refrigerated and reheated.

2 tablespoons lemon juice
2 pears, peeled, halved, and cored
¼ cup butter or margarine, melted
3 tablespoons firmly packed dark
    brown sugar
½ cup butter or margarine,
    softened
¾ cup sugar

1 egg
1⅔ cups all-purpose flour
2 teaspoons baking powder
½ teaspoon salt
½ cup milk
2 teaspoons grated lemon rind
1 teaspoon vanilla extract
Raspberry Sauce

Sprinkle lemon juice over pears; set aside.

Combine ¼ cup melted butter and dark brown sugar in an 8-inch square pan. Arrange pear halves, cut side down, on sugar mixture. Set aside.

Cream ½ cup softened butter in a medium mixing bowl; gradually add sugar, beating well. Add egg, beating well. Sift together flour, baking powder, and salt; add to creamed mixture alternately with milk, beginning and ending with flour mixture; beat well after each addition. Stir in lemon rind and vanilla.

Spoon batter over pears in pan. Bake at 350° for 50 minutes or until a wooden pick inserted in center comes out clean. Cut into squares, and spoon Raspberry Sauce over top. Yield: 4 servings.

Raspberry Sauce

1 (10-ounce) package frozen
    raspberries, thawed
½ cup hot water
1 tablespoon lemon juice
⅓ cup sugar

1 tablespoon cornstarch
¼ teaspoon salt
2 tablespoons kirsch or other
    cherry-flavored liqueur

Drain raspberries, reserving liquid. Set aside.

Combine reserved raspberry liquid, water, lemon juice, sugar, cornstarch, and salt in a medium saucepan. Bring to a boil; reduce heat to medium, and stir constantly until mixture begins to thicken. Add raspberries; continue to cook 3 minutes. Remove from heat; stir in kirsch. Serve warm or chilled over cake. Yield: 2½ cups.

Note: Leftover cake may be tightly covered, refrigerated, and served at a later date; cake becomes more moist while standing. Raspberry Sauce may be covered and refrigerated until ready to use.

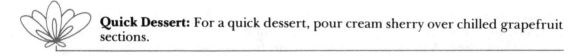

Quick Dessert: For a quick dessert, pour cream sherry over chilled grapefruit sections.

After Theater Chinese Supper

Pearl Balls
or
Egg Rolls
Pepper Steak
Frozen Orange Cream

Serves 8

A delightful meal to come home to! Freeze the uncooked egg rolls and dessert up to 1 month in advance. Pre-cook the beef and cut up the vegetables for the entrée before you go out. Then you can reheat or fry the egg rolls, cook the rice, and finish the entrée in a matter of minutes when you return.

Pearl Balls

1 cup glutinous rice
2 cups cold water
1 pound ground pork
2 scallions, minced
2 slices fresh gingerroot, minced
6 water chestnuts, minced
1 egg, beaten
2 tablespoons soy sauce

1 tablespoon sherry
1 tablespoon water
2 teaspoons cornstarch
1 teaspoon sugar
¼ teaspoon salt
Sweet and Sour Sauce (page 236)
Hot Mustard Sauce (page 236)

Soak rice in water for 1½ hours. Drain. Spread on paper towels to dry. Set aside.

Combine remaining ingredients. Shape into 1-inch balls. Spread rice on a flat plate. Roll pork balls in rice to cover meat.

Place paper towels in steamer basket; arrange balls 1½ inches apart on paper towels. Steam on rack 45 minutes to 1 hour.

Serve with Sweet and Sour Sauce and Hot Mustard Sauce. Yield: 8 servings.

Fresh Gingerroot: To preserve fresh gingerroot for later use, peel and slice or grate it. Place in an airtight container and store in the freezer until needed.

Egg Rolls

Uncooked egg rolls can be frozen; partially thaw in the refrigerator before cooking. Leftover egg roll wrappers may be frozen and reserved for later use.

¼ cup plus 2 tablespoons vegetable
    oil, divided
½ pound ground pork
½ pound uncooked medium
    shrimp, peeled and minced
¼ cup soy sauce
2 tablespoons sherry
½ teaspoon salt
2 cloves garlic, minced
Pinch of sugar
2 cups chopped celery

1 cup chopped water chestnuts
8 green onions, chopped
2 cups fresh bean sprouts, chopped
2 tablespoons cornstarch
2 tablespoons water
2 (1-pound) packages egg roll
    wrappers
Vegetable oil
Sweet and Sour Sauce
Hot Mustard Sauce

Place 2 tablespoons oil in a preheated wok, coating sides; allow to heat at medium-high (325°) for 2 minutes. Crumble pork into wok; stir-fry 2 minutes or until pork is lightly browned. Remove from wok and drain well on paper towels.

Combine shrimp, soy sauce, sherry, salt, garlic, and sugar in a small mixing bowl; add to preheated wok. Stir-fry 2 minutes or until shrimp is pink. Remove mixture from wok; set aside.

Heat remaining ¼ cup oil in wok. Add celery and water chestnuts; stir-fry 4 minutes. Add green onion and bean sprouts; stir-fry 2 minutes or until vegetables are crisp-tender.

Combine cornstarch and water, stirring well. Add pork, shrimp mixture, and cornstarch mixture to wok. Cook, stirring constantly, 1 minute or until mixture is slightly thickened. Remove mixture from wok; chill.

Spoon about 3 tablespoons of chilled filling in center of each egg roll wrapper. Fold top corner of wrapper over filling, then fold left and right corners over filling. Lightly brush exposed corner of wrapper with water. Tightly roll the filled end of the wrapper toward the exposed corner; gently press to seal. Repeat procedure until all egg rolls have been formed and sealed.

Fry egg rolls in deep, hot oil (375°) about 2 minutes or until golden brown; drain well on paper towels. Serve with Sweet and Sour Sauce and Hot Mustard Sauce. Yield: about 1½ dozen egg rolls.

Sweet and Sour Sauce

½ cup plus 2 tablespoons orange
    marmalade

2 tablespoons vinegar
2 teaspoons Worcestershire sauce

Combine all ingredients, stirring well. Yield: about ¾ cup.

Hot Mustard Sauce

¼ cup dry mustard
¼ cup beer

2 drops vinegar

Combine all ingredients, stirring well. Yield: about ¼ cup.

Pepper Steak

¼ cup plus 1 tablespoon vegetable
  oil, divided
¼ cup soy sauce
2 tablespoons sherry
1 teaspoon ground ginger
½ teaspoon sugar
1 (2-pound) boneless beef chuck
  roast, trimmed and cut across
  grain into ⅛-inch-thick strips
2 medium-size green peppers,
  seeded and cut into lengthwise
  strips

2 medium onions, quartered
2 stalks celery, thinly sliced
1 teaspoon salt
1 tablespoon plus 1 teaspoon
  cornstarch
1 cup water
2 tomatoes, cut into wedges
Hot cooked rice

Combine 2 tablespoons oil, soy sauce, sherry, ginger, and sugar in a medium mixing bowl; stir well to blend. Add meat, tossing lightly to coat well. Cover and marinate 1 hour.

Pour remaining oil around top of preheated wok, coating sides; allow to heat at medium (300°) for 2 minutes. Add beef, and stir-fry 2 to 3 minutes to brown. Reduce heat to low (275°); cover, and simmer 30 minutes, stirring occasionally. (Recipe can be made to this point several hours ahead; complete just before serving.)

Turn heat up to medium high (325°), and add green pepper, onion, celery, and salt. Toss vegetables in wok until crisp and tender (about 5 minutes). Blend cornstarch with water, and pour over vegetables and beef. Cook, stirring constantly, until slightly thickened. Stir in tomatoes; cook an additional 5 minutes. Serve immediately over rice. Yield: 8 servings.

Frozen Orange Cream

Light, easy and very attractive—fresh orange cream served in orange shells.

8 large oranges
½ cup orange juice
2 cups milk

2 cups whipping cream
1 cup sugar
Grated rind of 2 oranges

Slice tops from oranges, scalloping or notching edges, if desired. Gently remove fruit, leaving shells intact, and reserving ½ cup orange juice. Reserve fruit pulp for other recipes. Invert shells onto paper towels to drain.

Combine milk, cream, and sugar in a large saucepan. Bring to a boil; cover, reduce heat, and simmer 5 minutes, stirring frequently. Remove from heat, and stir in reserved orange juice and rind.

Freeze mixture in a shallow pan until partially set. Beat 1 minute at medium speed of electric mixer; spoon mixture into orange shells or into serving bowl. Freeze 2 hours or until firm. Yield: 8 servings.

Note: If lemon flavor is desired, substitute the grated rind and juice of 4 large lemons for orange rind and juice. Spoon into lemon shells.

Favorite Sunday Supper

Cabbage Rolls in Savory Sauce
Carrot-Apple Salad
Fresh Fruit Quick Cake

Serves 8

This is the kind of meal that fills the house with wonderful aromas. Make the savory sauce the day before, if you wish. The Fresh Fruit Quick Cake can be made from a variety of fruits—use whatever is available.

Cabbage Rolls with Savory Sauce

½ cup finely chopped onion
1 tablespoon butter or margarine
½ cup soft breadcrumbs
3 tablespoons milk
½ pound ground chuck
1 egg, lightly beaten
1 cup finely chopped parsley
¼ cup cooked rice

½ teaspoon salt
⅛ teaspoon pepper
⅛ teaspoon paprika
Pinch of red pepper
Pinch of garlic powder
1 large cabbage
Savory Sauce

Sauté onion in butter in a small skillet until tender; set aside.

Combine breadcrumbs and milk in a large mixing bowl, stirring until milk is absorbed. Add reserved sautéed onion, ground chuck, egg, parsley, rice, salt, pepper, paprika, red pepper, and garlic powder; mix well. Set aside.

Turn cabbage core side up. Make an incision across the base of the outermost leaf using a sharp knife. Gently peel away the leaf. Repeat this process until leaves can no longer be removed without tearing.

Make additional incisions around the base of the next outermost leaves. Place cabbage, stem side up, in a colander. Pour boiling water over cabbage until leaves can be easily removed. Repeat procedure until eight leaves have been removed.

Place cabbage leaves in a large Dutch oven with water to cover; bring to a boil. Reduce heat; cover, and simmer for 5 minutes until tender. Remove leaves from boiling water, and plunge quickly into cold water; remove and drain well.

Place 3 tablespoons meat mixture in the base of a cabbage leaf. Roll leaf, jellyroll fashion, until the mid-section is reached. Fold left side of leaf inward, and roll up remaining length of the leaf. Carefully stuff in the open end, using fingertips. Repeat with remaining meat mixture and cabbage leaves.

Place cabbage rolls in a 10- x 6- x 2-inch lightly greased baking dish. Pour 2½ cups Savory Sauce over cabbage rolls. (Remaining sauce may be refrigerated and used later.) Bake at 375° for 45 minutes. Serve immediately. Yield: 8 servings.

Savory Sauce

1 (24-ounce) can tomato juice	1 lemon, quartered
½ cup tomato puree	2 tablespoons apple cider vinegar
½ cup chili sauce	1 tablespoon honey
¼ cup catsup	¼ teaspoon chili powder
¼ cup firmly packed brown sugar	Dash of red pepper
1 medium tomato, quartered	1 bay leaf
1 orange, quartered	

Combine all ingredients in a Dutch oven, stirring well; bring to a boil. Reduce heat, and simmer 1 hour. Remove tomato, fruit, and bay leaf. Cover, and refrigerate until ready to use. Yield: about 1 quart.

Carrot-Apple Salad

6 medium carrots, shredded	½ cup chopped nuts
3 golden delicious apples, finely chopped	1 cup chopped celery
	Mayonnaise

Combine all ingredients in a large bowl. Stir in enough mayonnaise to blend ingredients. Yield: 4 to 6 servings.

Fresh Fruit Quick Cake

1½ cups biscuit mix	2 tablespoons butter or margarine, melted
½ cup plus 2 tablespoons sugar, divided	¼ cup firmly packed dark brown sugar
½ cup milk	½ teaspoon ground cinnamon
1 large egg, beaten	Commercial sour cream (optional)
1 teaspoon grated lemon rind	
2 cups peeled and sliced fresh peaches, nectarines, apples, or pears	

Combine biscuit mix, 2 tablespoons sugar, milk, egg, and lemon rind in a large mixing bowl; beat at medium speed of an electric mixer 30 seconds. Pour batter into a greased 9-inch square baking pan. Arrange fruit slices over batter; drizzle with melted butter.

Combine remaining granulated sugar, brown sugar, and cinnamon in a small mixing bowl; stir well. Sprinkle over fruit. Bake at 400° for 25 minutes or until browned and bubbly. Cut into squares, and serve warm with sour cream, if desired. Yield: 8 to 10 servings.

Quick Spaghetti Supper

Shrimp Italian
Tangy Salad
Italian Bread
Ice Cream with Bourbon Sauce
or
Chocolate Loaf Cake

Serves 8

Keep shrimp, bread, and cake in the freezer, spaghetti sauce on the shelf, and the salad dressing in the refrigerator to prepare this 30-minute meal on any busy night.

Shrimp Italian

2 medium onions, chopped
2 stalks celery, chopped
2 cloves garlic, minced
¼ cup butter or olive oil
1 (32-ounce) jar homestyle spaghetti sauce with mushrooms

½ cup water
2 tablespoons Worcestershire sauce
2½ pounds, uncooked medium shrimp, peeled and deveined
1 (12-ounce) package fettucine or thin spaghetti

Sauté onion, celery, and garlic in butter or olive oil in a large skillet until vegetables are tender. Add spaghetti sauce; rinse jar with ½ cup water, and add to sauce mixture. Stir in Worcestershire sauce and shrimp. Cover, and cook over medium heat 6 to 8 minutes.

Cook fettucine according to package directions. Drain, and place on a serving dish; spoon shrimp sauce over fettucine. Serve immediately. Yield: 8 servings.

Tangy Salad

¼ cup red wine vinegar
2 cloves garlic, minced
1½ teaspoons basil leaves
½ teaspoon dried oregano
½ cup vegetable oil
1 small zucchini, thinly sliced

1 head iceberg or romaine lettuce, torn into pieces
3 green onions, sliced
½ cup ripe olives, sliced (optional)
Salt and pepper

Combine wine vinegar, garlic, basil, oregano, and oil in a small bowl. Whisk until well combined. Pour over vegetables in a large serving bowl. Toss well; add salt and pepper to taste. Yield: 8 servings.

Bourbon Sauce

Delicious over ice cream or any plain cake.

½ cup butter or margarine
1½ cups sugar
1 (5.33-ounce) can undiluted
   evaporated milk

1 egg, beaten
3 tablespoons bourbon

Cream butter and sugar; add milk and beaten egg. Cook in double boiler until thickened. Cool. Add bourbon. Yield: 2 cups.

Note: Rum or sherry may be substituted for bourbon.

Chocolate Loaf Cake

Rich enough without frosting, but luscious with a dollop of ice cream or whipped cream.

¾ cup butter, softened
½ cup firmly packed dark brown
   sugar
½ cup sugar
1 teaspoon vanilla extract
2 eggs
1 cup coarsely chopped pecans or
   walnuts

1¾ cups unsifted all-purpose flour,
   divided
1 teaspoon baking powder
½ teaspoon baking soda
½ cup cocoa
1 (8-ounce) carton yogurt or ⅔ cup
   buttermilk

Cream butter; gradually add sugar and vanilla, beating well. Add eggs, one at a time, beating well after each addition. Beat on high speed for 2 minutes.

Combine nuts with 1 tablespoon flour; set aside. Combine remaining flour, baking powder, soda, and cocoa; add to creamed mixture alternately with yogurt, beginning and ending with flour mixture. Mix well after each addition. Stir in nuts.

Pour batter into a greased, floured, and waxed paper-lined 9- x 5- x 3-inch loafpan. Bake at 350° for 1 hour or until a wooden pick inserted in center comes out clean. Cool in pan 10 minutes; remove cake from pan, and let cool completely. Yield: one 9- x 5-inch loaf.

A Relaxed Evening

Chick-Pea Dip
or
Cucumber Yogurt Dip
Shrimp Balls with Rice
or
Shrimp Athenian
Sautéed Spinach
Double "O" Salad
Mocha Cup Custard
or
Palace White Chocolate Mousse

Serves 6 to 8

What's most relaxing about this colorful, informal dinner is that the timing is up to you. The dips and desserts will hold in the refrigerator for days. Shrimp Athenian cooks in less than 15 minutes; Shrimp Balls with Rice can be prepared the night before and completed at the last minute. Get salad ingredients ready, and clean the spinach early in the day to minimize last-minute fuss.

Chick-Pea Dip

1 (15-ounce) can chick-peas,
    drained, liquid reserved
3 tablespoons sesame seeds
    (optional)
2 tablespoons lemon juice
1 tablespoon salad olives, drained
1 tablespoon ripe olives with 1
    tablespoon juice

1 clove garlic, crushed
½ teaspoon curry powder
⅛ teaspoon red pepper
Pimiento strips for garnish
Pita bread

Combine all ingredients except pimiento and pita bread in food processor or blender; process until pureed. Add as much reserved chick-pea liquid as needed to moisten; process until smooth. Spoon into serving bowl; garnish with pimiento. Serve with pita bread cut into triangles. Yield: about 1½ cups.

Note: Dip can be covered and refrigerated up to 4 days.

Cucumber Yogurt Dip

2 tablespoons pine nuts, toasted
2 anchovies, rinsed and patted dry
1 clove garlic
¼ teaspoon ground cumin
1 cup yogurt
½ large cucumber, peeled, seeded, and cut into chunks
Pita bread

Combine all ingredients except cucumber in food processor or blender; process until smooth. Add cucumber; process until cucumber is chopped. Dip can be covered and refrigerated up to 2 days. Serve with pita bread cut into triangles. Yield: about 1½ cups.

Shrimp Balls with Rice

Make the shrimp balls and the sauce up to 1 day ahead and refrigerate separately. Combine and finish cooking just before serving.

4 slices white bread
2 pounds uncooked medium shrimp, peeled, and deveined
½ cup finely chopped onion
½ cup grated Parmesan cheese
⅓ cup chopped fresh parsley
1 egg, beaten
1 clove garlic, minced
½ teaspoon salt
Dash of pepper
¼ cup vegetable oil
1 small onion, finely chopped
1 clove garlic, minced
1 tablespoon olive oil
1 (6-ounce) can tomato paste
½ cup water
2 (15-ounce) cans tomato sauce
2 tablespoons sugar
Hot cooked rice

Soak bread in water to cover; place in colander, and press out excess water.

Finely chop raw shrimp. Combine shrimp, bread, ½ cup onion, cheese, parsley, egg, 1 clove garlic, salt, and pepper in a large mixing bowl; mix well. Shape mixture into 1-inch balls.

Heat ¼ cup vegetable oil in a large skillet over medium heat. Brown shrimp balls on all sides. Drain on paper towels.

Sauté finely chopped onion and minced garlic in 1 tablespoon olive oil in a Dutch oven until vegetables are tender. Add next 4 ingredients. Bring to a boil; reduce heat, and simmer, uncovered, 10 minutes. Add shrimp balls; simmer, uncovered, 30 minutes, stirring occasionally. Serve over rice. Yield: 8 servings.

 Too Salty Soup or Sauce: A dash of brown sugar won't sweeten the sauce or spoil the flavor, but it will reduce a too-salty taste in soup or sauce.

Shrimp Athenian

¼ cup butter or margarine
2 tablespoons all-purpose flour
1½ cups chicken broth, heated
2 tablespoons lemon juice
⅛ teaspoon ground mace
⅛ teaspoon red pepper

1 whole pimiento, diced
1½ pounds cooked shrimp, peeled
  and deveined
3 cups hot cooked rice
½ cup (4 ounces) shredded
  Longhorn cheese

Melt butter in a large skillet over low heat; add flour, stirring until smooth. Cook 1 minute, stirring constantly. Gradually add chicken broth; cook over medium heat, stirring constantly, until mixture is thickened and bubbly. Add lemon juice, mace, pepper, and pimiento; stir in shrimp.

Spoon shrimp mixture over rice on a serving plate. Sprinkle with shredded cheese. Yield: 6 to 8 servings.

Sautéed Spinach

The spinach will taste freshest if you pour off liquid from the pan as it accumulates. Clean the spinach in advance, and the cooking takes only a few minutes.

2 tablespoons olive oil
2 tablespoons vegetable oil
4 large cloves garlic, chopped
2 pounds spinach, well cleaned and
  thoroughly drained

Black pepper
Lemon wedges (optional)

Heat 1 tablespoon olive oil and 1 tablespoon vegetable oil in large, heavy skillet. Add half of garlic; cook over medium heat 2 minutes. Increase heat to high. Add one-fourth of spinach; cook, tossing to coat with oil, until wilted. Push cooked spinach to sides of skillet; add another one-fourth of spinach and cook until wilted. Remove spinach to serving plate with slotted spoon; keep warm in low oven. Pour off liquid from skillet and wipe dry. Repeat with remaining oil, garlic, and spinach. Sprinkle with freshly ground pepper and garnish plate with lemon wedges, if desired. Yield: 6 to 8 servings.

Double "O" Salad

8 Boston lettuce leaves, cleaned
    and dried
8 navel oranges, peeled and
    sectioned

1 large red onion, sliced into rings
Lemon Sherry Dressing

Place lettuce leaves on a large serving plate. Arrange orange sections and onion rings over lettuce. Cover with Lemon Sherry Dressing. Serve immediately. Yield: 8 servings.

Lemon Sherry Dressing

¾ cup fresh lemon juice
¾ cup golden sherry

¾ cup sugar
½ teaspoon salt

Combine all ingredients in a jar; shake vigorously. Refrigerate. Yield: about 2 cups.

Mocha Cup Custard

A light dessert with the tempting bouquet of chocolate and coffee.

2 cups boiling water
2 cups half-and-half
⅔ cup grated sweet baking
    chocolate
1 tablespoon plus 1 teaspoon
    instant coffee granules
4 eggs

2 egg yolks
½ cup plus 2 tablespoons sugar
¼ teaspoon salt
Sweetened whipped cream
1 tablespoon grated sweet baking
    chocolate

Combine boiling water, half-and-half, ⅔ cup chocolate, and coffee in a heavy saucepan; cook over medium heat until mixture reaches 180° on a candy thermometer.

Combine eggs, egg yolks, sugar, and salt in a large mixing bowl; mix well. Add coffee mixture to egg mixture; stir well.

Pour custard into eight 6-ounce custard cups. Place cups in a pan of hot water, and bake at 325° for 45 minutes or until a knife inserted in center comes out clean. Transfer individual custards to a cooling rack. Cool to room temperature; chill thoroughly.

Garnish each serving with a dollop of sweetened whipped cream, and sprinkle with remaining tablespoon of chocolate. Yield: 8 servings.

 To Make Chocolate Curls: Use a vegetable peeler to make chocolate curls. Pull the peeler firmly down the flat surface of a chocolate bar.

Palace White Chocolate Mousse

1 pound white chocolate, grated	2 cups whipping cream
½ cup sugar	Strawberry Sauce
¼ cup water	Fresh strawberry slices (optional)
4 egg whites	Fresh mint leaves (optional)

Place white chocolate in top of a double boiler over simmering, not boiling, water. Heat, stirring constantly, until chocolate melts. Remove from heat, and set aside.

Combine sugar and water in a small saucepan. Cook over medium heat, stirring frequently, until mixture comes to a boil and sugar is dissolved. Continue cooking mixture, stirring frequently, until candy thermometer registers soft ball stage (240°).

Beat egg whites (at room temperature) in a large mixing bowl until soft peaks form. Slowly pour hot syrup in a thin stream over beaten egg whites while beating at medium speed of electric mixer.

Continue beating at medium speed of electric mixer, and slowly add reserved white chocolate. Turn mixer to high speed, and continue beating until stiff peaks form and mixture is thick. Cool to room temperature.

Beat whipping cream in a large mixing bowl until soft peaks form; gently fold into egg white mixture.

Line eight individual dessert plates or bowls with Strawberry Sauce; attractively pipe or mound mousse in center. Chill 4 hours or until set.

Garnish mousse with strawberry slices and mint leaves, if desired. Serve immediately. Yield: 8 servings.

Strawberry Sauce

1 quart fresh strawberries, washed, hulled, and pureed	2 tablespoons kirsch or other cherry-flavored brandy
¼ cup sugar	

Combine all ingredients in a small mixing bowl; stir well. Cover and chill thoroughly. Yield: 8 servings.

Page 247: *Combine the varied textures of Winter Vegetable Salad and Honey Wheat Bread with the creamy smoothness of Canadian Cheese Soup for a Hearty Soup Supper (page 228). A quick Apple Pie completes the meal.*

Page 248: *Invite friends to come for coffee, and set out a tempting array of sweets. From top: Chocolate Pound Cake (page 267), sliced Brown Bread (page 253), Lemon Cream Loaf (page 253), Miniature Apricot Almond Tarts (page 260), Cran-Apple Bread (page 252), and whipped cream cheese for spreading.*

Come For Coffee And . . .

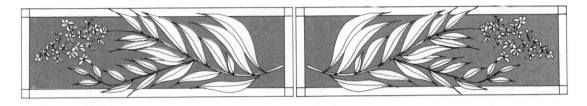

There's no need to forego company just because there's no time to prepare a whole meal. Indeed, there are many occasions for getting together when lunch or dinner would not be appropriate. Yet, a little something to eat remains the symbol of welcome all over the world. And in America, hospitality also means a waiting pot of coffee.

There are all kinds of ways to turn this formula into comfortable invitations to sit and talk. The classic mode is the morning coffee break—a cozy interlude highlighted by a warm-from-the-oven sweet bread or cake. Afternoon tea is gaining popularity here for the same reason it's long been enjoyed abroad—a snack in late afternoon really does revive energy between lunch and a late dinner. If the British notion of tea with tiny sandwiches and sweets sounds too alien, consider the afternoon pastime of Paris, Vienna, and Rome—a cup of hot coffee with a delectable piece of cake.

Translate the custom into an evening gathering, and you're more likely to be able to round up working friends. The principle remains the same as that followed in Europe where rich pastries are rarely served with a meal. You can better appreciate a dense, chocolaty pie or a butter-moist cake if it plays a starring role. And you can delight guests with a choice of such treats if there are no other culinary claims on your time or their appetites.

There's always been an American penchant for dessert parties during the holiday season, when greetings are often exchanged over eggnog or punch with fruitcake and cookies. But there's no reason to limit the season for such festivities. The logistics of serving beverages and do-ahead sweets allows you to accommodate a large group at a flexible hour year-round.

Browse through this chapter and you'll find that "Come for Coffee and . . ." can be concluded with temptations as diverse as Cran-Apple Bread, Chocolate Mousse Pie, and Miniature Apricot Almond Tarts. The batter breads, fruitcakes, and Christmas cookies will no doubt remind you that treats that go well with coffee also make mouthwatering gifts.

Grandmother's Eggnog

This delectable recipe has been served in our family for over 100 years. It came from Grandmother Garner and was always used to toast the New Year.

1 dozen eggs, separated
¾ cup sugar, divided
1½ cups brandy

2 cups whipping cream, whipped
Ground nutmeg

Beat egg whites (at room temperature) until foamy. Gradually add ¼ cup plus 2 tablespoons sugar; continue beating until stiff peaks form.

Beat egg yolks until lemon colored in a large bowl. Gradually add remaining sugar, beating until thick; stir in brandy.

Fold beaten whites and whipped cream into yolk mixture. Spoon into punch cups and sprinkle with nutmeg. Chill. Yield: 24 servings.

Percolator Hot Spiced Cranberry Punch

An invigorating punch for a cold winter's night and festive enough for a holiday gathering.

2 quarts unsweetened pineapple
  juice
2 quarts cranberry juice cocktail
4¼ cups water
2 or 3 drops red food coloring
  (optional)
1 cup firmly packed dark brown
  sugar

1 tablespoon plus 1 teaspoon whole
  cloves
4 (3-inch) sticks cinnamon, broken
  into pieces
¼ teaspoon salt

Place first 4 ingredients in bottom of 30-cup percolator. Place remaining 4 ingredients in percolator basket. Allow mixture to percolate 30 to 35 minutes; serve hot.

If you do not have a large percolator, tie the cloves and cinnamon in a cheesecloth bag. Place remaining ingredients in a large Dutch oven and cook over medium heat until mixture begins to boil. Lower heat and allow punch to simmer for at least 30 minutes. Taste for spicy flavor; if necessary, cook 5 or 10 additional minutes. Remove cheesecloth bag. Yield: 1½ gallons.

Hot Cocoa

¼ cup plus 1 tablespoon cocoa
½ cup sugar
Dash of salt

2 tablespoons hot water
1 quart milk
¾ teaspoon vanilla extract

Combine dry ingredients; place in a saucepan and stir in water. Stir and bring to a boil. Boil 2 minutes, stirring constantly. Add milk and stir, but do not let mixture boil. Remove from heat and add vanilla. Beat mixture with a wire whisk until foamy. Yield: 4 cups.

Peppermint Patty

3 packages hot cocoa mix or
   4 cups hot cocoa
½ cup peppermint schnapps

Whipped cream
Maraschino cherries

Dissolve cocoa mix in boiling water. Pour hot cocoa into four cups. Add 2 tablespoons schnapps to each cup. Garnish with whipped cream and a cherry. Yield: 4 servings.

Hot Buttered Rum

1 tablespoon brown sugar
Cinnamon
2 cloves
¼ cup water

2 teaspoons butter
2 tablespoons applejack or apple
   brandy
2 tablespoons rum

Combine brown sugar, a pinch of cinnamon, cloves, water, and butter in a brandy snifter. Add applejack and rum; mix well. Fill snifter with hot water. Yield: 1 serving.

Homemade Lemonade Mix

To make 1 glass of lemonade, put 3 tablespoons of mix in a glass, add ice, and fill with water; stir. To make 1 gallon of lemonade, combine entire recipe with 1 gallon of water, add ice, and stir well.

2 cups fresh lemon juice
½ cup sugar

1 cup light corn syrup

Combine all ingredients in a quart jar. Shake well, cover, and store in refrigerator; shake well before using. This may be used in mixed drinks also. Yield: 3½ cups.

Margaret Mosley's Easy Fruit Punch

2 tablespoons citric acid
2½ cups sugar
4 cups boiling water
8 cups cold water
3 cups unsweetened pineapple
   juice

1 (6-ounce) can frozen orange juice,
   thawed
½ cup cranberry juice cocktail
1 (23-ounce) bottle ginger ale,
   chilled

Dissolve citric acid and sugar in boiling water. Combine citric acid-sugar mixture with cold water, pineapple juice, orange juice, and cranberry juice; stir well. Add ginger ale just before serving, stirring well. Serve punch over ice. Yield: about 6 quarts.

Applesauce Nut Bread

1 cup sugar
2 cups all-purpose flour
1 tablespoon baking powder
½ teaspoon baking soda
1 teaspoon salt

½ teaspoon ground nutmeg
1 cup coarsely chopped pecans
1 cup unsweetened applesauce
¼ cup vegetable oil
2 large eggs, beaten

Combine sugar, flour, baking powder, soda, salt, and nutmeg in a small mixing bowl; stir in pecans to coat well. Set aside.

Combine applesauce, oil, and eggs in a medium mixing bowl; mix until well blended. Gradually stir in dry ingredients, stirring just until blended. Pour mixture into a greased and floured 8½- x 4½- x 3-inch loafpan. Bake at 350° for 1 hour or until a wooden pick inserted in center comes out clean. Cool 10 minutes in pan. Remove from pan, and cool completely on a wire rack. Yield: 1 loaf.

Cran-Apple Bread

¼ cup butter or margarine,
    softened
1 cup sugar
1 egg
2 cups sifted all-purpose flour,
    divided
1½ teaspoons baking powder
½ teaspoon baking soda
½ teaspoon salt

½ teaspoon ground cinnamon
¼ teaspoon ground mace
1 tablespoon grated orange rind
¾ cup orange juice
1 medium cooking apple, peeled,
    cored, and chopped
1 cup fresh cranberries, chopped
1 cup chopped pecans or walnuts

Cream butter; gradually add sugar, beating well. Add egg, beating well. Set aside 2 tablespoons flour. Combine remaining flour, baking powder, soda, salt, cinnamon, and mace in a medium mixing bowl; stirring well. Add to creamed mixture alternately with orange juice, beginning and ending with flour mixture.

Dredge chopped apple, cranberries, pecans, and orange rind in remaining flour; fold into batter. Spoon batter into a greased and waxed paper-lined 9- x 5- x 3-inch loafpan. Bake at 350° for 1 hour and 10 minutes or until a wooden pick inserted in the center comes out clean. Cool in pan 10 minutes; remove from pan, and cool completely on wire racks. Yield: 1 loaf.

Note: This bread tastes even better if allowed to stand overnight. It also freezes well.

Teatime Tips: Tea comes in so many blends that you can easily delight guests by offering a choice of two or three. For best flavor, follow the classic English brewing formula: Rinse the teapot with boiling water; then add fresh tea leaves (1 teaspoon per cup and 1 for the pot) and 1 inch of boiling water. Let the leaves steep for a few minutes before filling the pot with boiling water. Pour through a tea strainer. Provide another potful of boiling water to dilute the tea if it becomes too strong on standing.

Louise Mayhall's Brown Bread

Serve thin slices of Brown Bread spread with softened cream cheese.

3 tablespoons sugar
2 cups whole wheat flour
2 teaspoons baking powder
1 teaspoon salt
1 cup wheat bran cereal

½ teaspoon baking soda
2 cups buttermilk
1 cup molasses
1 cup raisins

Sift together sugar, flour, baking powder, and salt into a large mixing bowl; stir in cereal, mixing well.

Add soda to buttermilk, stirring to dissolve soda; add buttermilk mixture and molasses to flour mixture, beating well. Fold in raisins.

Pour batter into two greased and waxed paper-lined 7½- x 3- x 2-inch loafpans. Bake at 350° for 1 hour and 10 minutes or until a wooden pick inserted in center comes out clean. Cool in pans 10 minutes; remove from pans, and cool on wire racks. Yield: 2 loaves.

Note: After bread has cooled, wrap airtight and store in a cool place. It freezes well and can be frozen for 3 months.

Lemon Cream Loaf

½ cup finely chopped pecans
1 tablespoon grated lemon rind
2½ cups all-purpose flour, divided
½ cup shortening
1 (8-ounce) package cream cheese,
  softened

1⅓ cups sugar
2 eggs
1 tablespoon baking powder
1 teaspoon salt
1 cup milk
Lemon Glaze

Dredge pecans and lemon rind in 1 tablespoon flour in a small mixing bowl; stir well and set aside.

Cream shortening and cream cheese in a large mixing bowl; gradually add sugar, beating well. Add eggs, one at a time, beating well after each addition.

Combine remaining flour, baking powder, and salt; add to creamed mixture alternately with milk, beginning and ending with flour mixture. Mix well after each addition. Stir in reserved dredged mixture.

Pour batter into two well-greased 8½- x 4½- x 3-inch loafpans. Bake at 350° for 1 hour or until a wooden pick inserted in center comes out clean. Brush Lemon Glaze over loaves immediately. Cool in pans 20 minutes; remove from pans, and cool completely on wire racks. Yield: 2 loaves.

Lemon Glaze

1 tablespoon grated lemon rind
¼ cup lemon juice

¼ cup sugar

Combine all ingredients in a small mixing bowl; stir well. Yield: about ¼ cup.

Mandelbrot

A delectable, crunchy round to serve with coffee or sherry.

1 cup chopped almonds or pecans	4 eggs
1½ cups all-purpose flour, divided	½ cup vegetable oil
¾ cup sugar	¼ cup butter or margarine, melted
2 teaspoons baking powder	2 teaspoons vanilla extract
⅛ teaspoon salt	1 teaspoon almond extract

Seal the ends of 2 greased baguette pans with aluminum foil. Set aside.

Dredge almonds in 1 tablespoon flour; set aside. Combine remaining flour, sugar, baking powder, and salt in a large mixing bowl. Add eggs; beat on medium speed of electric mixer until blended. Add vegetable oil, butter, and flavorings; beat until blended. Stir in nuts.

Pour batter evenly into prepared baguette pans; bake at 350° for 30 minutes or until a wooden pick inserted in the center comes out clean. Cool in pans 10 minutes; remove from pans and cool completely. Slice each loaf into ¾-inch-thick slices and place rounds on 2 ungreased cookie sheets in a single layer. Bake at 250° for 30 minutes. Turn each round over, and bake an additional 45 minutes. Cool completely and store in an airtight container. Yield: about 3 dozen slices.

Laurin Stamm's Raisin Bran Muffins

This delicious muffin batter keeps for 6 weeks refrigerated. Store in a covered plastic container and scoop out the amount you need to bake fresh muffins for any meal.

1 (15-ounce) box raisin bran cereal	2 teaspoons salt
3 cups sugar	4 eggs, lightly beaten
5 cups all purpose flour	1 cup vegetable oil
5 teaspoons baking soda	1 quart buttermilk

Combine first 5 ingredients in a large bowl. Add eggs, vegetable oil, and buttermilk; blend well. If not baking at once, pour mixture into plastic container; cover and refrigerate. When ready to bake, spoon batter into well-greased muffin pans, filling two-thirds full. Bake at 400° for 20 minutes. Yield: about 5 dozen.

 Dredging: To prevent fruit or nuts from sinking to the bottom of bread or cake batter, shake them in a bag with a small amount of flour to coat lightly before adding to batter.

Strawberry Muffins

½ cup butter or margarine,
   softened
1 cup sugar
2 eggs
2 cups all-purpose flour
1½ teaspoons baking powder

¼ teaspoon salt
½ cup milk
1 teaspoon lemon extract
1 cup fresh strawberries, chopped
1 tablespoon cinnamon sugar

Cream butter; gradually add sugar and eggs; cream until light and fluffy. Sift together flour, baking powder, and salt; add to creamed mixture alternately with milk, beginning and ending with flour mixture. Add lemon extract, and gently fold in strawberries.

Spoon batter into well-greased muffin pans, filling two-thirds full. Sprinkle with cinnamon sugar. Bake at 375° for 15 to 18 minutes. Yield: about 2 dozen.

Kugelhopf

1 cup white raisins
5 tablespoons kirsch
4 cups all-purpose flour, divided
1 package yeast
½ teaspoon sugar
1¾ cups warm milk (105° to 115°),
   divided

1 cup butter, melted
2 eggs, lightly beaten
¾ cup sugar
⅛ teaspoon salt
½ cup toasted slivered almonds

Soak raisins in kirsch for 30 minutes; drain and roll in 2 tablespoons flour.

Dissolve yeast and ½ teaspoon sugar in ¼ cup warm milk. Stir well; cover and let stand at room temperature 5 minutes or until bubbly. Combine remaining warm milk, melted butter, and remaining flour; stir well. Add yeast mixture and eggs; mix well.

Add raisins, ¾ cup sugar, and salt to the flour mixture. Beat about 20 minutes or until the dough leaves the sides of the bowl.

Grease a 12-cup Bundt pan; sprinkle the bottom with almonds and pour in the batter. Cover, and let rise in a warm place (85°), free from drafts, 1 hour or until doubled in bulk. Bake at 350° for 1 hour or until a wooden pick inserted in center comes out clean. Cool in pan for 10 minutes; remove from pan and cool completely. Yield: 12 to 14 servings.

Honeycomb Coffee Cake

This salt-free coffee cake has a delicious flavor!

½ cup unsalted butter or
   margarine, softened
½ cup sugar
1¾ cups all-purpose flour
2 teaspoons baking powder

2 eggs
⅓ cup milk
½ teaspoon almond extract
½ teaspoon orange extract
Topping

Cream butter and sugar in large bowl of electric mixer, beating until light and fluffy.
Combine flour and baking powder; add to creamed mixture with eggs, milk, and flavorings. Beat on medium speed for 2 to 3 minutes, scraping sides of bowl often. Spread batter into a greased 9-inch square cake pan. Set aside and quickly make Topping.
Pour Topping evenly over cake. Bake at 350° for 25 to 30 minutes. Yield: 12 servings.

Topping

½ cup unsalted butter or margarine
½ cup chopped pecans
¼ cup sugar
¼ cup honey
½ teaspoon nutmeg

½ teaspoon ground cinnamon
1 tablespoon milk
1 teaspoon orange extract
1 teaspoon grated orange peel

Combine all ingredients in a heavy saucepan, and cook over medium heat, stirring occasionally until mixture comes to a full boil, about 6 minutes. Allow mixture to boil 2 to 3 minutes. Pour over coffee cake. Yield: topping for one 9-inch coffee cake.

Tahitian Coffee Cake

Lots of fruit flavor in an unusual yeast cake.

1 (8-ounce) can crushed pineapple,
   undrained
¾ cup butter or margarine, divided
½ cup firmly packed dark brown
   sugar
1 teaspoon ground cinnamon
1 teaspoon light corn syrup
½ cup flaked coconut
2 bananas, cut into ½-inch slices

2 cups bread flour, divided
½ cup sugar
½ teaspoon salt
1 package dry yeast
¼ cup milk
¼ cup water
3 eggs
Maraschino cherries, halved
   (optional)

Combine pineapple and juice, ¼ cup butter, brown sugar, cinnamon, and corn syrup in a medium saucepan. Bring mixture to a boil. Remove from heat, and spoon into an ungreased 9-inch square baking pan. Sprinkle evenly with coconut; arrange bananas over coconut.

Combine ½ cup flour, sugar, salt, and yeast in a large mixing bowl. Combine milk, water, and remaining butter in a small saucepan; heat to 130°. Gradually add milk mixture to yeast mixture, beating constantly. Beat at medium speed of electric mixer 2 minutes. Add eggs and remaining flour; beat at high speed of electric mixer 2 minutes.

Pour batter evenly over bananas in pan. Let rise in a warm place (85°), free from drafts, 1 hour or until doubled in bulk.

Bake at 375° for 30 minutes or until wooden pick inserted in center comes out clean. Cool in pan 15 minutes; invert onto serving dish. Garnish with cherries, if desired. Cut into 2-inch squares, and serve warm. Yield: 16 servings.

Becky Hoggard's Orange Rolls

1 (13¾-ounce) package hot roll mix
¼ cup lukewarm water (105° to 115°)
1 (8-ounce) carton commercial sour cream
1 egg, lightly beaten
2 teaspoons baking powder
2 teaspoons orange juice concentrate, thawed

½ cup sugar
½ cup chopped pecans
¼ cup butter or margarine, melted
2 tablespoons grated orange rind
2 cups sifted powdered sugar
2 tablespoons milk
1 tablespoon butter or margarine, melted

Dissolve yeast package from roll mix in lukewarm water in a small mixing bowl, stirring well; let stand 5 minutes or until bubbly.

Combine sour cream, egg, baking powder, and orange juice concentrate in a large mixing bowl, stirring well. Stir in yeast mixture and hot roll mix; turn dough out onto a floured surface, and knead 8 to 10 times.

Combine sugar, pecans, ¼ cup melted butter, and orange rind in a small mixing bowl, stirring well. Roll dough to a 16- x 12-inch rectangle; sprinkle sugar mixture evenly over surface of dough, leaving about a 1-inch margin on all sides.

Roll dough up, jellyroll fashion, beginning at long side; moisten edges with water to seal. Cut roll in 1-inch slices; twist each slice into a figure 8 shape, and place in a greased 13- x 9- x 2-inch baking pan. Cover and let rise in a warm place (85°), free from drafts, 1 hour or until doubled in bulk.

Bake at 350° for 20 minutes or until lightly browned. Combine powdered sugar, milk, and 1 tablespoon melted butter, mixing well; drizzle over warm rolls. Immediately remove from pan, and serve. Yield: 1½ dozen.

Dessert Wines to Sip with Sweets: Sherry and dessert wines can taste delicious with cakes and cookies that aren't too sweet. Offer both a cream and a dry sherry to please all palates. Choose a sparkling dessert wine, such as an Italian asti spumanti or German sekt, if the occasion is festive.

Florence Wallace's Black Bottom Pie

The recipe makes 5 pies. These freeze beautifully and make wonderful gifts.

5 cups milk
10 eggs, separated
2½ cups sugar, divided
1½ teaspoons all-purpose flour
6 envelopes unflavored gelatin
1 cup cold water
8 (1-ounce) squares semi-sweet
   chocolate

2 tablespoons vanilla extract,
   divided
5 (9-inch) Gingersnap Piecrusts
½ teaspoon cream of tartar
1½ (12-ounce) cartons frozen
   whipped topping, thawed

Place milk in the top of a double boiler; cook over simmering water until bubbles appear around the edge of the pan. Remove from heat.

Beat egg yolks in a large mixing bowl until light and lemon colored. Add 1½ cups sugar and flour, mixing well. Gradually stir ½ cup of the hot milk into yolk mixture; add to remaining milk in top of double boiler. Cook over simmering water, stirring constantly, until mixture thickens and coats a metal spoon. Remove from heat.

Dissolve gelatin in cold water; add to hot mixture, stirring well. Remove 1½ cups hot mixture; place in small mixing bowl. Chill remaining mixture.

Melt 7½ squares chocolate in top of a double boiler; reserve remaining chocolate. Stir melted chocolate into reserved 1½ cups custard; add 1 tablespoon vanilla extract, mixing well. Pour filling into prepared piecrusts; tilt pans to coat sides of crusts with the filling. Chill until set.

Beat egg whites (at room temperature) until foamy; gradually add remaining sugar, cream of tartar, and remaining vanilla, beating until stiff peaks form. Fold into chilled custard. Spoon filling over chocolate mixture; cover with plastic wrap and refrigerate overnight. Two hours before serving, top with whipped topping; grate remaining chocolate and sprinkle over pies. Refrigerate until serving. Yield: five (9-inch) pies.

Gingersnap Piecrusts

8 cups gingersnap crumbs   1 cup butter or margarine, melted

Combine gingersnap crumbs and butter in a medium mixing bowl; mix well. Press mixture into bottom and sides of five lightly greased 9-inch pieplates. Bake at 350° for 8 minutes. Cool. Yield: five (9-inch) piecrusts.

Betty Kruger's Chocolate Mousse Pie

4 (1-ounce) squares semisweet
   chocolate
3 ounces milk chocolate
½ cup plus 2 tablespoons butter or
   margarine
8 large eggs, separated

¼ cup Cognac
Chocolate Crumb Crust
1 cup whipping cream
3 tablespoons sugar
½ teaspoon vanilla extract
Grated chocolate

Combine semisweet chocolate, milk chocolate, and butter in the top of a double boiler placed over simmering water. Stir constantly until melted. Add egg yolks, one at a time, beating well after each addition; remove from heat. Cool slightly; stir in Cognac.

Beat egg whites (at room temperature) in a large mixing bowl until stiff but not dry; fold chocolate mixture into beaten egg whites.

Spoon mixture into Chocolate Crumb Crust; cover and refrigerate overnight.

Beat whipping cream in a small mixing bowl until foamy; gradually add sugar and vanilla, beating until soft peaks form. Spread over chocolate mixture; sprinkle with grated chocolate. Yield: one 10-inch pie.

Chocolate Crumb Crust

1 (8½-ounce) package crisp chocolate wafers, finely crushed

½ cup butter or margarine, melted
¼ cup sifted powdered sugar

Combine all ingredients in a medium mixing bowl; mix until well blended. Firmly press mixture into bottom and sides of a lightly greased 10-inch pieplate. Bake at 350° for 8 minutes. Cool. Yield: one 10-inch piecrust.

Catherine Hagaman's Brownie Pie

2 squares unsweetened chocolate
½ cup butter
1 cup sugar
¼ cup all-purpose flour
2 large eggs

¼ teaspoon salt
1 teaspoon vanilla extract
½ cup chopped pecans
Whipped cream
Maraschino cherries

Melt chocolate and butter in a heavy saucepan over low heat; remove from heat. Combine sugar and flour; stir into chocolate mixture. Add eggs and mix thoroughly. Add salt, vanilla, and pecans. Pour into buttered 9-inch piepan and bake at 325° for 25 to 30 minutes. Filling should still be moist. Serve warm topped with whipped cream and maraschino cherries. Yield: 8 servings.

Chocolate Chess Pie

Chocolaty and heavenly—calorie watchers, beware!

1 cup sugar
¼ cup cocoa
¼ cup butter or margarine, melted
⅛ teaspoon salt
2 large eggs, lightly beaten

1 (5.33-ounce) can evaporated milk, undiluted
2 teaspoons vanilla extract
¾ cup coarsely chopped pecans
1 (9-inch) unbaked pastry shell

Blend sugar, cocoa, melted butter, and salt in large mixing bowl. Add beaten eggs and beat by hand or on medium speed of electric mixer for 2 to 3 minutes. Add milk and vanilla; stir in pecans and pour mixture into pastry shell. Bake at 350° for 45 minutes. Cool before cutting. Yield: one 9-inch pie.

Miniature Apricot Almond Tarts

1 cup all-purpose flour
¼ cup plus 3 tablespoons sifted
    powdered sugar, divided
¼ cup plus 2 tablespoons butter
1 large egg, separated
2 teaspoons water
¼ teaspoon almond extract

½ cup almond paste
¼ cup butter or margarine,
    softened
1 tablespoon Grand Marnier or
    other orange-flavored liqueur
½ cup apricot preserves, divided

Combine flour and 3 tablespoons powdered sugar in a medium mixing bowl; cut in ¼ cup plus 2 tablespoons butter with a pastry blender until mixture resembles coarse meal. Combine egg yolk, water, and almond flavoring in a small mixing bowl; beat well. Add to crumbled mixture, stirring with a fork until all dry ingredients are moistened.

Divide dough into 18 equal portions. Place each in a 1¾-inch muffin tin, pressing and molding pastry to line each tin. Set aside.

Crumble almond paste in a medium mixing bowl. Add ¼ cup softened butter, remaining powdered sugar, and Grand Marnier; beat until well blended.

Beat egg white (at room temperature) until stiff peaks form; fold into almond paste mixture.

Spoon 1 teaspoon filling into prepared pastry shells. Bake at 350° for 30 minutes or until pastry is browned. Melt apricot preserves over low heat; spoon over tarts in pans. Allow tarts to cool in pans. Yield: 1½ dozen.

Fournou's Ovens Praline Ice Cream Pie

An elegant dessert—time-consuming but worth all the effort. The praline ice cream filling can be made anytime, and the meringue will hold up to 2 hours. Spread the meringue over the pie and place under the broiler just before serving.

½ cup firmly packed brown sugar
½ cup whipping cream
2 tablespoons butter or margarine,
    melted
2 teaspoons vanilla extract, divided
½ cup finely chopped pecans
1½ quarts vanilla ice cream,
    softened

1 baked (9-inch) pastry shell
3 egg whites
1 tablespoon water
¼ teaspoon cream of tartar
¼ cup plus 2 tablespoons sugar
⅛ teaspoon salt
Rum Sauce

Place brown sugar in a small iron skillet; cook over medium heat, stirring constantly, until sugar dissolves and becomes a golden syrup. Gradually add whipping cream and melted butter, stirring to blend well. Stir in 1 teaspoon vanilla and pecans.

Immediately combine praline mixture and softened ice cream in a large mixing bowl; stir until well blended. Spoon mixture into pastry shell, spreading with a spatula to smooth top. Cover and freeze overnight.

Combine egg whites (at room temperature), water, and cream of tartar in a medium mixing bowl; gradually add sugar, and beat at high speed of an electric mixer 3 minutes or until soft peaks form. Spread meringue over top of frozen pie, sealing to edge of pastry.

Place pie 6 inches from heating element, broiling just long enough to lightly brown the meringue. Drizzle top of pie with warm Rum Sauce; immediately cut into wedges and serve with additional Rum Sauce, if desired. Yield: 8 servings.

Rum Sauce

¼ cup plus 2 tablespoons butter
3 tablespoons sugar
Grated rind of 1 lemon

⅓ cup lemon juice
Dark rum to taste

Melt butter in a small saucepan over low heat. Add sugar, lemon rind, and juice; continue to cook until sugar dissolves, stirring constantly. Remove from heat, and stir in rum. Serve warm. Sauce can be made and held at room temperature. Stir over low heat before serving. Yield: ¾ cup.

Zollie Kimbrough's Coconut Pie

Quick and easy, yet rich and delicious!

3 large eggs, well beaten
1 cup sugar
1 (6-ounce) package frozen grated
    coconut, thawed

¼ cup butter or margarine, melted
3 tablespoons buttermilk
1 unbaked (9-inch) pastry shell

Combine eggs and sugar in a large mixing bowl; beat until light and fluffy. Add coconut, butter, and buttermilk, beating well.

Pour mixture into pastry shell. Bake at 350° for 55 minutes, or until set. Cool slightly before cutting into wedges. Yield: 6 servings.

Coffee to Sip with Sweets: Coffee is most people's first choice with sweets. You can make a fresh potful of regular or decaffeinated coffee even more tantalizing by mixing cardamom pods, whole cloves or allspice, broken cinnamon sticks, or pieces of orange rind (orange part only) into the coffee grounds when you brew them. For mocha coffee, mix equal parts of brewed coffee and hot cocoa in a pot or individual mugs. For after-dinner sipping, lace cups of coffee with coffee-flavored, peppermint, or chocolate liqueur; or use the liqueur to flavor whipped cream to dollop into each serving.

Food Processor Almond Macaroons

A joy to make in the food processor. These macaroons will keep fresh in a sealed container for 2 weeks. If they begin to dry out, quarter an apple and place on top of macaroons.

1 cup (8 ounces) almond paste, divided
1 cup sugar
3 large egg whites
½ teaspoon vanilla extract

1 teaspoon almond extract
3 tablespoons sifted all-purpose flour
⅓ cup powdered sugar, sifted
⅛ teaspoon salt

Position knife blade in food processor bowl; add half of almond paste. Pulse 5 or 6 times until paste is broken down into fine particles; place in a small mixing bowl. Repeat procedure with remaining almond paste.

Combine almond paste, sugar, egg whites, and flavorings in food processor bowl; process about 30 seconds. Add flour, powdered sugar, and salt; process about 1 minute or until mixture is thoroughly blended.

Drop mixture by rounded teaspoonfuls onto brown paper-covered baking pans. Flatten each macaroon with wet fingers. Let stand uncovered for 1 hour. Bake at 300° for 25 to 30 minutes. Remove from oven and slide brown paper onto a damp towel. The macaroons will come up easily with a spatula and can then be placed on a wire rack to cool. Yield: approximately 36 (2-inch) macaroons.

Ladyfingers

4 large eggs, separated
½ cup sugar
½ teaspoon vanilla extract

⅔ cup all-purpose flour, divided
2 tablespoons sifted powdered sugar

Place parchment or waxed paper on two large cookie sheets. Beat egg yolks and sugar until very thick and pale yellow in a small narrow, deep mixing bowl, using high speed of electric mixer.

Beat whites (at room temperature) until very stiff in small bowl. Take half of egg whites and fold into yolk mixture. Fold in flour, a small amount at a time. Fold in remaining whites.

Form 4-inch long fingers on parchment paper using a pastry bag and plain tube. Sprinkle with powdered sugar and bake at 350° for 10 to 15 minutes or until ladyfingers are lightly colored. These do not brown. Yield: approximately 48 ladyfingers.

Priscilla Everett's Rich Chocolate Brownies

2 cups chopped pecans
1½ cups plus 1 tablespoon all-purpose flour, divided
3 cups sugar
8 large eggs

2 teaspoons vanilla extract
¾ cup milk chocolate morsels
¾ cup semisweet chocolate morsels
1 cup unsalted butter, melted and divided

Dredge pecans in 1 tablespoon flour; set aside.

Combine sugar, eggs, and vanilla in a large mixing bowl; beat on high speed of an electric mixer 10 minutes.

Combine milk chocolate morsels, semisweet morsels, and 1 tablespoon melted butter in top of a double boiler. Place over simmering water; cook until chocolate melts, stirring frequently. Cool slightly, and add to beaten egg mixture.

Add remaining flour and melted butter; beat on medium speed until blended. Fold in pecans. Pour batter into greased and floured 15- x 10- x 1-inch jellyroll pan. Bake at 350° for 35 minutes or until a wooden pick inserted in the center comes out clean. Cool and cut into 2-inch squares. Yield: about 3 dozen.

Noel's Crunchy Cookies

A hit-the-spot snack!

½ cup butter or margarine,
   softened
1 cup sugar
1 large egg
1 cup all-purpose flour

1 teaspoon baking powder
¼ teaspoon salt
1 teaspoon vanilla extract
4 cups high-protein rice and wheat
   cereal, crushed and divided

Combine butter, sugar, and egg in a medium mixing bowl; beat at high speed of an electric mixer for 4 minutes.

Sift together flour, baking powder, and salt. Add to creamed mixture, mixing well. Stir in vanilla and 1 cup crushed cereal, mixing well.

Drop batter, 1 tablespoon at a time, into remaining cereal; roll to coat evenly. Place on ungreased cookie sheets, 2 inches apart; bake at 375° for 15 minutes or until lightly browned. Cool on wire racks. Yield: 2 dozen.

Mrs. R. L. Luckey's Coconut Crispies

A lacy cookie with the delicious flavor of coconut.

¼ cup butter, softened
¼ cup shortening
½ cup sugar
½ cup firmly packed light brown
   sugar
1 large egg, lightly beaten
1 teaspoon vanilla extract

1 cup all-purpose flour
½ teaspoon salt
½ teaspoon baking powder
½ teaspoon baking soda
1 cup flaked coconut
1 cup oven toasted rice cereal

Cream butter, shortening, and sugar until light and fluffy, about 4 minutes on medium speed of electric mixer. Add beaten egg and vanilla; beat well. Sift flour, salt, baking powder, and soda into mixture; mix well. Stir in coconut and rice cereal. Drop by teaspoonfuls onto greased cookie sheet; space at least 2 inches apart as batter tends to run. Flatten top of each dropped teaspoonful with bottom of glass dipped in water. Bake at 325° about 12 minutes or until golden brown. Yield: about 4 dozen.

Jo Nicholson's Nürnburger Lebkuchen

The donor of the recipe and her granddaughter, Susan Gear, bake these unusual cookies immediately after Thanksgiving every year. They stay fresh in the pantry through the holidays and can be decorated any way you wish.

1 cup dark brown sugar
1 cup honey
1 cup molasses
½ cup butter or margarine, softened
2 teaspoons baking soda
1½ teaspoons ground cinnamon
1½ teaspoons ground cloves

1 (8-ounce) carton commercial sour cream
½ cup citron
½ cup candied lemon peel
½ cup candied orange peel
½ cup chopped pecans (optional)
7 to 8 cups all-purpose flour
Fresh Lemon Juice Glaze

Combine brown sugar, honey, molasses, and butter in a large mixing bowl; mix well. Add soda, cinnamon, cloves, and sour cream, mixing well. Stir in citron, lemon peel, orange peel, and pecans (if desired). Add flour, mixing well. (Dough will be very sticky.) Cover and refrigerate overnight.

Roll one-fourth of dough to ¼-inch thickness on a lightly floured surface; keep remaining dough chilled. Cut dough into assorted holiday shapes with cookie cutters. Place on lightly greased cookie sheets and bake at 350° for 10 to 12 minutes or until lightly browned. Place cookies on a wire rack; spread Fresh Lemon Juice Glaze over warm cookies. Repeat with remaining dough. Yield: about 6 dozen cookies.

Fresh Lemon Juice Glaze

3½ cups sifted powdered sugar
¼ cup freshly squeezed lemon juice

2 tablespoons water

Combine all ingredients in a small mixing bowl; mix well. Yield: about 1½ cups.

Lib Hollers' Scotch Shortbread

This recipe came from Scotland about 50 years ago.

1 cup butter, softened
½ cup sifted powdered sugar

2 cups sifted all-purpose flour

Blend butter and sugar with pastry blender. Slowly add flour and knead until batter is thoroughly blended. Turn onto a marble slab or working area, and knead until well blended. Divide dough in half, and shape each half into a roll about 2½ to 3 inches in diameter. Place in double waxed paper, roll tightly and twist at both ends. Chill in refrigerator for 1 hour and 30 minutes, no longer. Slice ¼-inch thick and place on ungreased cookie sheet. Bake at 375° for 5 minutes; reduce heat to 325° and bake 20 minutes longer. Cool on wire rack. Place in a tightly sealed container. Keep about 10 days before using for best taste results. Yield: about 40 slices.

Sally C. Walker's Speculaas

A family favorite that comes from old King William Street in San Antonio.

3½ cups all-purpose flour
1 teaspoon baking powder
1 teaspoon cinnamon
1 cup butter, softened
2 cups sugar

3 large eggs, lightly beaten
1 tablespoon lemon juice
Grated rind of 1 lemon (about 1
    rounded tablespoon rind)

Sift flour, baking powder, and cinnamon into a large mixing bowl. Cut in butter with two knives or with pastry blender until dough resembles small peas. Add sugar and work in with pastry blender. Add eggs, lemon juice, and rind; work thoroughly into batter. (This is very sticky dough.) Chill in refrigerator for several hours. Roll dough very thin on marble or floured board.

Using a doughnut cutter or using different cookie cutters, cut shapes of stars or lambs, etc. Place on greased cookie sheet and bake at 350° for 8 to 10 minutes until golden brown around edges. Remove from pan immediately. Store in metal containers when cool. The recipe makes a large amount; you can save some of the dough and finish baking it several days later. Yield: about 8 dozen.

Ruth Boyl's Teacakes

Deliciously crisp, these teacakes will keep a month or two in a sealed container. Sprinkle them with colored sugar or other decorations for the holidays.

½ cup butter, softened
½ cup shortening
1¼ cups sugar
2 large eggs
1 tablespoon milk

3¼ cups all-purpose flour
1 tablespoon baking powder
¼ teaspoon salt
Green and red sugar sprinkles
    (optional)

Cream butter and shortening in a large mixing bowl; gradually add sugar, beating well. Add eggs and milk; beat well.

Sift flour, baking powder, and salt together in a small mixing bowl; gradually add to creamed mixture, stirring well after each addition. Shape dough into a ball. Wrap in waxed paper, and chill at least 30 minutes.

Shape dough into 1-inch balls; place about 2 inches apart on greased cookie sheets. Flatten slightly with palm of hand; sprinkle with green and red sugar, if desired. Bake at 325° for 15 to 20 minutes. Remove to wire racks to cool. Yield: 6 dozen.

Zucchini Treasures

2 cups chopped pecans or walnuts
1 cup white raisins
3 cups all-purpose flour, divided
1 cup softened butter or margarine
2 cups firmly packed dark brown
    sugar
1 teaspoon baking soda
¼ cup cold water

1 teaspoon ground allspice
2 teaspoons ground cinnamon
1 teaspoon ground nutmeg
2 eggs
1½ cups coarsely grated zucchini,
    patted dry
3 tablespoons wheat germ
1 teaspoon vanilla extract

Dredge nuts and raisins in 2 tablespoons flour in a small bowl.

Cream butter and brown sugar in large bowl at medium speed of electric mixer until light and fluffy.

Dissolve soda in cold water. Combine spices with remaining flour, and gradually add to creamed mixture alternating with soda and water mixture. Add eggs one at a time, and beat well after each addition. Add zucchini, wheat germ, and vanilla on low speed; fold in pecans and raisins.

Drop batter by heaping teaspoonfuls onto greased baking sheet. Bake at 350° for 12 to 15 minutes. Remove to wire rack at once and allow to cool completely; then place in tightly sealed canisters. The cookies will keep fresh for a month. Yield: about 7 dozen cookies.

George Belle Cottingham's Angel Food Cake Supreme

1½ cups sifted cake flour
1¾ cups plus 2 tablespoons sugar,
    divided
12 large egg whites
1¼ teaspoons cream of tartar
¼ teaspoon salt

1 teaspoon vanilla extract
¼ teaspoon almond extract
Creamy Seven Minute Frosting
1 (2½-ounce) package sliced
    almonds, toasted

Combine flour and ½ cup sugar in a small mixing bowl; set aside. Combine egg whites (at room temperature), cream of tartar, salt, and flavorings in a large mixing bowl. Beat on high speed of electric mixer until soft peaks form. Add remaining sugar, 2 tablespoons at a time, beating until stiff peaks form.

Sprinkle flour mixture over egg white mixture, ¼ cup at a time; fold in carefully. Pour batter into an ungreased 10-inch tube pan, spreading evenly with a spatula. Bake at 375° for 40 minutes or until cake springs back when lightly touched. Remove from oven, and invert pan. Cool 40 minutes; remove cake from pan, and place on cake stand. Spread frosting over cooled cake, and sprinkle with toasted almonds. Yield: one 10-inch cake.

Creamy Seven Minute Frosting

1½ cups sugar, sifted
2 large egg whites
¼ teaspoon cream of tartar
¼ cup plus 1 tablespoon cold water

1 teaspoon almond extract
1 cup whipping cream, whipped
1 tablespoon amaretto

Combine sugar, egg whites (at room temperature), and cream of tartar in the top of a double boiler. Add water and almond extract; beat on low speed of electric mixer for 30 seconds or just until blended.

Place over rapidly boiling water; beat constantly on high speed of electric mixer about 7 minutes or until stiff peaks form. Remove from heat.

Transfer mixture to a large mixing bowl; place over a bowl of ice. Cool 1 hour, stirring every 30 minutes. Gently fold whipped cream and amaretto into cooled mixture. Use immediately. Yield: enough frosting for one 10-inch cake.

Chocolate Pound Cake

1 cup butter, softened
½ cup shortening
2¼ cups sugar
5 eggs
1 tablespoon vanilla extract

3 cups sifted cake flour
½ cup cocoa
½ teaspoon baking powder
1 cup milk

Cream butter and shortening in large bowl of an electric mixer; gradually add sugar, beating well. Add eggs, one at a time, beating well after each addition. Stir in vanilla.

Sift together cake flour, cocoa, and baking powder; add to creamed mixture alternately with milk, beginning and ending with flour mixture. Mix well after each addition.

Pour batter into a well-greased and floured 10-inch tube pan. Bake at 325° for 1 hour and 40 minutes or until a wooden pick inserted in center comes out clean. Cool in pan 15 minutes; remove cake from pan to wire rack, and let cool completely. Yield: one 10-inch cake.

Mrs. John C. Banks's Date Nut Cake

A delectable cake that stays moist for several weeks sealed in a tin container.

4 cups pecans or walnuts, chopped
1 pound dates, chopped
1 pound candied cherries, chopped
4 cups all-purpose flour, divided
½ cup butter, softened

2½ cups sugar
4 large eggs, well beaten
2 tablespoons lemon extract
1 teaspoon vanilla extract

Combine nuts, dates, and candied cherries; dredge with 1 cup flour, stirring to coat well. Set aside.

Cream butter; gradually add sugar, beating until light and fluffy. Add eggs, one at a time, beating well after each addition. Add remaining 3 cups flour and flavoring; mix well. Stir in fruit-nut mixture.

Spoon batter into 3 waxed paper-lined and greased 9- x 5- x 3-inch loafpans. Cover pans tightly with foil. Place on middle rack of oven, and place a large pan of boiling water on lower oven rack. Bake at 300° for 1 hour. Remove foil, and bake an additional 30 minutes or until a wooden pick inserted in center comes out clean. Cool 10 minutes in pans. Remove loaves from pans; place on wire racks, and cool completely. Yield: 3 loaves.

Mama Hatton's Pineapple Pound Cake

1 cup unsalted butter, softened
½ cup shortening
2¾ cups sugar
6 large eggs, at room temperature
3 cups all-purpose flour
2 teaspoons baking powder

¼ teaspoon salt
¼ cup milk
1 teaspoon vanilla extract
¾ cup crushed pineapple with juice
Pineapple Glaze

Cream butter and shortening; gradually add sugar, beating at medium speed of electric mixer until light and fluffy. Add eggs, one at a time, beating well after each addition.

Combine flour, baking powder and salt; add to creamed mixture alternately with milk, beginning and ending with flour. Mix just until blended after each addition. Stir in vanilla and pineapple. Pour batter into a greased and floured 10-inch tube pan. Bake at 325° for 1 hour and 15 minutes or until a wooden pick inserted in center comes out clean. Cool cake in pan 10 to 15 mintues; remove from pan and cool completely. Pour glaze over cake while hot. Yield: one 10-inch cake.

Pineapple Glaze

1½ cups sifted powdered sugar   1 cup crushed pineapple in juice

Mix ingredients and pour over hot cake. Yield: about 2 cups.

George Reynold's Bakeless Fruitcake

Easy to make but requires time. The end result is worth every minute it takes.

1 pound pecan halves, divided
½ (1-pound) box vanilla wafers, crushed
½ (1-pound) box graham crackers, crushed
1 (9-ounce) box raisins
1 (8-ounce) package pitted dates, finely chopped

1 (6-ounce) bottle maraschino cherries, drained and chopped
1 (14-ounce) can sweetened condensed milk
¼ cup bourbon
Whipped cream

Reserve 40 pecan halves to place on top of cake; chop remaining pecans, and set aside.

Combine vanilla wafers and graham crackers in a large mixing bowl. Stir in raisins, dates, cherries, and reserved chopped nuts, mixing well. Add sweetened condensed milk and bourbon; stir well.

Line a 9-inch loafpan with waxed paper, allowing enough waxed paper to cover top. Press the cake mixture tightly into pan. Arrange reserved pecan halves on top. Cover cake with excess waxed paper. Chill overnight; slice and serve with whipped cream. Yield: one 9- x 5- x 3-inch cake.

Hot Water Gingerbread

⅓ cup shortening
⅔ cup boiling water
1 cup molasses
1 egg, beaten
2¾ cups all-purpose flour

1½ teaspoons baking soda
½ teaspoon salt
1 teaspoon ground cinnamon
1½ teaspoons ground ginger
¼ teaspoon ground cloves

Melt shortening in boiling water; add molasses and egg. Combine the dry ingredients; add to molasses mixture. Pour batter into a greased 9-inch square pan. Bake at 350° for 30 to 35 minutes or until a wooden pick inserted in center comes out clean. Cool before cutting into 3-inch squares. Yield: 9 squares.

Note: For a more elegant dessert, top each serving with Lemon Sauce.

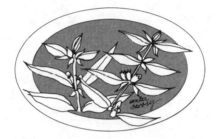

Lemon Sauce

Delicious served with blueberry pudding or gingerbread.

1 cup sugar
1 tablespoon butter or margarine
1¼ cups plus 3 tablespoons cold
   water, divided
¼ cup cornstarch

1 teaspoon grated lemon rind
¼ cup plus 2 tablespoons lemon
   juice
3 egg yolks, beaten
2 tablespoons milk

Combine sugar, butter, and 1¼ cups water in a small stainless steel, glass, or enamel saucepan; cook over low heat, stirring constantly, until sugar dissolves.

Combine cornstarch and remaining water in a small mixing bowl, mixing well with a wire whisk; add to syrup mixture, mixing well. Cook over low heat, stirring constantly until mixture clears and thickens.

Add lemon rind and juice; cook, stirring constantly, 2 minutes.

Combine egg yolks and milk in a small mixing bowl, mixing well; add a small amount of warm sauce, mixing well. Add back to sauce mixture in saucepan, mixing well. Bring to a boil, stirring constantly; remove from heat. Yield: about 2 cups.

Note: Sauce may be stored in refrigerator and reheated. It may be necessary to beat with a wire whisk before reheating.

Index

TABLESCAPES

Library of Congress Catalog Number: 88-061280
ISBN: 0-8487-0808-3
Manufactured in the United States of America
Fourth Printing

Material in *Tablescapes* is adapted from articles that have appeared in the
"Tablescapes" column of *Southern Accents*® magazine.

Southern Accents®

Editor: Karen Phillips Irons
Production Coordinator: Diane D. Burrell
Associate Editors: Sallie S. Stevens, Shelby Neely
Assistant Editor: Susannah M. Wilson
Senior Copy Editor: Trinket Shaw
Copy Editor: Tami C. Arnold
Editorial Assistants: Christine A. Wenning, Karen D. McElroy
Contributing Editors: Laura C. Lieberman (Visual Arts), Carol Haley
(Design Sources), Laura Cerwinske, David Dillon, Susan Stiles Dowell,
Palmer Graham, Jane G. Hollis, Nan Booth Simpson, Bonnie Warren
"Tablescapes" Contributors: Leslie E. Benham, Helen C. Griffith, Susan L.
Hewitt, Roberta Klein, Susan Percy, Karen M. Smith, Randall Wallace

Oxmoor House
Executive Editor: Candace N. Conard
Production Manager: Jerry Higdon
Associate Production Manager: Rick Litton
Art Director: Bob Nance

Tablescapes

Editor: Vicki L. Ingham
Copy Chief: Mary Jean Haddin
Designer: Earl Freedle

CONTENTS

China: Nineteenth-century English, possibly by Henry Daniel of Spode
Candlesticks: American silver, circa 1900
Shades: Silver filigree with silk underlining
Porcelain fruit basket: Nineteenth-century French

Introduction

Good table settings are creative works of art, collages assembled by the host or hostess to bring an additional dimension of pleasure to dining. To be sure, the accepted rules of placement are usually followed. But there remains an opportunity to give imagination free rein — to create an unusual vignette designed to complement the surrounding decor while sustaining an atmosphere of congeniality that will delight the eye and heighten the senses.

Tablescapes may be composed of a variety of elements: silver, porcelain, crystal, earthenware, fabric, flowers, plants, or whatever happens to strike a chord of creative fancy. Aesthetic success in arranging these elements depends on the individual's imagination, talent, and taste, those qualities that enable one to envision what is good and what is not. The final arbiter, taste, is that indefinable sense that signals an alarm when enough is enough. When this alarm sounds, the wise table arranger will always retreat several steps and consider whether less is not indeed more.

On the pages that follow, you will find tablescapes expressing a wide array of moods, from elegant and sophisticated to light-hearted, casual, and even whimsical. Each has been assembled according to certain design principles: harmony and contrast in colors, variety balanced with repetition in patterns, appropriate scale and size for flowers or other table decoration. Each also bears the stamp of its designer, whose personality inevitably emerges in the way artwork, flowers, china, and linens are combined and presented. That individuality is both the charm and the challenge of tablescapes. In creating a carefully crafted setting, a host conveys to his guests that the gathering is special — a celebration of friendship.

SPRINGTIME SETTING

An attractive table is a gracious compliment to guests, and the meticulous host or hostess leaves no detail unattended. For this springtime luncheon, the garden offers a perfect backdrop. Placing the table in front of a window wall allows guests to enjoy the massed banks of ivory roses, pink geraniums, begonias, and lavender petunias flourishing outside. Above the fireplace, a landscape painting brings a sense of the garden indoors — and provides the color key for the setting. The blue of the upholstery on the nineteenth-century Federal-style chairs and the plum and aqua in the floral-print cloth on the table seem drawn from the canvas, which also offers the note of rose found in the antique Rose Canton china. The china, in turn, suggests a scheme ranging from lavender to mauve, rose, and red for flowers and table linens. Even the menu is devised with an eye to color: bright red

radishes and tomatoes and orange-red lobsters introduce a lively warmth that, far from clashing with the cooler tones, accents and enhances them. Such fastidious attention to detail yields a tablescape that delights the eye with its harmony — and half of the pleasure of food is in its visual appeal.

In addition to carefully orchestrating color, this host gives his tablescapes a distinctively personal quality by incorporating collectibles and precious objects. Here a pair of antique Chinese figures enhances the impact of the flower arrangement, a spray of tulips, alstroemeria, and carnations.

China: antique Rose Canton
Flatware: antique American
Crystal: Cristal d'Arques
Table cover: Custom-made with Select Pleats fabric by Van Luit
Designer: John Leigh Spath, Albert Van Luit & Company

ARTFUL CARVINGS

A stunning centerpiece can set the tone for a gathering, and when one element — such as the container — is unexpected, a lively dinner conversation is assured. These table settings, in two posh Coconut Grove hotels, feature the watermelon vases of Art Smith, chef to Florida Governor Bob Graham. Drawing on food-carving skills perfected during an apprenticeship

China and candlesticks: "Old Imari" from Royal Crown Derby
Flatware: "Golden Medici" from Gorham
Crystal: "Maître" from Rosenthal

at The Greenbrier in West Virginia, Smith carves relief designs into the rind of the melon. Birds in flight, foliage, and flowers ornament the shapes that emerge as sculpted vases through his artistry. The original shape of the fruit is left intact, providing a slant here, a turn there — a touch that underscores the uniqueness of each piece. Flowers are secured directly in the flesh of the watermelon, whose sugary juice keeps the flowers fresh.

Although such intricate carving demands more time and skill than most hosts and hostesses can devote, the idea of building an arrangement in a watermelon vase is one that can be readily adapted. With fruit-filled melon halves almost a cliché at summer parties, using the melon as a vase for flowers is simply the next imaginative step.

A TOUCH OF WHIMSY

Because a sense of humor adds spice to life, there is no better way to enliven a dinner party than to give the setting a touch of whimsy. As an alternative to the usual simple centerpiece, this collection of ceramic fruits and vegetables is combined with vases of florists' flowers to create a lighthearted mood. In the same spirit of unconventionality, classic silver candlesticks are paired with Italian ceramic ones shaped like palm trees, and each place setting includes an assortment of silver patterns. To balance variety with repetition, napkins pick up the pink note in flowers and fruit, and china accents the yellow.

Such a fanciful table setting can succeed in any home, particularly if classic shapes are used. But it seems especially appropriate in a home whose interiors suggest the presence of a lively wit. Here a crayon drawing by Freyburger reveals a hostess with a firm grasp of the lighter side of life.

China: "Morning Glory" from Ceralene, Limoges
Flatware: Various patterns, including Kirk and Tiffany & Co.
Napkins: Porthault
Designer: Terry Alexander, Very Terry, Atlanta

Fine Functionalism

When the table is set with handcrafted dinnerware, other embellishments are superfluous: the table itself becomes a collage of art.

The best in contemporary American design combines inspiration from a variety of sources, successfully integrating influences as disparate as Japanese decorative art and bold Memphis designs. The pieces should be used in equally astute yet casual combinations. By mixing contemporary crafts with fine antiques, ethnic handwoven fabrics, oriental pieces, and post-modern art, the connoisseur can create striking arrangements for any fashionable occasion. A bright yellow teapot with a short spout and fat curves, for example, presents

Dinnerware and (on sideboard) fruit bowl and platter: by Sherry Steinway
Handblown glasses, goblets, and (on sideboard) candlesticks: by John and Jan Gilmor
High-legged bowl and (on sideboard) tall vase: by Kathy Triplett
Butter dish: by Joe Chasnoff and Judy Azulay
Table linens and (on sideboard) table runner: by Catharine Ellis Muerdter
Oil painting: Expansion Series #4 *by Ted Potter*
Table: by Robert Kopf
Tablescapes photographed at the Southeastern Center for Contemporary Art, Winston-Salem, North Carolina

an Art Deco flair as the eye-catching centerpiece for a table serenely set with black-and-white dinnerware. Unexpected fusions offer endless possibilities for personal stylishness, and the individual character of each design adds its own certain eccentricity within the setting.

For fireside or alfresco dining, finely crafted clay, glass, wood, and fiber combine to create high art. The function is feeling.

Dinner plates, bowls, and (on mantel) painted bowls: by Silvie Granatelli
Goblets: by John and Jan Gilmor
Fish plates: by Janet Belden
Napkins: by Kathrin Weber Scott
Teapot and (on mantel) vase: by Kathy Triplett

FLAVOR OF PROVENCE

In a home where rooms flow into one another and the dining room is readily accessible to living areas, a tablescape is highly visible. Therefore it must be treated as an integral part of the interior decor. In this house, French furnishings, tile and heart pine floors, and clean white walls create a country French setting in which antique Delft and Chinese export porcelain establish a dominant blue and white theme. The flavor of Provence carries into the dining area, where painted French chairs covered in a blue-and-white oversize plaid are drawn up to a table set with French faience and damask napkins. Wheat-colored burlap accented with a painted border from Colefax & Fowler offers a rustic backdrop for the dinnerware, but rusticity need not preclude elegance. Silver candlesticks, etched crystal, and English silver flatware dress up the table without ruffling its casual informality. In keeping with the mood of the setting, the centerpiece is appropriately simple: a pot of narcissus in an eighteenth-century Chinese-export punch bowl is flanked by bunches of delphinium in antique Delft vases, giving emphasis to the blue-and-white scheme.

*Dinner plates: French faience "Normandie" from Frank McIntosh at
Henri Bendel
Pewter service plates: from Pierre Deux*

TABLETOP TOPIARY

Enjoyable dining involves a combination of appreciative friends, excellent food presented with charm and insight, an inviting setting that encourages and sustains animated conversation, and last — but by no means least — unusual, fragrant, and colorful flowers and plants. Flowers are such an important ingredient for entertaining at the dining table that few formal meals are served without them.

Even a rather ordinary arrangement of roses can make a table special when it is accompanied by something more imaginative. Here the trunks of miniature ficus trees have been woven together, and kumquats have been fastened to the branches. The result is trompe l'oeil fruit trees, a witty allusion to the art of bonsai. Nineteenth-century handpainted wooden pigeons complete the table decoration.

Serving plates: "Athlone Blue" from Coalport
Dessert/salad plates: "Hong Kong" from Coalport
Flatware: "Louis XV" from Birks
Trompe l'oeil fruit trees: by Scott Blonder, Atlanta

A SOPHISTICATED WINTERTIME SETTING

Simplicity is the key to elegance in this table setting. White and gold establish a formal mood, warmed by the rich contrast of red and green. The subtle repetition of these accent colors also harmonizes them with the setting. Individual ashtrays and cigarette holders, for example, repeat the malachite-green of the Louis XV-style chairs, which welcome guests to sit on what appear to be Flemish floral paintings that include notes of red. (The upholstery is in fact hand-painted with acrylics.)

For the focal point, the host chose anthuriums, a difficult flower because its unyielding form does not lend itself easily to conventional arrangements. Thus, he took a more contemporary approach, inserting the stems into glass beaker vases. This technique is simple but effective because it uses the plant's characteristically straight stem and stiff shape to advantage. To tie the individual vases into a single composition, most of them are grouped in a deep glass bowl that is filled with water and smooth black stones, giving the arrangement visual weight at its base. To complete the centerpiece, the remaining containers and Chinese blanc-de-chine figures are placed in an orderly circle around the bowl. The result is a strikingly sophisticated tablescape that extends a glittering invitation to shed winter doldrums.

Service plates: "Platine d'Or" from Fitz and Floyd
Soup bowls: "Fleur et Nuages" from Fitz and Floyd
Champagne flutes: Waterford
Flatware: "Aristocrat" from Towle
Candlesticks: "Odilon" from Baccarat
Designer: Max Eckert

ANNIVERSARY DINNER

Anniversaries mark not only years but also memories. A romantic dinner for two that builds on happy remembrances sets the stage for an unforgettable evening.

Designer and author Alexandra Stoddard began her tablescape with a special table covering. Taking her cue from a rich childhood image — masses of purple and yellow pansy faces smiling up from her mother's flower beds — Stoddard wove together a collection of ribbons to make this tablecloth for her first wedding anniversary. The cloth has become a tradition, a colorful foundation for an imaginative assortment of ornaments and tabletop accessories — porcelain fruits and flowers, green Wedgwood dishes, and handpainted pansy candlesticks by English ceramic artist Lady Anne Gordon. Gold-rimmed crystal from the Cristalleries de Saint-Louis adds a celebratory sparkle: each piece is hand blown and hand cut to the exacting traditions of France's oldest crystal manufacturer, a company founded in 1586.

Dinnerware: Wedgwood
Crystal: Cristalleries de Saint-Louis

OLD-WORLD CHARM

      Poinsettias are the only homage paid to traditional Christmas decorations in this intimate dinner-party setting. Instead of the usual green and red, the designer chose shades of rose, red, and fuchsia, accented by gold. And instead of conventional Christmas fabric, he chose a carnation-strewn Brunschwig & Fils material for tablecloth, napkins, and chair cushions. A simple and charming centerpiece was quickly constructed with pots of fuchsia-colored cyclamen and antique Chinese dolls perched on miniature chairs. Tall silver candlesticks hold short red candles, an unexpected combination that respects the scale of the centerpiece and the dimensions of the table. With the glitter of gold-rimmed antique china, Venetian champagne glasses, and gilded ballroom chairs, an air of festivity prevails.

Service plates: Tiffany
Tablecloth, napkin, and cushion fabric: Brunschwig & Fils
Designer: J. Allen Murphy

THE MORE THE MERRIER

Any dinner party with a guest list exceeding forty or so requires a special approach to create a warm, convivial atmosphere. Few homes can accommodate such a large gathering, so planning often includes deciding on a location, usually a restaurant, hotel, or private club. The best thing about entertaining away from home is that many of the details are handled by the chosen establishment. And while this certainly alleviates a number of worries — sufficient dinnerware, preparing and serving the meal, and so on — it also results in certain limitations, such as the choice of tablecloths, china, crystal, and silver. Nonetheless, the host or hostess still has several avenues for imprinting his or her style on the setting.

One important way is through table arrangements, which set the mood for the evening. These centerpieces should be either low enough that guests can see over them or high enough that they can see under them. And when heights are varied on different tables, the overall effect is dramatic.

On those occasions when two different generations will be celebrating, each group can be made to feel at home with specially designed decorations. For the younger crowd, tall arrangements with colorful balloons create an upbeat mood. Where the adults will gather, more traditional flower arrangements bring a Victorian elegance to tables. Flowers and greenery that might be found in an English country garden — roses, gerbera daisies,

hydrangeas, and ferns — are combined in low containers, either wicker or French wire ones. Tall arrangements featuring Queen Anne's lace make a striking show, held aloft on bamboo poles anchored in terra-cotta pots. Soaring arrangements are particularly effective in the high-ceilinged ballrooms of clubs and hotels, offering a lively antidote to the potentially cold grandeur of such spaces.

PHOTOGRAPHY CREDITS

page 4
TINA FREEMAN

pages 6, 7
MAX ECKERT

pages 8, 9
DAN FORER

pages 10, 11
DELOYE R. BURRELL

pages 12, 13
GARY WARNIMONT

page 14
DELOYE R. BURRELL

page 15
STEVE HOGBEN, ATLANTA

page 1 /
MAX ECKERT

page 18
DAVID PHELPS

page 19
NPC

pages 20, 21, 22
STEVE HOGBEN, ATLANTA